SOUTH CAROLINA

REVOLUTIONARY WAR INDENTS:

A SCHEDULE

BY

JOHN LENNELL ANDREWS, JR.

Heritage Books
2025

HERITAGE BOOKS

AN IMPRINT OF HERITAGE BOOKS, INC.

Books, CDs, and more—Worldwide

For our listing of thousands of titles see our website
at
www.HeritageBooks.com

A Facsimile Reprint
Published 2025 by
HERITAGE BOOKS, INC.
Publishing Division
5810 Ruatan Street
Berwyn Heights, MD 20740

Library of Congress Catalog Card Number: 2001 132865

— Publisher's Notice —
In reprints such as this, it is often not possible to remove
blemishes from the original. We feel the contents of this
book warrant its reissue despite these blemishes and
hope you will agree and read it with pleasure.

International Standard Book Number
Paperbound: 978-0-7884-5099-0

INTRODUCTION

The documentation of the South Carolina patriots who provided military service, supplies, aid, or assistance to the cause of independence has been the subject of numerous articles, pamphlets, and books. Information is also available from a variety of primary sources including muster rolls, bounty land grants, stub indent books, and the South Carolina Audited Accounts. However, even with this wide variety of sources available, the documentation does not always provide information as to the section of the state in which an individual lived. This becomes problematic when there are two or more individuals with the same or similar names. Often additional research must be undertaken to properly separate the different individuals.

Within the records of the Commissioners to Adjust the Public Accounts (Series S126055 South Carolina Department of Archives and History) are three pamphlet volumes which help to tie an individual to a particular geographic location within South Carolina. These Schedules of Indents, dated 1791, contain summarized information on an individual's claim for services or materials provided the state during the Revolutionary War. Most of the information concerning the military service or assistance provided can be easily ascertained from the sources mentioned above. However, one column on these Schedules of Indents lists the district in which the individual patriot lived. Using this information, it is now possible to easily tie an individual to a particular district, thus making a correct identification more certain.

After the fall of Charles Town in 1780 the American forces within the state faced the problem of how to pay those who served in the military as well as those who provided supplies. A system of credit was established which relied upon an issuance of receipts in return for military service or supplies. The State of South Carolina promised to redeem these receipts when normalcy was reestablished. On March 26, 1783, six commissioners were elected by the Privy Council to collect the claims from each of the circuit court districts outside of Charleston (the commissioner from Charleston was already serving at this time). The claims were filed in the district the claimant lived and these receipts were later collected by the Auditor General's office. As each account was audited, interest-bearing indents were issued in payment. Each indent was cut in an irregular manner (to prevent forgery) from its stub and issued to those who had submitted approved claims. Each stub contained a summary of the information contained on its matching indent. This information included a letter and number designation, the date of issue, the name of the claimant, the principal amount of the claim, the annual interest due, and the service or supplies that had been rendered. Stubs were retained in letter-designated books, letters A through FEC. The initial deadline for submission of claims, September 26, 1784, was extended to October 1, 1785. The indents quickly became a type of substitute currency and speculators collected large numbers of them in hopes of either the Federal Government assuming South Carolina's debt or using the indents to purchase land from the state. Indents were issued between March 1783 and October 1791.

The State of South Carolina soon established a system in which the indents could be used to purchase land. During the 1780's many South Carolinians took advantage of this system and used their indents to purchase real property for themselves, while some individuals sold or assigned their indents to others for the same purpose. The process of an individual using an indent to purchase state land can be tracked by using the records of the South Carolina Commissioners of the Treasury, Secretary of State, and Comptroller General. In many cases it is possible to tie an individual patriot to a particular tract of land. This is a very useful exercise when confronted with different individuals with similar names. A successful search requires a familiarity with the treasury records and the Italian accounting system used during the eighteenth century. To establish that a particular Revolutionary War patriot used his indent to purchase a certain tract of land from the State of South Carolina it is necessary to consult these South Carolina Department of Archives and History records: South Carolina Treasury Ledger (S 218107), Treasury Journal (S 218106), Accounts of Land Paid for Since Opening the Land Office, 1784 – 1793 (S 218118), Daybook Accounts of Land Paid (S 218104), Accounts Audited of Claims Growing Out of the Revolution in South Carolina (S 126003), South Carolina Land Grants (Columbia Series S 213022 and Charleston Series S 213024), and South Carolina State Plats (Charleston Series S 213190 and Columbia Series S 213192).

In 1790 the United States Congress set in motion the process of Federal assumption of the debts incurred by the states during the Revolutionary War. The State of South Carolina, by an act of the General Assembly dated February 19, 1791, submitted all the indents it had in its hands to the Federal government and called for all privately held indents to be turned in. The three Schedules of Indents presented in this book apparently were made in response to this call. One schedule covered the three lower districts of South Carolina, Beaufort, Charleston, and Georgetown. The other two schedules provide information from all districts in South Carolina and are, with the exception of the end pages, duplicates of each other. For the purpose of this book, the information on these three schedules has been combined and presented by Indent number, beginning with the Book A designation and continuing through the Book FEC designation. At the end of Beaufort, Charleston, Georgetown schedule is listed additional information containing an aggregate of indents as well as notes on individual indents. Similar information is listed on one of the remaining schedules. This information is also included in this work.

With any work of this type, certain judgments must be made in regard to the spelling of names. Care was taken to compare names in question to the published *Stub Entries to Indents*. When a difference in spelling was present, the spelling on the Schedule of Indents was used. The same procedure was used to reconcile monetary differences between the Schedule of Indents and the published *Stub Entries to Indents*. In instances when a name or monetary amount could not be deciphered from the Schedule of Indents, the name or amount on the published *Stub Entries to Indents* was used. Other editorial changes were made in order to facilitate research: All district names are fully spelled out and all instances of "Ditto" (do. and ") have been eliminated and the word or name referred to has been substituted. Two specific items were omitted from this work, a series of accounting notes and two pages of ledger-like writings. Both these items were at the end of one of the Schedules of Indents and are not within the context of this work.

In many instances the previously published series *Stub Entries to Indents* noted that some of the stubs or pages were missing from the existing record. Information from forty-two missing stubs has been found on the Schedule of Indents. These include stubs L-194; W-337, 350, 363, 380, 403, 411, 417, 418, 420; X-1007, 1324, 1326, 1564, 1577, 1578, 1579, 2164, 2165, 2166, 3345, 3346, 3347, 3360, 3362, 3363, 3416, 3417, 3419, 3420, 3424, 3441, 3445, 3446, 3460, 3463, 3467, 3469, 3473, 3647, 3652, and 3664.

John Lennell Andrews, Jr.
Hartsville, South Carolina
May 30, 2001

Acknowledgements

I wish to thank several individuals and groups who have given their assistance and support during the preparation of this book. Several members of the South Carolina Department of Archives and History have freely given of their time, knowledge, and expertise. Dr. Charles H. Lesser generously provided information concerning the history of the South Carolina indent system. He was able to give accurate and reliable answers to my many questions. The staff of the Archives Reference Room made valuable contributions to the completion of this book. Steve Tuttle, supervisor, and the entire staff were always willing to produce obscure records from within the Archives stacks. I am grateful to Robert Mackintosh for ensuring that the copies of the Schedules of Indents were of high quality and the best that could be obtained from the fragile documents.

GeLee Corley Hendrix provided several helpful suggestions and is truly a professional genealogist in every way. Those who have South Carolina Revolutionary War ancestors owe her a debt of gratitude for her contributions to genealogical methodology. The officers and members of the Old Darlington District Chapter, South Carolina Genealogical Society were very supportive of this project. Without their encouragement I would not have undertaken this project. Brent H. Holcomb has also provided much support and encouragement. He enthusiastically agreed to publish this book in a joint effort with the Old Darlington District Chapter, SCGS, thus ensuring a wider audience.

Finally, I thank each of the members of my family for their understanding and support. My wife Debbie and my two children, Thomas and Sarah, have been the foundation that enabled me to complete this work. Their love has sustained me.

NORTH CAROLINA

GEORGETOWN DISTRICT

Pee Dee River

Georgetown

Santee River

CHERAWS DISTRICT

Long Bluff

Lynches River

CHARLESTON DISTRICT

Charleston

Beaufort

CAMDEN DISTRICT

Camden

Congaree River

Orangeburg

Combahee River

ORANGEBURG DISTRICT

BEAUFORT DISTRICT

Broad River

NINETY-SIX DISTRICT

Ninety-Six

GEORGIA

Savannah River

Indian Land

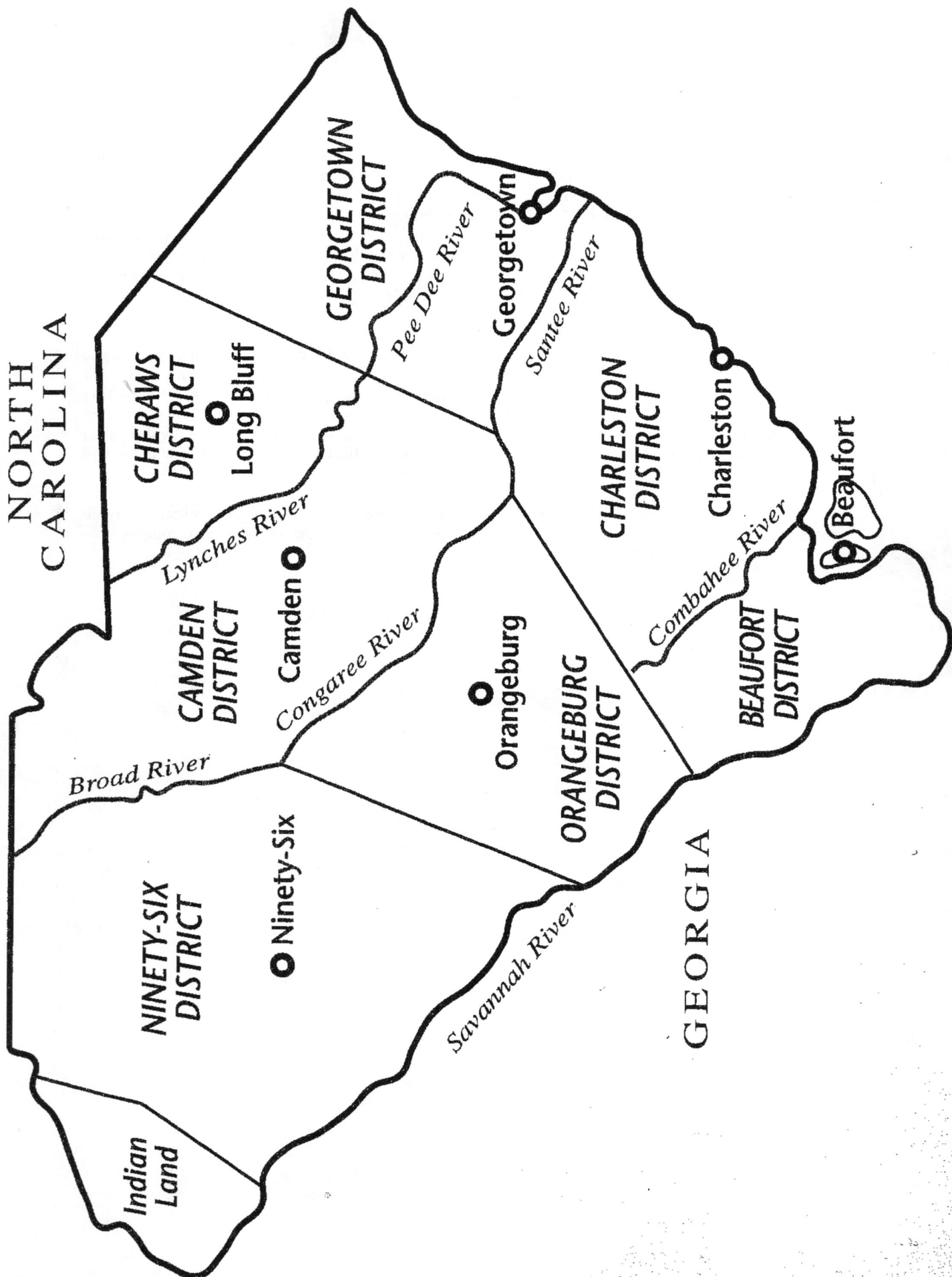

Map used by permission of the South Carolina Department of Archives and History

Numb. & Book	To whom Granted	For what Granted			District	Amount Indent
257 A	Wilson, John for self & Estᵃ Algernon Wilson	Supplies		St. Commʸ.		£ 62. 9.
267 A	Farr, Thomas	Supplies		St. Commʸ.	Charleston	£ 21.14.1
253 B	Wood, John & Cuyler, Abraham	Monies loaned				£ 59.3 . 5
254 B	Rohde, Levin Jorgen	Monies loaned				£ 81. .11
255 B	Magens, Johannes	Monies loaned				£ 124.17. 6
256 B	Beyer, Hans Peter	Monies loaned				£ 78.17.11
304 B	Adams, David & Co.	In lieu of Indent 21, B, lost				£ 29.
352 B	Young, Benjamin	Monies loaned				£ 123.11.10 ¾
540 B	Chalmers, Martha	Monies loaned			Charleston	£ 40. 1. 7
541 B	Huger, Senʳ. Isaac for Huger, Junʳ. Isaac	Monies loaned				£ 4.11.3 £ 4.11. 3
573 B	Thomas, Mary Lamboll for Baucart, Mary	Monies loaned			Charleston	£ 6.15.10
581 B	Lane, Catherine	Monies loaned				£ 11.17. 6
1086 B	Miller, William Assnee Richd. Winn	In lieu of Indent 172, Q, for Duty & Provisions			Charleston	£ 23.10. 4¼
9 C	Holman, Mary	Supplies		St. Commʸ.		£ 2. 7. 6
51 C.	Hunter, Henry	Supplies		St. Commʸ.		£ 6.19. 3
53 C	Wittaker, William	Supplies		St. Commʸ.		£ 61. 7.10
86 C	Smith, John	Supplies		St. Commʸ.		£ 27. 9. 3
129 C	Gerardeau, Peter	Supplies		St. Commʸ.		£ 19. 5.
250 C	Hall, Daniel	Supplies		St. Commʸ.		£ 4. . 7
299 C	Collins, Harakin John	Supplies		St. Commʸ.		£ 3.16. 1½
303 C	Giddens, ~~John~~ James	Supplies		St. Commʸ.		£ 3.16. 1½
304 C	Griner, Mʳˢ.	Supplies		St. Commʸ.		£ 3.16. 1½
305 C	Crusie, Jesse	Supplies		St. Commʸ.		£ 3.16. 1½

Numb. & Book	To whom Granted	For what Granted		District	Amount Indent
308 C	Bowers, Mrs.	Supplies	St. Commy.		£ 3.16. 1½
309 C	Swicard, George	Supplies	St. Commy.		£ 3.16. 1½
310 C	Richards, James	Supplies	St. Commy.		£ 3.16. 1½
311 C	Lamar, Susanna	Supplies	St. Commy.		£ 7.12. 3
314 C	Grant, John	Supplies	St. Commy.		£ 11. 8. 4
318 C	Williams, Ezekiel	Supplies	St. Commy.		£ 11. 8. 4
323 C	Clanton, David	Supplies	St. Commy.		£ 1.15.
324 C	Clark, William	Supplies	St. Commy.		£ 2. 1. 0
334 C	Douglas, David	Supplies	St. Commy.		£ 3. 1.10
335 C	Neeland, William	Supplies	St. Commy.		£ 21.19. 7
352 C	Smith, Francis	Supplies	St. Commy.		£ 5.13. 8
358 C	Bellinger, William	Supplies	St. Commy.		£ 3. 7. 2
359 C	Bellinger, John	Supplies	St. Commy.		£ 29.16. 8
376 C	Muncrief, Richard	Supplies	St. Commy.		£ 2.11. 4
384 C	Stroman, Jacob	Supplies	St. Commy.		£ 12.16. 8
385 C	Citts, George	Supplies	St. Commy.		£ 1.17. 6
387 C	Edwards, Elizabeth	Supplies	St. Commy.		£ 8.17. 7
388 C	Clifford, Elizabeth	Supplies	St. Commy.		£ 56.13. 7
390 C	Goddard Esta., Francis	Supplies	St. Commy.		£ 102.13. 4
404 C	Houston, John	Supplies	St. Commy.		£ 5. 5. 2
407 C	Grove, Francis	Supplies	St. Commy.		£ 2.11. 4
449 C	Searson, William	Supplies	St. Commy.		£ 15.13. 1½
487 C	Cobia, Nicholas	Supplies	St. Commy.		£ 4.14.10
491 C	Wells, Matthew	Supplies	St. Commy.		£ 9. 2.
553 C	Grant, Mary	Supplies	St. Commy.		£ 3.17.
558 C	Dupont, Gideon	Supplies	St. Commy.		£ 4. 1. 8
580 C	Reed, Mary	Supplies	St. Commy.		£ 11. 8. 4
586 C	Moore, Levi	Supplies	St. Commy.		£ 5.17.10
665 C	Darrington, Thomas	Supplies	St. Commy.		£ 25.18. 6
108 D	Frierson, Robert	Supplies	St. Commy.	Georgetown	£ 5. 7.
112 D	Grimsley, George	Supplies	St. Commy.		£ 5.19.
115 D	Hyrne, Henry	Supplies			£ 3. 4. 2

Numb. & Book	To whom Granted	For what Granted		District	Amount Indent
117 D	Hardyman, Thomas	Supplies		Camden	£ 3.10. 7
119 D	Hogg, William	Supplies		Beaufort	£ 9.12. 6
133 D	Muckleduff, Adam	Supplies			£ 13. 4. 4
134 D	McGinney, Charles	Supplies		Camden	£ 5. . 3
149 D	Rippon, Isaac	Supplies			£ 2.17. 6
176 D	Bradley, John	Supplies		Camden	£ 2.11. 4
178 D	Brunson, David	Supplies		Camden	£ 10.11. 9
38 E	Allison, Dorothea	Supplies		Charleston	£ 2. 6. 2
43 E	Blackmond, Esta. Thos.	Supplies	Marion's Brigade		£ 30.16.
108 E	Hustess, John	Supplies			£ 5. 5
110 E	Izard Jun, Ralph	Supplies		Charleston	£ 6.16. 7
152 E	Pendarvis, Esta. Thomas	Supplies			£ 3.13. 2¼
176 E	Saunders, Roger Parker	Supplies		Charleston	£ 114.16.
197 E	Wood, Dempsey	Supplies		Cheraw	£ 5. 2. 8
14 F	Anderson, Henry	Militia Duty		Georgetown	£ 2. .
15 F	Anderson, John	Supplies		Georgetown	£ 4. 9.10
16 F	Anderson, Robert	Militia Duty		Georgetown	£ 2. 1. 4
19 F	Adkinson, James	Militia Duty		Georgetown	£ 2. 8.
31 F	Bellune, Francis	Militia Duty		Georgetown	£ 3. .
32 F	Butler, Esta. Thomas	Supplies		Georgetown	£ 10.17.10¾
55 F	Baxter, Robt., James, & John	Supplies		Georgetown	£ 228.15. 2
73 F	Bone, James	Militia Duty	Marion's Brigade		£ 6.16.
78 F	Burrows, Saml. Jun	Militia Duty	Marion's Brigade		£ 3. 8. 6
79 F	Burrows, Joseph	Militia Duty	Marion's Brigade		£ 4. 8. 6
83 F	Connor, Jonathan	Militia Duty	Marion's Brigade		£ 2. 1. 4
95 F	Chisham, Mary	Supplies	St. Helena Compy.	Beaufort	£ 1. 5. 8
108 F	Parker, John	Militia Duty			£ 6.17. 4
120 F	Farned, Hannah	A Horse			£ 10. 5. 8
126 F	Goddin, Ann	Supplies			£ 50.12. 8
183 F	Meggett, Margt.	Supplies			£ 2. 3. 7½
188 F	Neal, Thomas	Supplies		Camden	£ 14. 8. 7

Numb. & Book	To whom Granted	For what Granted		District	Amount Indent
195 F	Saltus, Samuel	Supplies			£ 12. 6. 7
197 F	Stevens, Isham	Supplies		Georgetown	£ 7.17.
200 F	Stevens, John	Supplies		Georgetown	£ .16.6
351 F	Crofts, Estᵃ. Edwᵈ.	Militia Duty		Camden	£ 3. 8. 6¾
384 F	Adams, John	Supplies		Camden	£ 9.17.
385 F	Adams, James	Militia Duty		Camden	£ 2.17. 1½
394 F	Burch, Charles	Supplies			£ 19.17. 7
412 F	Branden, John	Riding Express for Col. Brandon		Ninety Six	£ 7.12. 3
431 F	Cantey, William	Supplies		Camden	£ 3. 4. 2
435 F	Cooke, John	Militia Duty	Sumter's Brigade		£ 4. 8. 6¾
438 F	Cousart, James	Militia Duty	Major Thompson		£ 5. 10. 8
441 F	Commander, Samˡ.	Supplies			£ 8. 9. 4¾
59 G	Carr, John	Militia Duty		Georgetown	£ 6. .
60 G	Casey, Elizabeth	Supplies	Col. Davis's Regiment	Beaufort	£ 3. 4. 2
97 G	Cunningham, James	Supplies		Georgetown	£ 3.17.
122 G	Dehay, Andʷ.	Summᵍ & overlookᵍ Negroes		Georgetown	£ 3. 9. 4½
127 G	Edwards, John	Militia Duty		Georgetown	£ 6. 5. 4
175 G	Gaddis, Christ.	Supplies		Georgetown	£ 3. 6. 8
191 G	Grier, Samuel	Militia Duty	Marion's Brigade	Georgetown	£ 2. .
192 G	Grier, Joseph	Militia Duty	Marion's Brigade	Georgetown	£ 4. 4.
197 G	Gilchrist, John	Militia Duty	Marion's Brigade	Georgetown	£ 2. 1. 4
208 G	Harris, Timothy	Militia Duty	Marion's Brigade	Georgetown	£ 2.12. 0
216 G	Hancock, John	Saddle & Bridle for State Troops		Georgetown	£ 4. 2.10
218 G	Heartley, Amos	Militia Duty		Georgetown	£ 1.12.
219 G	Henning, Thomas	Supplies to Genˡ. Greene		Georgetown	£ 2.11. 4
220 G	Hartsfield, James	Militia Duty	Marion's Brigade	Georgetown	£ 2. .
229 G	Huggins, Estᵃ. Joseph	Supplies	Marion's Brigade	Georgetown	£ 2.11. 4
231 G	Horn, Mʳˢ	Supplies		Georgetown	£ 3. 4. 2
232 G	Huger, Estᵃ. Benjⁿ.	Supplies		Georgetown	£ 34. 8. 4

Numb. & Book	To whom Granted	For what Granted		District	Amount Indent
248 G	Kellsall, Agnes	Supplies		Beaufort	£ 1. 8.
252 G	Lynch, Esta Thomas	Supplies		Georgetown	£ 26. 2. 8
254 G	Meggett, William	Supplies		Georgetown	£ 64. 4. 6
255 G	Muckleduff, Adam	Supplies		Georgetown	£ 11. 5.5½
257 G	McCracken, Robert	Supplies & Duty as Sergt.		Georgetown	£ 8.18.10
273 G	Newman, Jonathan	Supplies		Georgetown	£ 10. 5. 4
274 G	Neeland, John	Supplies		Camden	£ 7. 4. 8
275 G	Neeland, William	Supplies		Camden	£ 9. 3. 2
289 G	Sanders, Esta. Willm	Supplies		Charleston	£ 10. 2. 4
297 G	Sansum, Esta. John	Negro hire		Charleston	£ 15. 6. 8
304 G	Theus, Randolph	Supplies		Georgetown	£ 6.10. 4
312 G	Walter, Richard	Supplies		Charleston	£ 37. 5.10
32 H	Laws, William	Militia Duty		Georgetown	£ 4.10.
43 H	Bourline, Esta. Joseph	Supplies		Charleston	£ 8.19. 8
49 H	Campbell, Alexander	Supplies		Camden	£ 22. 5. 8
51 H	Cowsant, James	Supplies		Camden	£ .14.
57 H	Dupont, Cornelius	Supplies		Charleston	£ 20.15. 8½
87 H	Horton, Robert	Militia Duty		Camden	£ 3. 4. 3½
104 H	Jayroe, Peter	Militia Duty		Georgetown	£ 36.10.
110 H	June, Peter	Supplies			£ 15. 9.10
119 H	Lawsey, William	Supplies			£ 7. 1. 2
125 H	Long, Joshua	Militia Duty			£ 2. 1. 4
128 H	Lamb, Ezekiel	Supplies			£ 9.17. 9½
131 H	Legear, James	Supplies			£ 3.10. 7
160 H	McCracken, John	Militia Duty			£ 8. 4.
169 H	Meyers, Margaret	Bounty Money due her son			£ 6. 8. 4
170 H	Martin, James	Supplies			£ .14.
179 H	McIntosh, Esta. George	Supplies	Error	State of Georgia	£ 30. .7
195 H	Mixon, Michael & Francis	Supplies		Georgetown	£ 2.16.
197 H	Mackleduff, Thomas	Supplies		Georgetown	£ 3.17.
200 H	McWattey, Esta. John	Supplies		Georgetown	£ 30.13. 5
202 H	Nell, Jun. William			Georgetown	£ 7.15. 8½

Numb. & Book	To whom Granted	For what Granted			District	Amount Indent
204 H	Neal, Samuel				Georgetown	£ 8. 5. 4
220 H	Port, Jun. Benjn.	Supplies			Georgetown	£ 3. .
221 H	Port, Peter	Supplies			Georgetown	£ 5.19. 3¾
225 H	Powers, Giles				Georgetown	£ 2. .
231 H	Perry, Est^a. John	Supplies				£ 33. 1 .10½
233 H	Postell, Jun. Ja^s.	Supplies			Georgetown	£ 22. 7. 5
236 H	Rouse, Sarah	Supplies			Orangeburgh	£ 2. 5.
245 H	Rowe, Edwd.	Militia Duty			Georgetown	£ 8. 4. 3¾
246 H	Reaves, Burgess	Militia Duty			Georgetown	£ 5.12.
252 H	Rees, Charles	Supplies			Georgetown	£ 14. 4. 8
258 H	Robertson, Willm.	Supplies			Camden	£ 1.14. 1
260 H	Guerard, Jacob	Supplies			Charleston	£ 6. 8. 4
266 H	Smith, Henry	Militia Duty			Georgetown	£ 2. .
4 I	Stricklan, William	Supplies			Georgetown	£ 1.18. 6
5 I	Squires, Andrew	Militia Duty			Georgetown	£ 5. 9. 4
8 I	Sweet, Anth^y.	A Horse			Georgetown	£ 2.13. 7½
24 I	Sullivan, John	Taylor's Work			Camden	£ 3.14. 7
25 I	Sessions, Solomon	Supplies			Georgetown	£ 15.19. 3½
29 I	Singleton, John	Supplies			Georgetown	£ .14.
30 I	Singleton, William	Militia Duty			Georgetown	£ 2. 1. 4
36 I	Terry, George	Militia Duty			Georgetown	£ 4. 8. 6
40 I	Tucker, Benjamin	Supplies			Georgetown	£ 3. 4. 2
72 I	White, Jun Anth^y.	Militia Duty			Georgetown	£ 2.18. 6¾
120 I	Bell, John	Supplies			Orangeburgh	£ . 8. 6¾
121 I	Bell, Thomas	Militia Duty	Ret^d by Capt Tate		Camden	£ 6.18. 6¾
130 I	Berry, Richard	Militia Duty	Ret^d by Capt Tate		Camden	£ 3. .
136 I	Barron, Est^a., Thomas	Militia Duty	Ret^d by Capt Tate		Camden	£ 3.14. 3
149 I	Booth, Joseph	Supplies		Lacey's Regiment	Camden	£ 1.12. 1½
152 I	Campbell, Thomas	Supplies & Militia Duty		Neil's Regiment	Camden	£ 9.10.
154 I	Campbell, Andrew	Militia Duty	Ret^d by Capt Tate	Sumter & Henderson	Camden	£ 5.17. 1½
167 I	Carsan, James	Militia Duty	Ret^d by Capt Tate	Capt. Wallace	Camden	£ 3.18. 6

Numb. & Book	To whom Granted	For what Granted			District	Amount Indent
171 I	Clark, James	Militia Duty	Retd by Capt Tate	Capt. Steel	Camden	£ 2. 2.10¼
180 I	Carter, John	Militia Duty	Retd by Capt Tate	Capt. Steel	Camden	£ 2. 2.10¼
181 I	Corkshadden, Robert	Supplies & Militia Duty		Cols. Hill & Bratton	Camden	£ 6.14. 1½
183 I	Creath, Junr. Willm.	Militia Duty	Retd by Capt Tate	Capt. Walker	Camden	£ 8. 5. 8½
186 I	Crawford, Nathl.	Militia Duty	Retd by Capt Tate	Capt. Hannah	State of Georgia	£ 6. 5. 8½
190 I	Cloud, James	Militia Duty	Retd by Capt Tate	Capt. Steel	Camden Dist.	£ 5. 1. 5
196 I	Chambers, John	Militia Duty	Retd by Capt Tate	Capt. Steel	Camden Dist.	£ 5. .
203 I	Castellaw, William	Supplies	Retd by Capt Tate	Col. Bratton	Camden Dist.	£ 1. 8. 6¾
212 I	Dunnam, James	Supplies	Retd by Capt Tate	Genl. Sumter	Camden Dist.	£ 7.18. 6¾
229 I	Elliotte, Esta. James	Supplies	Retd by Capt Tate	Capt. McClure	Camden Dist.	£ 36. 7. 1½
245 I	Ferguson, Samuel	Supplies	Retd by Capt Tate	Capt. Steel	Camden Dist.	£ 5. .
246 I	Ferguson, Elizabeth	Supplies	Retd by Capt Tate		Camden Dist.	£ 1.17. 1½
291 I	Hagartee, John	Militia Duty	Retd by Capt Tate		Camden Dist.	£ 11.11. 5
296 I	Hood, Esta. William	Supplies	Retd by Capt Tate	Genl. Sumter	Camden Dist.	£ 5.16. ¾
297 I	Harrison, Thomas	Militia Duty	Retd by Capt Tate	Capt. Potter	Camden Dist.	£ 4. 8. 6¾
298 I	Harper, Hance	Militia Duty	Retd by Capt Tate	Capts. Pegan & Mills	Camden Dist.	£ 6. .
299 I	Hail, Henry	Militia Duty	Retd by Capt Tate	Capt. Steel	Camden Dist.	£ 2. 2.10¼
303 I	Hanna, Jun. William	Militia Duty	Retd by Capt Tate	Capt. Hanna	Camden Dist.	£ 10. 1. 5
304 I	Hanna, Senr. William	Supplies	Retd by Capt Tate	Capt. Hanna	Camden Dist.	£ 3.15. 8½
309 I	Hart, Esta. Jacob	Militia Duty	Retd by Capt Tate	Capt. Mills	Camden Dist.	£ 5. .
315 I	Jeffers, Samuel	Militia Duty	Retd by Capt Tate	Bratton's & Hills Regts.	Camden Dist.	£ 11.16. 5
325 I	King, Kerby	Militia Duty	Retd by Capt Tate	Capt. Steel	Camden Dist.	£ 1. 8. 6¾
333 I	Kelsey or Kelly, James	Supplies	Retd by Capt Tate	Genl. Sumter	Camden Dist.	£ 3. 5. 8½
335 I	Kerr, Senr. John	Supplies	Retd by Capt Tate	Genl. Sumter	Camden Dist.	£ .13.11
336 I	Keleaugh, John	Militia Duty	Retd by Capt Tate	Col. Bratton	Camden Dist.	£ 8. 8. 6¾
343 I	Lauglen, Anthy.	Militia Duty	Retd by Capt Tate	Col. Bratton	Camden Dist.	£ 1.18. 6¾
352 I	Lott, Jun. John	Militia Duty	Retd by Capt Tate	Capt. Steel	Camden Dist.	£ 2. 2.10¼
354 I	Lipham, Daniel	Militia Duty	Retd by Capt Tate		Camden Dist.	£ 2.17. 1½
357 I	Lewis, Benjn.	Militia Duty	Retd by Capt Tate	Capt. Gill	Camden Dist.	£ 1.12.10¼
367 I	Barber, Mary	Supplies/Retd by Capt Tate	W. Arthur	Sumter's Brigade	Orangeburgh	£ 3. 4. 2
382 I	Bush, John	Supplies/Retd by Capt Tate	W. Arthur	Col. Thompson	Orangeburgh	£ 1.10.11¼

Numb. & Book	To whom Granted	For what Granted			District	Amount Indent
388 I	Cook, John	Supplies	W. Arthur	Henderson's Brigade	Orangeburgh	£ 2. 1.
395 I	Cullreaker, Joseph	Supplies	W. Arthur	Sumter's Brigade	Orangeburgh	£ 11.11.
397 I	Danseller, Henry John	Supplies	W. Arthur	Sumter's Brigade	Orangeburgh	£ 1.15. 1¾
399 I	Danseller, Henry	Supplies	W. Arthur	Col. Thompson	Orangeburgh	£ .18. 9
401 I	Eikester, or Eikesber, Mary	Supplies	W. Arthur		Orangeburgh	£ 1.17. 6
405 I	Fogle, Barbara	Supplies	W. Arthur		Orangeburgh	£ 3.17.
412 I	Green, William	Supplies	W. Arthur	Sumter's Brigade	Orangeburgh	£ 3. 4. 2
417 I	Harter, Nicholas	Supplies	W. Arthur	Sumter's Brigade	Orangeburgh	£ 7.19. 4½
423 I	Herlong, Jacob	Supplies	W. Arthur	Sumter's Brigade	Orangeburgh	£ 6. 7. 7½
440 I	Johnston, John	Supplies	W. Arthur	Henderson's B.	Orangeburgh	£ 4. 5. 8½
443 I	Keller, George	Supplies	W. Arthur	Col. J. Thomas, Jr.	Orangeburgh	£ .11. 3
445 I	Kennelley, Elizabeth	Supplies	W. Arthur	Col. J. Thomas, Jr.	Orangeburgh	£ 7. 1. 7
449 I	Keagler, Andrew	Supplies	W. Arthur	Henderson's Brigade	Orangeburgh	£ 8.11. ½
450 I	Kirkland, Susanna	Supplies	W. Arthur	Genl. Pickens	Orangeburgh	£ 8.11.11½
454 I	Lee or See, Nicholas	Supplies	W. Arthur	Genl. Pickens	Orangeburgh	£ 3.17.
455 I	Lee or See, Abraham	Supplies	W. Arthur	Genl. Pickens	Orangeburgh	£ 7. 1. 2
456 I	Libolt, John	Supplies	W. Arthur	Genl. Pickens	Orangeburgh	£ 1.11.
458 I	Lewis, George	Supplies	W. Arthur	Genl. Sumter	Orangeburgh	£ 1.18. 6
465 I	Morreau, Mary	Supplies	W. Arthur	Genl. Sumter	Orangeburgh	£ 8. 1.
469 I	Myers, John	Supplies	W. Arthur	Genl. Sumter	Orangeburgh	£ 1.10. ¾
472 I	Nevelen, Jacob	Supplies	W. Arthur	Genl. Sumter	Orangeburgh	£ 2.12. 6
473 I	Niblin, Philip	Supplies	W. Arthur		Orangeburgh	£ 3. 1. 7
475 I	Nuble, Philip	Supplies	W. Arthur	Genl. Sumter	Orangeburgh	£ 6. 8. 4
483 I	Pew, William	Supplies	W. Arthur	Genl. Sumter	Orangeburgh	£ 3.17.
487 I	Reed, Francis	Supplies	W. Arthur	Col. Postell	Orangeburgh	£ 2. 3. 7½
488 I	Reeves, Ann	Supplies	W. Arthur	Gl. Henderson	Orangeburgh	£ 3.17.
490 I	Rivers, John	Supplies	W. Arthur	Gl. Sumter	Orangeburgh	£ 2. 3. 7½
493 I	Rumph, David	Supplies	W. Arthur	Gl. Sumter	Orangeburgh	£ 6. 8. 4
516 I	Sandlen, Daniel	Supplies	W. Arthur	Gl. Henderson	Orangeburgh	£ 15.13. 1½
521 I	Tanseller, Mary	Supplies	W. Arthur		Orangeburgh	£ 3.17.
525 I	Walter, Jasper	Supplies		Col. Thompson	Orangeburgh	£ 1. 2. 6

Numb. & Book	To whom Granted	For what Granted			District	Amount Indent
546 I	Bell, Robert	Supplies & Militia Duty			Orangeburgh	£ 129.13.11
560 I	Adams, Thomas	Militia Duty		Col. Anderson	Ninety Six	£ 15. 5. 8½
568 I	Barksdale, Hickison	Militia Duty		Col. Anderson	Ninety Six	£ 1. . .
571 I	Brown, Est^a. John	Militia Duty & a Horse &c. lost		Col. Anderson	Ninety Six	£ 19. 7. 1½
581 I	Boyes, Charles	Militia Duty		Col. Anderson	Ninety Six	£ 10. 14. 3¾
597 I	Braziel, Wood	Militia Duty		Col. Anderson	Ninety Six	£ 1. . .
604 I	Bready, William	Militia Duty		Col. Anderson	Ninety Six	£ 5.14. 3¼
607 I	Burdel, William	Militia Duty		Col. Anderson	Ninety Six	£ 14. 8. 6¾
613 I	Blythe, Samuel	Militia Duty		Col. Anderson	Ninety Six	£ 2.12.10¼
618 I	Baggs, John	Militia Duty		Col. Anderson	Ninety Six	£ 5.11. 5
623 I	Bonner, James	Militia Duty		Col. Anderson	Ninety Six	£ 10.17. 1½
17 K	Bellinger, Jun. Edmund	Supplies			Charleston	£ 17.10.
32 K	Copelin, Est^a. John	Supplies			Charleston	£ 5.15. 6
42 K	Elliott, Est^a. Barnard				Charleston	£ 129. 2. 5
44 K	Forster, John	Militia Duty Guard^g Pub. Stores			Camden	£ 8.14. 2
115 K	Read, James	Supplies		Genl. Henderson	Orangeburgh	£ 3.16. 1
123 K	Shrewsberry & Lawrence	Twenty Oars			Charleston	£ 4.11.11½
124 K	Sommers, John	Supplies			Charleston	£ 37.17. 9¾
127 K	Werner, Est^a. Jacob	Supplies			Charleston	£ 1.18. 7
128 K	Watts, Est^a. John	Supplies for G. Town garrison			Georgetown	£ 4.12. 4¾
138 K	Askew, Thomas	Supplies	W^m. Wigg	Granville Co. Reg.	Beaufort	£ 2.11. 4
139 K	Allergottie, Anthony	Supplies	W^m. Wigg	Granville Co. Reg.	Beaufort	£ 2.19. 4½
146 K	Devant, Ann	Supplies	W^m. Wigg	Granville Co. Reg.	Beaufort	£ .19.10
149 K	Keal, Abraham	Supplies	W^m. Wigg	Genl. Wayne	Beaufort	£ 6.18. 6
151 K	Lewis, Winifred	Supplies	W^m. Wigg		Beaufort	£ 9.15.
152 K	McKee, John	Indigo Impressed	W^m. Wigg		Beaufort	£ 35. 7.
154 K	Mullett, Gideon	Supplies	W^m. Wigg	Genl. Wayne	Beaufort	£ 2.11. 4
158 K	Sealy, Biggin	Supplies	W^m. Wigg	Col. Stafford	Beaufort	£ 2.11. 4
161 K	Trezevant, Isaac Stephen	Caps for a Regt. of Horse			Charleston	£ 11.13. 4

Numb. & Book	To whom Granted	For what Granted		District	Amount Indent
201 K	Copacke, Joseph	Supplies	Gen¹. Pickens	Ninety Six	£ 1. 4. 3¼
210 K	Cox, James	Militia Duty	Col. Anderson	Ninety Six	£ 2.17. 1½
221 K	Cain, Estᵃ. James	Militia Duty	Col. Anderson	Ninety Six	£ 5. 7. 1½
228 K	Cowan, John	Militia Duty	Col. Anderson	Ninety Six	£ 8.11. 5
234 K	Clark, Sen. Alexander	Militia Duty	Col. Anderson	Ninety Six	£ 15. 2.10¼
236 K	Crosby, James	Militia Duty	Col. Anderson	Ninety Six	£ 15. .
238 K	Campbell, Henry	Militia Duty	Col. Anderson	Ninety Six	£ 4. 7. 1½
239 K	Campbell, Estᵃ. Patrick	Militia Duty	Col. Anderson	Ninety Six	£ 11.11. 5
244 K	Calhoun, Estᵃ. John	Militia Duty	Col. Anderson	Ninety Six	£ 4. .
262 K	Coughran, Estᵃ. Robert	Militia Duty	Col. Anderson	Ninety Six	£ 6. 2.10½
268 K	Crawford, Gilbert	Militia Duty	Col. Anderson	Ninety Six	£ 10. .
6 L	Altman, Sarah	Supplies		Camden	£ 2. 3. 6
26 L	Brown, James	Supplies & Militia Duty	Hill's, Wimm's Regiment	Camden	£ 5. 1. 4¾
29 L	Butler, Pierce	Supplies		Charleston	£ 57. 1.
48 L	Danel, Thomas	Supplies		Beaufort	£ 11.11.
64 L	Fleming, William	Militia Duty at Brier Creek	Capt. Black	Camden	£ 6. 5. 8½
65 L	Franklin, Benjamin	Supplies		Camden	£ 3.17.
73 L	Gore, Rachel	Supplies		Camden	£ 2. 5. 8½
78 L	Harris, Jesse	Militia Duty	Capt. Gray	Camden	£ 6. 7. 1½
81 L	Hannah, Richard	Militia Duty	Marion's Brigade	Geo Town	£ 5.12.10¼
83 L	Henderson, Archibald	Militia Duty	Capt. Cooper	Camden	£ 4.17. 1½
90 L	Hughes, Samuel	Militia Duty	Cˡ. Bratton	Camden	£ 4. 5. 8½
91 L	Jefferson, John	Militia Duty		Camden	£ 2.10.
94 L	Johnson, John	Militia Duty	Capt. Gray	Camden	£ 10.17.10¼
106 L	Lowder, Zilpha	Supplies	Gen¹. Marion	Camden	£ 3. 5.
114 L	Maston, Thomas	Cont. Duty		Camden	£ 18.13. 4
116 L	Mathews, Edmund	Supplies		Charleston	£ 31.18. 8
151 L	Paul, Mathew	Contˡ. Duty			£ 11.13. 4
152 L	Person, Enoch	Supplies	Gen¹. Pickens	Ninety Six	£ 14. 8. ½
157 L	Pen, Azariah	Supplies	Gen¹. Pickens	Ninety Six	£ 4.18. 9¼
160 L	Pierson, Edward	Supplies	Col. Wᵐ. Davis	Beaufort	£ 3. 5. 3

Numb. & Book	To whom Granted	For what Granted			District	Amount Indent
164 L	Demsey, Jesse Purkins, Willis	Cont^{l}. Duty				£ 118. 4. 3
166 L	Price, Daniel	Supplies		Genl. Sumter	Camden	£ 2. 6. 8¼
180 L	Saunders, Est^{a}. James	Supplies			Cha^{s}ton	£ 21. .
189 L	Bridges, Joseph	Militia Duty	p. paybill of Lieut. Danl. Smith	Col. Bratton	Camden	£ 3. 8. 6¾
190 L	Parker, John	Militia Duty	p. paybill of Lieut. Danl. Smith	Col. Bratton	Camden	£ 3. 8. 6¾
191 L	Harris, Thomas	Militia Duty	p. paybill of Lieut. Danl. Smith	Col. Bratton	Camden	£ 1.14. 3½
192 L	Logan, Thomas	Militia Duty	p. paybill of Lieut. Danl. Smith	Col. Bratton	Camden	£ 1.14. 3½
193 L	Dobbins, James	Militia Duty	p. paybill of Lieut. Danl. Smith	Col. Bratton	Camden	£ 1.14. 3½
194 L	Dover, Zeph^{a}.	Militia Duty	p. paybill of Lieut. Danl. Smith	Col. Bratton	Camden	£ 1.14. 3½
209 L	Walters, Mary	Supplies		Genl. Marion	Georgetown	£ 16.17. 4½
212 L	Wallace, Michael	Smith's Work		Col. Kershaw	Orangeburgh	£ 3.10. 6¼
217 L	Warren, Robert	Cont^{l}. Duty				£ 20. 4. 5½
218 L	Weas, William	Supplies			Camden	£ 4. 9.10
224 L	Wragg, John	Supplies			Charleston	£ 24.15. 3
228 L	Moorehead, William	Militia Duty	Ret^{d} by Capt Tate		Camden	£ 3. .
239 L	Moore, Jun. James	Militia Duty	Ret^{d} by Capt Tate	Capt. Wallace	Camden	£ 5. 8. 6¾
251 L	Miller, John	Sundries (Duty & Supp^{s}.)	Ret^{d} by Capt Tate	Capt. Bratton	Camden	£ 33. 2. 10¼
263 L	Martin, Edward	Militia Duty	Ret^{d} by Capt Tate	Capt. McCluer	Camden	£ 20. .
265 L	McCance, William	Militia Duty	Ret^{d} by Capt Tate	Col. Winn	Camden	£ 3. 7. 1½
280 L	McCowen, James	Militia Duty	Ret^{d} by Capt Tate	Capt. Steel	Camden	£ 6. .
289 L	Morrow, Joseph	Militia Duty	Ret^{d} by Capt Tate	Capt. McCluer & Jones	Camden	£ 46. 7. 1½
291 L	Morrow, Jun. Samuel	Militia Duty	Ret^{d} by Capt Tate	Col. Lacey	Camden	£ 22.17. 1½
300 L	McClearey, Robert	Supplies		Col. Moore	Camden	£ 2. 4.11
316 L	Nickells, Thomas	Militia Duty		Capt. Steel	Camden	£ 2. 2.10¼
317 L	Neely, Jun. Robert	Militia Duty		Capt. Hanna	Camden	£ 7. 15. 8½

Numb. & Book	To whom Granted	For what Granted			District	Amount Indent
321 L	Neely, John	Sundries			Camden	£ 4.15.
332 L	Patton, Benjamin	Militia Duty		Cols. Neel & Anderson	Camden	£ 8.11.5
334 L	Patton, Jacob	Militia Duty		Capts. Walker & Neeley	Camden	£ 10. 8. 6¾
346 L	Patterson, Joseph	Supplies		Genl. Henderson	Camden	£ .15.
353 L	Phelpes, Moses	Militia Duty		Capt. Henderson	Camden	£ 11. 8. 6¾
357 L	Robertson, Joseph	Militia Duty		Capt. Bell	Camden	£ 5.14. 3¾
358 L	Robinson, Patrick	Militia Duty		Capt. Barnet	Camden	£ .11.5
368 L	Ramsey, Robert	Militia Duty		Capt. Hillhouse	Camden	£ 3. 8. 6¾
382 L	Sellars, John	Supplies	Ret'd by Capt Tate		Camden	£ 4. .6
400 L	Sandiford, Samuel	Militia Duty	Ret'd by Capt Tate	Capt. Steel	Camden	£ 5. 1. 5
408 L	Shaw, William	Militia Duty	Ret'd by Capt Tate	Moffett	Camden	£ 4. 5. 8½
430 L	Thomson, William	Militia Duty	Ret'd by Capt Tate		Camden	£ 9.14. 3
433 L	Townsend, Henry	Militia Duty	Ret'd by Capt Tate		Camden	£ 13.11. 5
436 L	Taylor, Estd. William	Supplies	Ret'd by Capt Tate	Genl. Sumter	Camden	£ 2. 6. 5
444 L	Vance, William	Militia Duty	Ret'd by Capt Tate	Capt. Moffett	Camden	£ 4. 5. 8½
446 L	Whitehead, Daniel	Militia Duty	Ret'd by Capt Tate	Capt. Moffett	Camden	£ 4. 5. 8½
448 L	Wheeler, Mary	Supplies	Ret'd by Capt Tate		Camden	£ 1.15. 8½
457 L	Wright, Henry	Militia Duty	Ret'd by Capt Tate		Camden	£ 3. . .
466 L	Wyley, William	Sundries	Ret'd by Capt Tate	Capts. Walker & Neeley	Camden	£ 11.14. 3¾
475 L	Williamson, William	Supplies	Ret'd by Capt Tate	Col. Bratton	Camden	£ .5. 8½
13 N	Garlant, William	Militia Duty		Genl. Marion	Camden	£ 2.13.10
34 N	Henderson, (Genl.) William	Supplies & Ferriage			Camden	£ 16. 6. 3
58 N	Hewey, James	Supplies & Militia Duty &c.		Cols. Kershaw Marshall Kimball	Camden	£ 24. 4. 7½
72 N	Allston, Peter	Supplies	Powe's Return		Cheraw	£ 8.15.10½
75 N	Allen, Benjamin	Militia Duty	Powe's Return		Cheraw	£ 2.10.
85 N	Brown, Benjamin	Militia Duty	Powe's Return		Cheraw	£ 2. .
95 N	Burquett, Ephraim	Militia Duty	Powe's Return		Cheraw	£ 5. 7. 1½

Numb. & Book	To whom Granted	For what Granted		District		Amount Indent
97 N	Bridges, John	Militia Duty	Powe's Return	Cheraw		£ 2. 8. 6¾
98 N	Bridges, Mary	Supplies	Powe's Return	Cheraw		£ .12. 6
104 N	Ball, William	Militia Duty	Powe's Return	Cheraw		£ 9. . 4½
111 N	Bruce, Caleb	Supplies	Powe's Return	Cheraw		£ 6. 5. 9
119 N	Childs, John	Boat hire	Powe's Return	Cheraw		£ 14. .
123 N	Clayter, Laurence	Militia Duty	Powe's Return	Cheraw		£ 2.10.
126 N	Cherrey, William	Militia Duty	Powe's Return	Cheraw		£ 2.11. 5
129 N	Cox, Josiah	Militia Duty	Powe's Return	Cheraw		£ 2.11. 5
130 N	Cox, William	Militia Duty	Powe's Return	Cheraw		£ 5. 1. 5
135 N	Cole, Daniel David	Supplies	Powe's Return	Cheraw		£ 2.11. 8¾
142 N	Cane, Richard	Militia Duty	Powe's Return	Cheraw		£ 2. 2.10¼
143 N	Crummy, Stephen	Militia Duty	Powe's Return	Cheraw		£ 2.11. 5
146 N	Collins, Cary	Supplies	Powe's Return	Cheraw		£ 4. 9.10
149 N	Harman, Clarke Clarke, Harman	Militia Duty	Powe's Return	Cheraw		£ 2.11. 5
152 N	Cone, Matthew	Militia Duty	Powe's Return	Cheraw		£ 3. 1. 5
154 N	Coker, Nathan	Militia Duty	Powe's Return	Cheraw		£ 2.11. 5
158 N	David, Zekiel	Militia Duty	Powe's Return	Cheraw		£ 2. 1. 5
166 N	Douglas, Joshua	Militia Duty	Powe's Return	Cheraw		£ 5. .
178 N	Donham, Joseph	Sundries	Powe's Return	Cheraw		£ 3.14. 2
187 N	Fields, Samuel	Militia Duty	Powe's Return	Cheraw		£ 2.17. 1½
189 N	Flanagan, Mrs.	Supplies	Powe's Return	Cheraw		£ 1.18. 6
190 N	Faulkner, John	Militia Duty	Powe's Return	Cheraw		£ 2. 2.10½
194 N	Fitzpatrick, James	Militia Duty	Powe's Return	Cheraw		£ 2. 7. 1½
204 N	Gardner, William	Militia Duty	Powe's Return	Cheraw		£ 4. 8. 6¾
216 N	Gibson, Roger	Supplies	Powe's Return	Cheraw		£ 3.17.
225 N	Gilmore, Edward	Supplies	Powe's Return	Cheraw		£ .16. 4
254 N	McClellan, Samuel	Supplies		Genl. Sumter	Camden	£ 10.16. 2
255 N	Picket, Micajah	Supplies			Camden	£ 1.17. 4
267 N	Rivers, Benjamin	Militia Duty		Major Crawford	Camden	£ 4. .
278 N	Scott, Archd.	Militia Duty		Col. Bratton	Camden	£ 8.17. 1½
292 N	Tucker, John	Militia Duty		Capt. McCooll	Camden	£ 10. .
294 N	Tomlinson, Nathl.	Militia Duty		Major Crawford	Camden	£ 5. 1. 5

Numb. & Book	To whom Granted	For what Granted			District	Amount Indent
304 N	Wilson, James	Supplies		Col. S. Hammond	Ninety Six	£ 3.15.
305 N	Wigg, William Hazard	Supplies			Beaufort	£ 40.19. 2
308 N	Woodcock, Robert	Cont. Duty			~~George~~	£ 18.13. 4
318 N	Lynch, Est^a. Thomas	Supplies			Georgetown	£ 92. 9.9
324 N	Young, John	Supplies	Tate's Return		Camden	£ 2. 1.9½
332 N	Sanders, Est^a William	Supplies			Charleston	£ 33.12.
333 N	Thomson, Col. James	~~Militia-Duty~~ Supplies			Beaufort	£ 77. .
335 N	Addis, Richard	Supplies			Beaufort	£ 15. 5. 8½
17 O	Lesley, John					
18 O	Linn, Mary	Supplies		Genl. Sumter	Camden	£ 2. 2.10¼
30 O	Mayers, Elijah	Militia Duty		Col. Winn	Camden	£ 11.12. 3¾
32 O	Martin, Robert			Col. Maham	Cha^ston	£ 84.
48 O	McDowell, David	Supplies		Col. Thomas, Jun.	Ninety Six	£ 6.12. 8½
53 O	Middleton, Henry	Two Horses		Col. Maham	Charleston	£ 108.15.
59 O	Moultrie, William	Supplies		Genl. Marion	Charleston	£ 12. 3.10
74 O	Noble, Thomas	A Mare				£ 10.19.11
129 O	Johnson, Jacob	Cont^el. Duty				£ 12.17. 1½
175 O	Love, ~~James~~ John	Supplies		Col. Lacey	Camden	£ 13.19. 3½
184 O	~~Mathews~~ Matheney, James	Ferriage			Orangeburgh	£ 1. 7. 6
187 O	Marshall, William	Supplies		Genl. Sumter	Camden	£ 4. .
189 O	Mackey, Thomas	Militia Duty & a Gun lost		Col. Kimball	Camden	£ 10. .
190 O	Mabrey, Daniel	Militia Duty		Col. Taylor & Bratton	Camden	£ 24. 2.10¼
195 O	McCowen, Alex^r.	Supplies			Camden	£ 2.11 . 4
216 O	Martin, Jun. James	Ferriages &c			Georgetown	£ 8.16.11
223 O	Audey, Christ.	Cont^el. Duty			~~Camden~~	£ 27.15.10
242 O	Bacon, Thomas	Supplies			~~Camden~~	£ 4.13 . 4
244 O	Barnet, Est^a. Joseph	Supplies		Genl. Sumter	Camden	£ 21.15.
247 O	Brumfield, Elizabeth	Supplies			Camden	£ 3. 4. 2
248 O	Bacon, Thomas	Supplies			Camden	£ 27.11.10
249 O	Brown, Burrell	Militia Duty		Genl. Marion	Camden	£ 2.13.10
272 O	Clayton, Isaac	Militia Duty		Genl. Marion		£ 2. 2. 8

Numb. & Book	To whom Granted	For what Granted		District	Amount Indent
287 O	Carter, William	Cont¹. Duty			£ 6.13.10½
309 O	Drayton, Thomas	Supplies		Charleston	£ 15.10. 1
313 O	Dupont, Charles	Supplies		Beaufort	£ 19. 6. 6¾
316 O	Dean, Abner	Militia Duty	Capt. Liles		£ 6. 18. 6¾
318 O	Elliott, Estª. Barnard	Supplies		Charleston	£ 223.15. 0½
360 O	Davis, Jun. James	Militia Duty	Capt. Cowan	Ninety Six	£ 4. .
362 O	Davis, Thomas	Militia Duty	Capt. Pickens	Ninety Six	£ 2.14. 3¼
366 O	Davis, Gardner	Militia Duty	Capt. Cowan	Ninety Six	£ 6. 4. 3¼
370 O	Davis, Joseph	Militia Duty	Capt. Calhoun	Ninety Six	£ 2. 4. 3
373 O	Dardon, George	Militia Duty	Capt. Cowan	Ninety Six	£ 5.14. 3¼
374 O	Dardon, John	Militia Duty	Capt. Cowan	Ninety Six	£ 5.14. 3¼
376 O	Darling, Ephraim	Militia Duty	Capt. Freeman	Ninety Six	£ 4. 7. 1½
377 O	Damewood, Estª. Henry	Militia Duty	Capt. Liddle	Ninety Six	£ 18.14. 5
378 O	Delwood, William	Militia Duty		Ninety Six	£ 1.15. 8½
382 O	Donaldson, Mathew	Militia Duty	Capt. Pickens	Ninety Six	£ 2. 2.10¼
387 O	Doss, Joel	Militia Duty	Capt. Pickens	Ninety Six	£ 6. 2.10¼
398 O	Edds, John	Militia Duty		Ninety Six	£ 3.14. 3¼
399 O	Eddins, John	Militia Duty	Capt. Strain	Ninety Six	£ 2. 5. 8½
401 O	Elliott, William	Militia Duty	Capt. Calhoun	Ninety Six	£ 7. 1. 5

Numb. & Book	To whom Granted	For what Granted			District	Amount Indent
409 O	Finlay, Estᵃ. John	Militia Duty	Anderson's Return & Regiment	Capt. Pickens	Ninety Six	£ 39. 4. 3½
416 O	Ford, Edward	Militia Duty	Anderson's Return & Regiment	Capt. Dawson	Ninety Six	£ 4. 7. 6
429 O	Garrineau, Peter	Militia Duty Anderson's Return & Regiment	Anderson's Return & Regiment	Capt. Bouchillon	Ninety Six	£ 14.11. 5
433 O	Garner, Richard	Militia Duty Anderson's Return & Regiment	Anderson's Return & Regiment	Capt. Freeman	Ninety Six	£ 13.18. 6¾
434 O	Gentry, Cain	Militia Duty	Anderson's Return & Regiment	Capt. Dawson	Ninety Six	£ 5.11. 5
437 O	Giles, Robert	Militia Duty	Anderson's Return & Regiment	Capt. McGaw	Ninety Six	£ 1. 2.10¼
444 O	Gillespie, Andrew	Militia Duty	Anderson's Return & Regiment		Ninety Six	£ 4.11. 5
452 O	Griffin, Lane	Militia Duty	Anderson's Return & Regiment	Capt. Calhoun	Ninety Six	£ 12. 2.10¼
454 O	Griffin, William	Militia Duty	Anderson's Return & Regiment	Capt. Calhoun & Freeman	Ninety Six	£ 18.15. 8½
456 O	Griffin, James	Militia Duty	Anderson's Return & Regiment	Capt. Calhoun & Freeman	Ninety Six	£ 9.14. 3¼
464 O	Hannah, James	Militia Duty	Anderson's Return & Regiment	Capt. Anderson	Ninety Six	£ 42.14. 3¼
473 O	Hay, Charles	Militia Duty	Anderson's Return & Regiment	Capt. Baskins	Ninety Six	£ 6. 5. 8½
474 O	Harris, John	Militia Duty	Anderson's Return & Regiment	Capt. Cowan	Ninety Six	£ 1. .
477 O	Hall, Hugh	Militia Duty	Anderson's Return & Regiment		Ninety Six	£ 5. 8. 6¾
478 O	Haggard, Jonadab	Militia Duty	Anderson's Return & Regiment	Capt. Anderson	Ninety Six	£ 13.17. 1½
479 O	Harrard, Hardy	Militia Duty	Anderson's Return & Regiment	Capt. Norwood	Ninety Six	£ 18. 4. 3¼

Numb. & Book	To whom Granted	For what Granted			District	Amount Indent
494 O	Hill, Adam	Militia Duty	Anderson's Return & Regiment	Capt. Dawson	Ninety Six	£ 2. 2.10¼
497 O	Holland, John	Militia Duty	Anderson's Return & Regiment	Capt. Calhoun	Ninety Six	£ 7. 5. 8½
502 O	Hogwood, Reuben	Militia Duty	Anderson's Return & Regiment	Capt. Irwin	Ninety Six	£ 14. 4. 3¼
509 O	Hutchinson, Thomas	Militia Duty	Anderson's Return & Regiment	Capt. Cowan	Ninety Six	£ 3.14. 3¼
511 O	Hutson, Nath[l].	Militia Duty & Driving Cattle	Anderson's Return & Regiment	Capt. Herd	Ninety Six	£ 7. 7. 1½
512 O	Hutson, William	Militia Duty	Anderson's Return & Regiment	Capt. Willson	Ninety Six	£ 8. 8. 6¾
513 O	Hutson, David	Militia Duty & Driving Cattle	Anderson's Return & Regiment	Capt. Herd	Ninety Six	£ 7. 7. 1½
514 O	Hutson, James	Militia Duty	Anderson's Return & Regiment	Capt. Pickens	Ninety Six	£ 3. .
515 O	Hutson, Robert	Militia Duty	Anderson's Return & Regiment	Capt. Calhoun	Ninety Six	£ 1. 2.10¼
516 O	Hutson, James	Militia Duty	Anderson's Return & Regiment	Capt. Calhoun	Ninety Six	£ 8. .
528 O	Jones, John	Militia Duty	Anderson's Return & Regiment	Capt. M[c]Gaw	Ninety Six	£ 3. 7.10¼
537 O	Johnston, Est[a]. John	Militia Duty	Anderson's Return & Regiment		Ninety Six	£ 1. 5. 8½
543 O	Jordan, Est[a]. Adam	Militia Duty	Anderson's Return & Regiment		Ninety Six	£ 7. 8. 6¾
559 O	Kitts, Francis	Militia Duty	Anderson's Return & Regiment	Capt. Pickens & Strain	Ninety Six	£ 26. . 4¼
569 O	Spears, David	Militia Duty	Powe's Return	Marion's Brigade	Cheraw	£ 2.10.
570 O	Stevens, John & Darby, Jacob	Militia Duty	Powe's Return		Cheraw	£ 3.11. 5
572 O	Starks, Henry	Militia Duty	Powe's Return		Cheraw	£ 2.11. 5
586 O	Thorp, Eleazer	Militia Duty	Powe's Return		Cheraw	£ 9.14. 3¼

Numb. & Book	To whom Granted	For what Granted			District	Amount Indent
590 O	Tearel, Will[m].	Supplies	Powe's Return		Cheraw	£ .14.
601 O	Warren, John	Supplies	Powe's Return	Marion's Brigade	Cheraw	£ 26. 5.
605 O	Wise, James	Militia Duty	Powe's Return		Cheraw	£ 3. 1. 5
606 O	Wise, James	Militia Duty	Powe's Return		Cheraw	£ 2. 1. 5
612 O	Wood, Benj[a].	Militia Duty	Powe's Return		Cheraw	£ 2.15. 8½
617 O	Whitfield, Benj[a].	Militia Duty	Powe's Return		Cheraw	£ 2.11. 5
643 O	Windham, Jesse	Militia Duty	Powe's Return		Cheraw	£ 2.17. 1½
662 O	Gray, James	Militia Duty		Capt. Wilson	Ninety Six	£ 6. 3. 3¾
671 O	Harbour, Walter	Supplies	Anderson's Return		Ninety Six	£ .15. 8½
2 P	Andress, Israel	Militia Duty				£ 20. 5. 4¾
3 P	Adams, David	Suplies			Camden	£ 5. 9. 2
9 P	Bennet, Hugh	Supplies		Marion's Brigade	Georgetown	£ 4.18. 9
16 P	Blair, James	Waggon hire			C	£ 17. 1.
18 P	Benbow, Martha	Supplies			Camden	£ 3.11.10
19 P	Bellinger, Est[a]. Will[m].	Supplies			Charleston	£ 3.10.
24 P	Carter, Robert	Supplies		Col. Lee	Camden Georgetown	£ 8.17. 4
36 P	Clarke, Bartly	Supplies		Col. Lee	Georgetown	£ 1. 8.
43 P	Donald, John	Militia Duty		Marion's Brigade	Georgetown	£ 7.12.10¼
54 P	Gourdine, Est[a]. Theodore	Supplies		Marion's Brigade	Charleston	£ 33.16. 8
56 P	Greenwood's Wharf	Wharfages			Charleston	£ 2.13. 6¾
67 P	Hood, Will[m].	Supplies			Camden	£ 2.11. 4
80 P	M[c]Queen, Alex[r].	Supplies		Col. Maham	Cha[s]ton	£ 11.19.
83 P	Malone, Will[m].	Supplies		Maj. Otterson	Camden	£ 1.10.
99 P	Murfey, Drury	A Mare lost				£ 9.12.10¼
100 P	Neilson, Isaac	Supplies		Marion's Brigade		£ 32.14. 6
108 P	Parker, Daniel	Saddle		Major Jackson		£ 3. 5. 3
110 P	Perret, Sen. John Est[a].	Supplies		Gen[ls]. Sumter & Marion		£ 19. 7. 2¾
124 P	Saunders, Charles	Supplies			Charleston	£ 37. 1. 9
130 P	Smith, Mary	Supplies			Georgetown	£ 7. 1. 2
145 P	Winders, Est[a]. James	Militia Duty		Col. Anderson	Ninety Six	£ 13.17. 1½

Numb. & Book	To whom Granted	For what Granted		St. Comm^y.	District	Amount Indent
147 P	Willawer, John	Supplies		St. Comm^y.	Cheraw	£ 3. 4. 2
150 P	Windham, Amos	Supplies			Cheraw	£ 6. 8. 4
168 P	Leach, Thomas	Militia Duty	Anderson's Return	Capt. Freeman	Ninety Six	£ 3. 2.10¼
169 P	Leech, John	Militia Duty	Anderson's Return	Capt. Calhoun	Ninety Six	£ 16. .
171 P	Liddle, Sen. James	Supplies	Anderson's Return		Ninety Six	£ 4.10. 4¼
192 P	Lyon, Joseph	Militia Duty	Anderson's Return	Capt. Pickens	Ninety Six	£ 5. 5. 8½
200 P	Luckie, Jun. Willm.	Militia Duty	Anderson's Return	Capt. Pickens	Ninety Six	£ 11.14. 3¼
217 P	Murray, James	Militia Duty	Anderson's Return	Capt. Herd	Ninety Six	£ 7. 7. 1½
221 P	Murray, Est^a. David	Militia Duty	Anderson's Return	Capt. Freeman	Ninety Six	£ 18.11. 5
237 P	Morris, Garret	Militia Duty	Anderson's Return	Norwood	Ninety Six	£ 2. 2.10¼
241 P	McFadden, Arch^d.	Militia Duty	Anderson's Return		Ninety Six	£ 4.10.
242 P	McFadden, Andrew	Militia Duty	Anderson's Return			£ 4. 5. 8½
248 P	Mitchell, Thomas	Militia Duty	Anderson's Return	Capt. Herd	Ninety Six	£ 6. 8. 6¾
249 P	Mitchell, Solomon	Militia Duty	Anderson's Return	Capt. Freeman	Ninety Six	£ 3.15. 8½
256 P	Morrow, Est^a. Willm.	Militia Duty	Anderson's Return		Ninety Six	£ 26. 5. 8½
260 P	Maxwell, Jun. John	Militia Duty	Anderson's Return		Ninety Six	£ 36. .
261 P	Maxwell, Nicholas	Militia Duty	Anderson's Return	Capt. Norwood	Ninety Six	£ 26. 5. 8½
262 P	Maxwell, Willm.	Militia Duty	Anderson's Return	Capt. Norwood	Ninety Six	£ 2.14. 3¼
263 P	Maxwell, Alex^r.	Militia Duty	Anderson's Return		Ninety Six	£ 22.17. 1½
267 P	Moore, Willm.	Militia Duty	Anderson's Return	Capt^s. Irwin & Rosamond	Ninety Six	£ 13.10.
268 P	Moore, William	Militia Duty	Anderson's Return		Ninety Six	£ 13.15. 8½
269 P	Moore, Est^a. John	Militia Duty	Anderson's Return		Ninety Six	£ 7. 8. 6¾
270 P	Moore, Joseph	Militia Duty	Anderson's Return		Ninety Six	£ 22.11. 5
281 P	Magary, Edward	Militia Duty	Anderson's Return	Capt. Pickens	Ninety Six	£ .14. 3
294 P	Mulherrin, Charles	Militia Duty	Anderson's Return	Capt. Freeman	Ninety Six	£ 4.10.
296 P	McCord, Sen. John	Militia Duty	Anderson's Return	Capt. Pickens	Ninety Six	£ 2. .
297 P	McCord, Jun. John	Militia Duty	Anderson's Return	Capt. Pickens	Ninety Six	£ 11. 2.10¼
310 P	McKee, Adam	Militia Duty	Anderson's Return	Capt. Rosamond	Ninety Six	£ 1.14. 3¼
323 P	McGill, John	Militia Duty	Anderson's Return	Capt. Carrithers	Ninety Six	£ 5. 2.10¼
332 P	Norris, Est^a. Robert	Militia Duty	Anderson's Return		Ninety Six	£ 4. 2.10¼
333 P	Norris, Andy	Militia Duty	Anderson's Return		Ninety Six	£ 1. 2.10¼
339 P	Bates, Thomas	Militia Duty &c.	Horry's Return.	Marion's Brigade	Georgetown	£ 5. 4. 3¼

Numb. & Book	To whom Granted	For what Granted			District	Amount Indent
343 P	Buchanan, John (Doctr.)	Sundries	Horry's Return.	Marion's Brigade	Georgetown	£ 16. 8. 6
346 P	Barton, William	Ferriage	Horry's Return.		Georgetown	£ .18.10½
351 P	Derry, Lieut. John	Sundries				£ 28.11. 5
356 P	Melven, Capt. George	Pay as A D Q M G & 2 Horses				£ 173. 8. 6½
358 P	Spears, Esta. William	Militia Duty & Supplies		Marion's Brigade	Georgetown	£ 25. .6
359 P	Stead, Esta. Benjn.	Supplies			[Georgetown] Charleston	£ 7.
361 P	Smith, Francis	Supplies			Charleston	£ 35.18. 8
369 P	Campbell, Willm.	Supplies	Col. P. Horry	Marion's Brigade	Georgetown	£ 2. 9. 2
373 P	Dick, Robert	Supplies	Col. P. Horry	Marion's Brigade	Georgetown	£ 8. 1. 5½
384 P	Freeman, James	Supplies	Col. P. Horry	Marion's Brigade	Georgetown	£ 19.17.10
387 P	Ford, Jun. Stephen	Supplies	Col. P. Horry	Col. Washington	Georgetown	£ 179. 1.10
404 P	Clayton, Abraham	Supplies		Col. Harden	[Charleston] Beaufort	£ 11.11.
412 P	Bar, Esta. Christopher	Supplies			Beaufort	£ 2. 7.
419 P	Dupont, Josiah	Supplies			Charleston	£ 4.16. 6
435 P	LaBruce, Esta. Thomas	Supplies	Col. P. Horry		Georgetown	£ 3.11.10
444 P	Murrel, William	Militia Duty	Col. P. Horry		Georgetown	£ 10. 1. 4
447 P	McCracken, James	Militia Duty	Col. P. Horry		Georgetown	£ 4.16.
450 P	Mitchell, Thomas	Militia Duty & a Horse	Col. P. Horry		Georgetown	£ 147. 7. 5½
453 P	McCants, Thomas	Militia Duty & Supplies			Georgetown	£ 10.13. 5
462 P	Michau, Daniel	Supplies	Col. P. Horry		Georgetown	£ 16.16. 3
465 P	Maxwell, Samuel	Supplies	Col. P. Horry		Georgetown	£ 7. 4. 6¾
467 P	Perret, James	Supplies			Georgetown	£ 6. 7.10¾
469 P	Price, Samuel	Supplies	Col. P. Horry		Georgetown	£ 4. 9. 2
471 P	Port, Benja.	Supplies	Col. P. Horry		Georgetown	£ 5. 2. 8
479 P	Rhodes, John	Supplies	Col. P. Horry		Georgetown	£ 3. 4. 9
480 P	Rhodes, Henry	Militia Duty	Col. P. Horry		Georgetown	£ 5.13. 4
481 P	Rhodes, Solomon	Militia Duty	Col. P. Horry		Georgetown	£ 4.15. 8½
485 P	Reams, Jeremh.	Militia Duty	Col. P. Horry		Georgetown	£ 2. 4.
490 P	Rolleson, Benja.	Supplies		Marion's Brigade	Camden	£ 17. 9. 3
491 P	Richardson, Abraham	Militia Duty			Camden	£ 5. .

Numb. & Book	To whom Granted	For what Granted		District	Amount Indent
493 P	Simons, Estᵃ. Peter	Supplies	Col. P. Horry	Georgetown	£ 12.12.
495 P	Smith, Geoᵉ.	Militia Duty	Col. P. Horry	Georgetown	£ 2. 2. 8
503 P	Swicard, Jacob	Supplies	Col. Garden	Orangeburgh	£ 11.14.
508 P	Singleton, Benjⁿ.	Militia Duty	Genˡ. Marion	Georgetown	£ 2.13. 4
512 P	Swinton, Willᵐ.	Supplies	Col. P. Horry	Georgetown	£ 11.11.
514 P	Stewart, Thomas	Supplies	Gˡ. Marion	Cheraw	£ 42.15. 8
515 P	Tomplatt, John	Militia Duty & Supplies		Georgetown	£ 7.11. 7¼
530 P	Wells, Estᵃ John	Supplies		Charleston	£ 84.10.10¼
536 P	Burgess, William	Supplies	W. Hampton's Cavʸ.	Camden	£ 34. 1. 1
537 P	Clanton, Sen. Richard	Supplies		Camden	£ 11. 7. 7
544 P	Harrel, John	Militia Duty		Camden	£ 5.14. 8
552 P	Moses, John	Militia Duty		Camden	£ 3. 5. 4
555 P	McGarretty, James	Supplies & Duty	Lacey's Regiment	Camden	£ 9.17. 1½
566 P	White, George	Supplies	Maj. Crawford	Camden	£ 26. 8. 7½
607 P	Blair, James	Militia Duty	Colˢ. Hill & Bratton	Camden	£ 16.14. 4
623 P	Collins, Samuel	Militia Duty	Col. Bratton	Camden	£ 8.11. 5
649 P	Davis, John, Edwᵈ., Thomas	Militia Duty	Capt. Ramsay	Camden	£ 7. .
17 Q	Bean, Thomas	Militia Duty	Capt. Turner	Camden	£ 2.12.10¼
24 Q	Boone, Thomas	Supplies		Charleston	£ 4.19. 3
28 Q	Brown, Samˡ.	Supplies	Capt. Rumph	Orangeburgh	£ 4. 5. 8½
30 Q	Brailsford, Joseph	Supplies	Col. Harden	Beaufort	£ 13. 1. 4
59 Q	Crumley, Martin	Supplies			£ 6.18. 4
73 Q	Dill, Nichˢ.	Militia Duty	Capt. Rumph	Orangeburgh	£ 4. 5. 8½
142 Q	Huxford, Harlow	Militia Duty		Orangeburgh	£ 3.15. 8½
144 Q	Huger, Isaac	A Mortar & Pestle		Charleston	£ 1.17. 4
146 Q	Jones, Isaac	Supplies	Marion's Brigade	Georgetown	£ 3.17.
185 Q	Murray, William	Supplies		Orangeburgh	£ 3.17.
205 Q	Quinney, Joseph	Work for St. Cavalry			£ 3. 6.
211 Q	Rickenbacker, Jacob	Militia Duty	Capt. Rumph	Orangeburgh	£ 4. 5. 8½
228 Q	Sheaver, Francis	Supplies	Col. McCrery	Ninety Six	£ 4.11.10½
234 Q	Snell, John	Supplies		Orangeburgh	£ 7.11. 5

Numb. & Book	To whom Granted	For what Granted			District	Amount Indent
240 Q	Stanley, John	Supplies		Henderson's Brigade	Orangeburgh	£ 2.19.
246 Q	Thomas, Mary Lamboll	Supplies			Charleston	£ 1.13. 5½
259 Q	Ward, Susanna	Supplies		Col. Murphy	Cheraw	£ 2. .
270 Q	Wooters, Lilly	Supplies			Georgetown	£ 3. 6. 8
273 Q	Wragg, Estª. William	Wood & Schooner hire			Charleston	£ 16.19. 6¾
285 Q	Cockfield, James Joseph	Supplies	Powe's Return		Cheraw	£ 4.12. 4¼
293 Q	Davis, William	Militia Duty	Powe's Return		Cheraw	£ 2.10.
295 Q	Evans, John	Militia Duty	Powe's Return		Cheraw	£ 4.10.
301 Q	Ellerbie, Jun. Willᵐ.	Militia Duty	Powe's Return		Cheraw	£ 5. 7. 1½
308 Q	Filend, Peter	Militia Duty	Powe's Return		Cheraw	£ 4. 5. 8½
310 Q	Goodman, David	Militia Duty	Powe's Return		Cheraw	£ 4.11. 5
316 Q	Gilbert, Uriah	Militia Duty	Powe's Return		Cheraw	£ 2.18. 6¾
317 Q	Gainey, William	Militia Duty	Powe's Return		Cheraw	£ 8. 4. 2
329 Q	Niel, Elisha	Militia Duty	Anderson's Return	Col. Anderson	Ninety Six	£ 4.14. 3¼
332 Q	Cooper, Ezekiel	Contl. Duty				£ 18. 5.
340 Q	Delstoche, Michael	Supplies & Duty			Beaufort	£ 3.17.
369 Q	Stokes, William	Supplies & Duty		Genl. Sumter	Camden	£ 28.11. 5
398 Q	Wilson, Jun. James	Supplies				£ 36.16. 5
411 Q	Altman, Sarah	Supplies			Camden	£ 16.14.10
416 Q	Bowers, Sylvan	Supplies			Beaufort	£ 11.11.
418 Q	Benson, Andrew	Militia Duty		Capt. Stewart	Camden	£ 3.17. 1½
422 Q	Boull, William	Militia Duty		Lieut. Gray	Camden	£ 2.17. 1½
423 Q	Boyd, Hardy	Supplies			Georgetown	£ 2.16.5½
446 Q	Dickson, John	Supplies		Brandon's Regiment	Camden	£ 4. 9.10
447 Q	Dowdle, James	Supplies & Duty		Neel's Regiment	Camden	£ 6.14. 3½
448 Q	Dover, John	Supplies			Camden	£ .16. 4
454 Q	Eacheson, John	Militia Duty		Capt. Martin	Camden	£ 11.14. 3¾
460 Q	Frederick, James	Supplies	Arthur's Return	Genl. Pickens	Orangeburgh	£ 4.15. 5
461 Q	Favers, Theopˢ.	Supplies			Orangeburgh	£ 2. 2.
466 Q	Gillelan, Elenor	Supplies		Brandon's Regiment	Orangeburgh	£ 1. 6. 3

Numb. & Book	To whom Granted	For what Granted		District	Amount Indent
471 Q	Gibbons, Michael	Supplies & Militia Duty			£ 1.12. 1½
472 Q	Goodman, Willm.	~~Militia Duty~~ Contl. Duty			£ 18.13. 4
474 Q	Goyen, John	Militia Duty & a Horse lost	Capt. Lewis	Camden	£ 1.10.
477 Q	Gough, John	Supplies		Charleston	£ 48.17. 4½
481 Q	Graham, Chas.	Militia Duty	Lt. Hollis	Camden	£ 1.12.10¼
482 Q	Green, Abm.	Supplies	Col. Bratton	Camden	£ .17. 6
483 Q	Grindrat, Henry	Supplies		Charleston	£ 4. 7.10½
492 Q	Hull, Willm.	Militia Duty			£ 10. 3. 4
496 Q	Henson, Obedh.	Militia Duty	Capt. Lewis	Camden	£ 4. 5. 8
497 Q	~~Hall~~ Wall, Howell	Militia Duty & a Horse lost	Col. Jas. Thompson	Beaufort	£ 19. 1. 7¾
505 Q	Helms, Mary	Militia Duty	Capt. Lewis	Camden	£ 2. 2.10¼
507 Q	Hornsby, Moses	Militia Duty	Capt. Lewis	Camden	£ 2.18. 6½
516 Q	King, Esta. John	Supplies	Col. H. Hampton	Camden	£ 3. 7. 9½
518 Q	Kindermier, Henry	Supplies			£ 1. 9. 9
525 Q	Martin, William	Supplies	Lt. Gray	Camden	£ 7. 2.10
553 Q	Palmer, Charles	Supplies		Beaufort	£ 36.11. 1½
559 Q	Perdriau, John	Supplies	Col. Horry	Georgetown	£ 25. 4. 8
560 Q	Pierson, Edward	Supplies	Col. Harden	Beaufort	£ 15.11. 2
562 Q	Peyre, John	Supplies		Charleston	£ 1.16.
572 Q	Reed, Murray	Waggon & Team			£ 13.14. 8½
576 Q	Ritchman, John	Militia Duty & Supplies	Col. Lacey	Camden	£ 9. 3. 6¾
583 Q	Robinson, John	Supplies	Col. Lacey	Camden	£ 3. 7. 9
588 Q	Smith, Reuben	Supplies	Col. Bratton	Camden	£ .14.
591 Q	Smith, Joel	Militia Duty	Col. Bratton	Camden	£ 2.10.
598 Q	Smith, Ralph	Militia Duty & Supplies	Sumter's Brigade	Camden	£ 16. 5. 9
600 Q	Stewart, James	Supplies	Sumter's Brigade	Camden	£ 6. 7. 9
609 Q	Vallo, Nicholas	Contl. Duty			£ 18.13. 4
612 Q	Wadkins, Abhabel	Militia Duty			£ 2.14. 3¾
614 Q	West, William	Contl. Duty			£ 18.13. 4
615 Q	Whitfield, Thomas	Militia Duty	Genl. Marion W. Wigg	Georgetown	£ 1.13. 4
624 Q	Wilson, Willm.	Militia Duty	Capt. Jenkins	Camden	£ 2.10.
627 Q	Wilson, Ulman	Militia Duty	Capt. Jenkins	Camden	£ 2.10.

Numb. & Book	To whom Granted	For what Granted		District	Amount Indent
633 Q	Bowman, Estᵃ. Thoˢ.	Supplies	W. Wigg	C̶h̶a̶s̶t̶o̶n̶ Beaufort	£ 50. 1. 0
639 Q	Dopson, Joseph	Supplies	W. Wigg	Col. Harden	Beaufort	£ 7. 4. 8
640 Q	De Traville, John B.	Supplies	W. Wigg	Col. Garden	Beaufort	£ 2.16.
641 Q	Dawson, Richard	Supplies	W. Wigg	Col. Garden	Beaufort	£ 11.13. 6
643 Q	Doharty, James	Supplies	W. Wigg	Col. Garden	Beaufort	£ 2.19.3¼
645 Q	Ellis, Elizʰ.	Supplies	W. Wigg		Beaufort	£ 3. 2.10
647 Q	Felts, Capt. John	Supplies & Duty	W. Wigg	Col. Harden	Beaufort	£ 4.14.3¼
649 Q	Giroud, Estᵃ. David	Supplies	W. Wigg	Col. Garden	Beaufort	£ 1.18. 3
650 Q	Heyward, Estᵃ. Daniel	Supplies	W. Wigg		Beaufort [Charleston]	£ 110. 9. 7
652 Q	Heyward, Jun. Thoˢ.	Supplies	W. Wigg		Beaufort [Charleston]	£ 2.10.11
4 R	Alison, Estᵃ. James H.	Supplies & Militia Duty			£ 28. 9. 2
14 R	Allen, Estᵃ. Sallathiel	Supplies		Georgetown	£ 2.17. 9½
17 R	Buckholts, Peter	Supplies		Georgetown	£ 3. 4. 2
23 R	Boughman, Joseph	Militia Duty	Capt. Fridig	Orangeburgh	£ 2.18. 6¾
28 R	Brazell, James	Supplies		Camden	£ 2. 1.
38 R	Babilitman, Zora	A Mare		Georgetown	£ 5.14. 3¼
76 R	Davis, Jun. Henry	Supplies	Genˡ. Marion	Georgetown	£ 5. 2. 8
86 R	Dove, Jacob	Militia Duty	Capt. Andrⁿ. Thomas	Camden	£ 9. 7. 1½
88 R	Driggers, Julius	Supplies & Duty	Genˡ. Marion	Georgetown	£ 5. 5. 7¼
96 R	Elliott, Estᵃ. William	Supplies		Charleston	£ 81. 9.11¼
108 R	Fail, Lieut. Thomas	Militia Duty			£ 8.10.
121 R	Gassert, John	Militia Duty	Capt. Fridig	Orangeburgh	£ 2. 8. 7
132 R	Gessindaner, Henry	Supplies	Capt. Rumph	Orangeburgh	£ 2.15. 2
134 R	Gates, Christian	Militia Duty	Capt. Kelly	Orangeburgh	£ 2. 4.3¼
135 R	Gates, Jacob	Militia Duty	Capt. Kelly	Orangeburgh	£ 2. 4.3¼
143 R	Holsey, Willᵐ.	Militia Duty	Capt. A. Thomas	Camden	£ 8.11. 5
146 R	Hasford, Samuel	Indigo Impressed			£ 32.14. 7½
147 R	Holmes, Estᵃ. James	A Mare & Saddle			£ 11.17. 4

Numb. & Book	To whom Granted	For what Granted			District	Amount Indent
151 R	Hill, Thomas	Supplies			Camden	£ .12.11¾
155 R	Hassan, George	Supplies & Militia Duty		Genl. Winn	Camden	£ 7.12.10¼
157 R	Hogg, ,James	Supplies & Militia Duty		Col. Bratton	Camden	£ 6.10. 4¼
158 R	Hogg, John	Militia Duty		Col. Bratton	Camden	£ 7. 5. 8½
164 R	Houston, John	Supplies			Beaufort	£ 5. 5. 2¾
166 R	Hier, Chris^{r}.	Supplies			Beaufort	£ 3.11.10¼
174 R	Harman, Ab^{m}.	Militia Duty			Charleston	£ 38. 8. 6¾
180 R	Hatcher, Est^{a}. Benj. (Capt.)	A Horse				£ 15. .
192 R	Jordan, Moses	A Horse & Bell			Camden	£ 5.17. 2¼
203 R	Kelley, Daniel	Militia Duty		Capt. G. Kelly	Orangeburgh	£ 5.14. 3¼
215 R	Lankford, Est^{a}. Willm.	Waggon hire & Supp^{s}.			Cheraw	£ 15. 1. 6
240 R	Mackie & Cameron	Cooperage			Charleston	£ 51. 9.11
244 R	Moore, Thomas	Militia Duty		Capt. Amos Davis	Camden	£ 5. .
245 R	Moore, Eliab & Est^{a}. Samuel	Two Horses		~~Capt. John~~	Camden	£ 50. .
256 R	Myers, Ab^{m}.	Militia Duty & a Saddle		Capt. John McCooll	Camden	£ 3.18. 6½
268 R	Nesmith, Nathl.	Supplies		Genl. Marion	Georgetown	£ 5. 2. 8
293 R	Potts, Thomas	A Boat burnt		Genl. Marion	Georgetown	£ 15. .
306 R	Bryant, Thomas	Militia Duty	Powe's Ret^{n}		Cheraw	£ 4.14. 3¼
307 R	Botsford	Supplies	Powe's Ret^{n}	Col. Benton	Cheraw	£ 1. .10¾
309 R	Burkett, John	Militia Duty	Powe's Ret^{n}	Marion's Brid^{e}.	Cheraw	£ 1.19. 8
311 R	Benthen, Samuel	Supplies	Powe's Ret^{n}		Cheraw	£ 8.19. 8
312 R	Baron, Willm.	Supplies	Powe's Ret^{n}		Cheraw	£ 3. 4. 2
314 R	Blackwell, Abraham	Militia Duty	Powe's Ret^{n}	Marion's Brid^{e}.	Cheraw	£ 2.11. 5
318 R	Arnold, Willm.	Militia Duty	Powe's Ret^{n}	Marion's Brid^{e}.	Cheraw	£ 2. 5. 8½
322 R	Clements, Joseph	Militia Duty	Powe's Ret^{n}	Marion's Brid^{e}.	Cheraw	£ 3. . 8½
326 R	Casettee, Willm.	Militia Duty	Powe's Ret^{n}	Marion's Brid^{e}.	Cheraw	£ 2. 1. 5
328 R	Collier, John	Militia Duty	Powe's Ret^{n}	Marion's Brid^{e}.	Cheraw	£ 2. 8. 6¾
347 R	Bush, John	Militia Duty		Capt. Wommock	Orangeburgh	£ 16. 7. 1½
351 R	Baldwin, Isaac	Militia Duty				£ 23.15.
352 R	Buchanan, Thomas	Militia Duty				£ 35. 2.10¼
361 R	Bolton, John	Militia Duty			Georgetown	£ 3. 8. 6¾
362 R	Bolton, Spencer	Militia Duty			Georgetown	£ 2. 4. 3¼
366 R	Brewton, George	Militia Duty				£ .17. 1½

Numb. & Book	To whom Granted	For what Granted			District	Amount Indent
373 R	Bradford, Rich^d.	A Horse			Camden	£ 26.10. 8½
395 R	Corbett, James	Militia Duty		Marion's Brid^e.	Camden	£ 2. 8. 6¾
407 R	Cooley, John	Militia Duty		Capt. Wommock	Orangeburgh	£ 15.11. 5
410 R	Clayton, Est^a. Isham	Supplies			Orangeburgh	£ 23.15. 4¾
414 R	Christian, Philip	Supplies				£ 13. 9. 6
419 R	Crossley, Jarmon	Militia Duty			Georgetown	£ 2. 2.3½
424 R	Davis, Jesse	Militia Duty			Beaufort	£ 9. 5. 8½
438 R	Martin, John & Dasher, Est^a. Christ^n.	Militia Duty				£ 17. 8. 6½
466 R	Gillam, James	Supplies	Tate's Return		Camden	£ 38.11. 5
478 R	Greer, Willm.	Supplies	Tate's Return		Camden	£ 12. 8. 7
505 R	Johnson, John	Supplies	Tate's Return		Camden	£ 7.17. 2
506 R	Johnston, John	Supplies	Tate's Return		Camden	£ 10.19. 8
528 R	Leard, John	Supplies	Tate's Return		Camden	£ 9. 2.10
538 R	McCance, Charles	Supplies	Tate's Return	Capt. Hanna	Camden	£ 4. 5. 9
539 R	McCullough, Samuel	Supplies	Tate's Return		Camden	£ 2.10.
541 R	Morris, Thomas	Supplies	Tate's Return		Camden	£ 5.13. 9
542 R	Morris, James	Supplies	Tate's Return		Camden	£ 6.10.
566 R	McLilly, John	Supplies	Tate's Return		Camden	£ .16. 5
590 R	Moorehead, Edward	Supplies	Tate's Return		Camden	£ 16.15.
595 R	Neel, Est^a. Thos.	Supplies	Tate's Return		Camden	£ 13. 5. 8½
597 R	Neel, Hugh	Militia Duty			Camden	£ 2.17. 2
659 R	Gieger, John	Supplies	Arthur's Return		Orangeburgh	£ 12. 7. 6¾
660 R	Griffith, Joshua	A Bay Mare	Arthur's Return		Orangeburgh	£ 8.11. 6
16 S	Robison, Robert	Militia Duty	Anderson's Return	Anderson's Regiment	Ninety Six	£ 10.11. 5
23 S	Rogan, Philip	Militia Duty	Anderson's Return	Anderson's Regiment	Ninety Six	£ 5. .
27 S	Rochateer, Robert	Militia Duty	Anderson's Return	Anderson's Regiment	Ninety Six	£ 2. 2.10¼
33 S	Saunders, M^rs.	Militia Duty by her husband		Anderson's Regiment	Ninety Six	£ 3. 1. 5

Numb. & Book	To whom Granted	For what Granted			District	Amount Indent
38 S	Sharp, Estᵃ. Francis	Militia Duty	Anderson's Return	Anderson's Regiment	Ninety Six	£ 3.14. 3¼
67 S	Stevens, Burrell	Militia Duty	Anderson's Return	Anderson's Regiment	Ninety Six	£ 3.14. 3¼
71 S	Stewart, Alexʳ.	Militia Duty	Anderson's Return	Anderson's Regiment	Ninety Six	£ 5.17. 1½
87 S	Thompson, Moses	Militia Duty	Anderson's Return	Anderson's Regiment	Ninety Six	£ 1. 8. 6¾
88 S	Thomas, Evan	Militia Duty	Anderson's Return	Anderson's Regiment	Ninety Six	£ . 8. 7
104 S	Vicary, Sen. Willᵐ.	Militia Duty	Anderson's Return	Anderson's Regiment	Ninety Six	£ 3. .
113 S	Watt, Samuel	Militia Duty & Supplies		Anderson's Regiment	Ninety Six	£ 2. 5.
125 S	Weams, Thomas	Militia Duty	Anderson's Return	Anderson's Regiment	Ninety Six	£ 1. .
127 S	Weams, Willᵐ.	Militia Duty	Anderson's Return	Anderson's Regiment	Ninety Six	£ 3. .
140 S	White, Estᵃ. Andʷ.	Militia Duty	Anderson's Return	Anderson's Regiment	Ninety Six	£ 20.14. 3¼
149 S	Willson, Estᵃ. Robᵗ.	Militia Duty	Anderson's Return	Anderson's Regiment	Ninety Six	£ 2. 4. 3¼
150 S	Wiley, John	Militia Duty	Anderson's Return	Anderson's Regiment	Ninety Six	£ 11. 5. 8½
161 S	York, Richᵈ.	Militia Duty	Anderson's Return	Anderson's Regiment	Ninety Six	£ 33.11. 5
168 S	Owen, Archᵈ.	Militia Duty	Anderson's Return	Anderson's Regiment	Ninety Six	£ 13. 2.10¼
182 S	Prator, Philip	Militia Duty	Anderson's Return	Anderson's Regiment	Ninety Six	£ 13. 2.10¼
183 S	Prator, Philip	Militia Duty	Anderson's Return	Anderson's Regiment	Ninety Six	£ 15.11. 5

Numb. & Book	To whom Granted	For what Granted			District	Amount Indent
207 S	Puckett, Willm.	Militia Duty		Anderson's Regiment	Ninety Six	£ 17. 7. 1½
215 S	Baxter, Robert	Supplies			Georgetown	£ 8.19. 8
228 S	Cannon, Samuel	Supplies		Casey's Regiment	Ninety Six	£ . 8. ¼
242 S	Faulkenbery, Jacob	Supplies			Camden	£ 4.19. 2
247 S	Gaillard, Chas.	Militia Duty			Charleston	£ 4. 8. 6¾
250 S	Hazleton, Richard	Militia Duty		Marion's Brigade	Georgetown	£ 23. 8. 6¾
262 S	Jolley, Joseph	Militia Duty		Marion's Brigade	Georgetown	£ 4.11. 5
273 S	Myers, Est^a. Rich^d	Militia Duty		Col. Marshall	Camden	£ 5. 2. 8
278 S	Van Marjenhoff, John	Militia Duty		Capt. Youngblood	Charleston	£ 12.17. 1½
292 S	Perdriau, John	Supplies		Marion's Brigade	Georgetown	£ 4.16. 7¼
294 S	Printer, Marg^t.	Supplies				£ 4. 9.10
295 S	Patterson, Willm.	Supplies			Charleston	£ 2.11. 4
307 S	Strange, Mitchel	Supplies				£ 2.11.10
308 S	Simons, Est^a. Peter	Indigo Impressed			Georgetown [Charleston]	£ 109.13. 2½
326 S	Wiley, Peter	Militia Duty		Capt. Turner	Camden	£ 8. 2.10¼
329 S	Yonge, Francis	A Pettiauger			Charleston	£ 81.13. 1
330 S	Young, Est^a. Benjn.	Indigo Impressed			Charleston	£ 179. 7. 1½
333 S	Allison, James	Militia Duty	Anderson's Return	Casey's Regiment	Ninety Six	£ 27. 2.10¼
336 S	Atkins, Joseph	Militia Duty	Anderson's Return	Casey's Regiment	Ninety Six	£ 8. 6¾
343 S	Allen, Est^a. Joel	Militia Duty	Anderson's Return	Casey's Regiment	Ninety Six	£ 10. 5. 8½
351 S	Adair, Sarah	Waggon hire &c.	Anderson's Return	Casey's Regiment	Ninety Six	£ 3. 5. 5½
368 S	Bean, Jun. William	Militia Duty & a Horse	Anderson's Return	Casey's Regiment	Ninety Six	£ 12.14. 4¼
370 S	Barlain, Babister	Militia Duty	Anderson's Return	Casey's Regiment	Ninety Six	£ 5.12.10¼
371 S	Beekes, Samuel	Militia Duty	Anderson's Return	Casey's Regiment	Ninety Six	£ 3. .
372 S	Brookes, Bartlett	Militia Duty	Anderson's Return	Casey's Regiment	Ninety Six	£ 8. .
376 S	Bishop, Samuel	Militia Duty	Anderson's Return	Casey's Regiment	Ninety Six	£ 2. 2.10¼
381 S	Briggs, John	Militia Duty	Anderson's Return	Casey's Regiment	Ninety Six	£ 1.14. 3¼
383 S	Blakely, John	Militia Duty	Anderson's Return	Casey's Regiment	Ninety Six	£ 3. 5. 8½
387 S	Black, Willm.	Militia Duty	Anderson's Return	Casey's Regiment	Ninety Six	£ 5.11. 5
388 S	Barrett, Nathl.	Militia Duty	Anderson's Return	Casey's Regiment	Ninety Six	£ 58. 4. 3¼
390 S	Burdit, Fred^k.	Militia Duty	Anderson's Return	Casey's Regiment	Ninety Six	£ 3. 1. 5

Numb. & Book	To whom Granted	For what Granted			District	Amount Indent
391 S	Beaseley, Henry	Militia Duty	Anderson's Return	Casey's Regiment	Ninety Six	£ 2. 4. 3¼
392 S	Bonds, Elisha	Militia Duty	Anderson's Return	Casey's Regiment	Ninety Six	£ 8.17. 1½
399 S	Couch, Millington	Militia Duty	Anderson's Return	Casey's Regiment	Ninety Six	£ 8.11. 5
401 S	Carter, Robt.	Militia Duty	Anderson's Return	Casey's Regiment	Ninety Six	£ 2.15. 8½
408 S	Cummins, Willm.	Militia Duty	Anderson's Return	Casey's Regiment	Ninety Six	£ 2. 7. 1½
413 S	Cannon, Robt.	Militia Duty	Anderson's Return	Casey's Regiment	Ninety Six	£ 3. 2.10¼
415 S	Cannon, Willm.	Militia Duty	Anderson's Return	Casey's Regiment	Ninety Six	£ 4. 7. 1½
434 S	Cheat, Ellice	Militia Duty	Anderson's Return	Casey's Regiment	Ninety Six	£ 3. 8. 6¾
437 S	Dickison, Jun. Robt.	Militia Duty	Anderson's Return	Casey's Regiment	Ninety Six	£ 3. 5. 8½
446 S	Dunlap, Est^a. John	Waggon Hire	Anderson's Return	Casey's Regiment	Ninety Six	£ 4.11. 5
449 S	Durham, Arthur	Supplies	Anderson's Return	Casey's Regiment	Ninety Six	£ .11.
456 S	Eddy, Henry	Militia Duty	Anderson's Return	Casey's Regiment	Ninety Six	£ 2.17. 1½
460 S	East, Josiah	Supplies	Anderson's Return	Casey's Regiment	Ninety Six	£ . 7.10¼
463 S	Fowler, John	Militia Duty	Anderson's Return	Casey's Regiment	Ninety Six	£ 5. .
464 S	Findley, Paul	Militia Duty	Anderson's Return	Casey's Regiment	Ninety Six	£ 9. .
469 S	Fowler, Richard	Prov^s.	Anderson's Return	Casey's Regiment	Ninety Six	£ .16. ¾
470 S	Fowler, Willm.	Prov^s.	Anderson's Return	Casey's Regiment	Ninety Six	£ 2.11. 5
471 S	Farmer, Willm.	Militia Duty	Anderson's Return	Casey's Regiment	Ninety Six	£ 2. 7. 1½
472 S	Ford, Robt.	Militia Duty	Anderson's Return	Casey's Regiment	Ninety Six	£ 15.14. 3¼
480 S	Gunter, Chas.	Militia Duty	Anderson's Return	Casey's Regiment	Ninety Six	£ 2. 2.10¼
481 S	Gunter, Willm.	Militia Duty	Anderson's Return	Casey's Regiment	Ninety Six	£ 2.17. 1½
488 S	Goodwin, Harris	Militia Duty	Anderson's Return	Casey's Regiment	Ninety Six	£ 5.10.
489 S	Geary, John	Supplies	Anderson's Return	Casey's Regiment	Ninety Six	£ 2. 6. 5
505 S	Griffith, Ezekiel	Supplies	Anderson's Return	Casey's Regiment	Ninety Six	£ .12.10¼
509 S	Griffin, Anth^y.	Supplies	Anderson's Return	Casey's Regiment	Ninety Six	£ 4. 3. 6¾
516 S	Glenn, James	Militia Duty	Anderson's Return	Casey's Regiment	Ninety Six	£ 6. 1. 5
517 S	Glenn, Joseph	Militia Duty & Supp^s.	Anderson's Return	Casey's Regiment	Ninety Six	£ 5.14. 7½
539 S	Ford, Nathl.	Militia Duty		Col. Taylor	Camden	£ 8.11. 5
548 S	Finkley, Chas.	Supplies		Marion's Brigade	George Town	£ 3. 4. 4¾
549 S	Foxworth. Zach^h.	Militia Duty		Marion's Brigade	George Town	£ 2. 1. 5
554 S	Green, Jacob	Militia Duty		Marion's Brigade	George Town	£ 4.19.11¾
557 S	Garvey, Mich^l.	Supplies			Beaufort	£ 5. 2. 8
568 S	Godbold, James	Militia Duty		Marion's Brigade	Georgetown	£ 2. 1. 5

Numb. & Book	To whom Granted	For what Granted		District	Amount Indent
569 S	Garsington, Chris[r].	Supp[s].		Cheraw	£ 3.17.
571 S	Ginn, Mesheck	Militia Duty	Marion's Brigade	Georgetown	£ 2.11. 5
583 S	Haselton, W[m].	Militia Duty		Georgetown	£ 3.15. 8½
585 S	Hext, Thomas	Militia Duty		Georgetown	£ 4.11. 5
588 S	Hamilton, David	Militia Duty	Capt. Edw[d]. Martin	Camden	£ 5.11. 5
591 S	Hutson, Joseph	Militia Duty		Georgetown	£ 50.11. 5
595 S	Hilton, James	Militia Duty		Georgetown	£ 2.10.
606 S	Hogg, Est[a]. George	Supplies			£ 17.19. 4
610 S	Hughes, Capt. William	Supplies	Gen[l]. Winn	Camden	£ 45.12. 1½
612 S	Hicklin, John	Militia Duty	Col[s]. Kershaw & Kimball	Camden	£ 12. 2.10¼
630 S	Ravencraft, Will[m].	Militia Duty	Anderson's Return Purvis's Regiment	Ninety Six	£ 6. .
631 S	Randolph, James	Militia Duty	Anderson's Return Purvis's Regiment	Ninety Six	£ 24. 5. 8½
637 S	Rambee, Nich[s].	Militia Duty	Anderson's Return Purvis's Regiment	Ninety Six	£ 9.12.10¼
645 S	Reed, Job	Militia Duty	Anderson's Return Purvis's Regiment	Ninety Six	£ 2. 2.10¼
647 S	Reeves, James	Militia Duty	Anderson's Return Purvis's Regiment	Ninety Six	£ 1.10.
651 S	Richardson, John	Militia Duty & Supplies	Purvis's Regiment	Ninety Six	£ 24.18. 4¾
662 S	Roebuck, John	Militia Duty	Anderson's Return Purvis's Regiment	Ninety Six	£ 2. .
665 S	Rogers, Est[a]. George	Militia Duty	Anderson's Return Purvis's Regiment	Ninety Six	£ 3.19. 7½
3 T	Hoofman, Martin	Supplies	Anderson's Return	Orangeburgh	£ 14. 4. 6
8 T	Hartsuch, John	Supplies	Anderson's Return	Orangeburgh	£ 6. 3. 2¼
9 T	Inabner, Marg[t].	Supplies	Anderson's Return	Orangeburgh	£ 2.10. 3½
11 T	Kinslow, John	Supplies	Anderson's Return	Orangeburgh	£ 8. .6¾
17 T	Myers, Joseph	Supplies	Anderson's Return	Orangeburgh	£ 7.14.
23 T	Miller, M[rs]	Supplies	Anderson's Return	Orangeburgh	£ 2. 6. 8½
26 T	Noble, Martin	Supplies	Anderson's Return	Orangeburgh	£ 21. 3. 6
29 T	Pen, Eliz[h].	Supplies	Anderson's Return	Orangeburgh	£ 4.17.
36 T	Stocker, Sam[l].	Supplies	Anderson's Return	Orangeburgh	£ 5.12. 8¼
38 T	Smith, Christ[n].	Supplies	Anderson's Return	Orangeburgh	£ 7.14.
46 T	Spiel, Jacob	Supplies	Anderson's Return	Orangeburgh	£ 5.14. 2¾
47 T	Smith, Robert	Gunflints	Anderson's Return	Orangeburgh	£ .17.
51 T	Toller, Mary	Supplies	Anderson's Return	Orangeburgh	£ 3.13. 4

Numb. & Book	To whom Granted	For what Granted			District	Amount Indent
54 T	Wingart, Mich^{l}.	Supplies	Anderson's Return		Orangeburgh	£ 2. 3. 7½
59 T	Zann, Christ^{r}.	Supplies	Anderson's Return		Orangeburgh	£ 70. 8.11½
62 T	Harvey, Charles	Militia Duty	Anderson's Return	Casey's Regiment	Ninety Six	£ 5.10.
67 T	Harden, John	Militia Duty	Anderson's Return	Casey's Regiment	Ninety Six	£ 12.17. 1½
83 T	Hollingsworth, Joseph	Militia Duty	Anderson's Return	Casey's Regiment	Ninety Six	£ 1.11. 5
85 T	Hutchinson, Robt.	Militia Duty	Anderson's Return	Casey's Regiment	Ninety Six	£ 4. 5. 8½
87 T	Hogan, John	Militia Duty	Anderson's Return	Casey's Regiment	Ninety Six	£ 4. 8. 6¾
88 T	Hodges, Benjn.	Militia Duty	Anderson's Return	Casey's Regiment	Ninety Six	£ . 8. 6¾
90 T	Holmes, John	Militia Duty	Anderson's Return	Casey's Regiment	Ninety Six	£ 10. 5. 8½
93 T	Hunter, And^{w}.	Supplies	Anderson's Return	Casey's Regiment	Ninety Six	£ 1. 1. 5
94 T	Johnson, Mathew	Militia Duty	Anderson's Return	Casey's Regiment	Ninety Six	£ 3. 7. 1½
98 T	Johnston, Robt. & James	Supplies	Anderson's Return	Casey's Regiment	Ninety Six	£ 3.12.10¼
106 T	Kirk, James	Supplies	Anderson's Return	Casey's Regiment	Ninety Six	£ 2.15.
107 T	Lewis, John	Militia Duty	Anderson's Return	Casey's Regiment	Ninety Six	£ 4. 8. 6¾
108 T	Lewis, Ross	Militia Duty	Anderson's Return	Casey's Regiment	Ninety Six	£ 8.11. 5
110 T	Lang, James	Militia Duty	Anderson's Return	Casey's Regiment	Ninety Six	£ 2. 2.10¼
129 T	Miller, Hans	Supplies	Anderson's Return	Casey's Regiment	Ninety Six	£ . 9. 3¼
150 T	McCarney, Owens	Militia Duty	Anderson's Return	Casey's Regiment	Ninety Six	£ 2. 7. 1½
151 T	Magill, John	Militia Duty	Anderson's Return	Casey's Regiment	Ninety Six	£ 5.14. 3¼
163 T	McFarsin, Willm.	Militia Duty	Anderson's Return	Casey's Regiment	Ninety Six	£ 3. 8. 6¾
165 T	Messer, James	Militia Duty	Anderson's Return	Casey's Regiment	Ninety Six	£ 2.17. 1½
169 T	McDaniel, Matthew	Militia Duty	Anderson's Return	Casey's Regiment	Ninety Six	£ 2.17. 1½
170 T	McClure, James	Supplies	Anderson's Return	Casey's Regiment	Ninety Six	£ .10.
171 T	McGloughling, George	Militia Duty	Anderson's Return	Casey's Regiment	Ninety Six	£ 18. 7. 1½
172 T	McDonald, Thos.	Militia Duty	Anderson's Return	Casey's Regiment	Ninety Six	£ 3.11. 5
173 T	McCree, John	Militia Duty	Anderson's Return	Casey's Regiment	Ninety Six	£ 3. 8. 6¾
175 T	McDead, James	Militia Duty	Anderson's Return	Casey's Regiment	Ninety Six	£ 3. 1. 5
181 T	Rouch, Thomas	Militia Duty		Capt. Owen	Orangeburgh	£ 3.15. 8½
185 T	Richardson, Benjn.	Militia Duty		Marion's Brigade	Camden	£ 4.17. 1½
186 T	Roberts, Lewis	Militia Duty		Genl. Winn	Camden	£ 2. 5. 8½
189 T	Snellgrove, John	Militia Duty		Capt^{a}. Owen	Orangeburgh	£ 4.11. 9

Numb. & Book	To whom Granted	For what Granted			District	Amount Indent
199 T	Snow, James	Militia Duty	Marion's Brigade		Georgetown	£ 33. 7. 4
200 T	Stemwinder, Fred^k.	Militia Duty	Capt. Oliver		Orangeburgh	£ 4.14. 7½
201 T	Slack, John	Militia Duty	Col. Thomson		Orangeburgh	£ 4. 5. 8½
205 T	Sommers, (Est^a.) Hump^y.	Supplies			Charleston	£ 6. 6.
231 T	Simons, Jesse	A Mare	Col. Kimball			£ 3.18. 6
252 T	Turil, Willm.	Militia Duty	Col. Kimball		Camden	£ 5. 5. 8½
262 T	Vivian, Est^a. John	Supplies of Arms			Georgetown	£ 24.18. 3
266 T	Waide, John	Militia Duty	Capt. Anderson Thomas		Camden	£ 3.15.
267 T	Waight, Ab^m.	Negro hire			Beaufort	£ 2.14. 3½
275 T	Winyert, Mathias	Militia Duty			Orangeburgh	£ 2.17. 1½
281 T	Woods, John	Supplies			Georgetown	£ 1. 8.
285 T	Williams, John	Militia Duty			Charleston	£ 17.10.
300 T	Neighbour, Willm.	Militia Duty	Casey's Regiment	Anderson's Return	Ninety Six	£ 4. 5. 8½
316 T	Park, Andrew	Supplies	Casey's Regiment	Anderson's Return	Ninety Six	£ 4. 5. 8½
317 T	Poole, John	Militia Duty	Casey's Regiment	Anderson's Return	Ninety Six	£ 12.17. 1½
321 T	Phegan, Philip	Supplies	Casey's Regiment	Anderson's Return	Ninety Six	£ 2. 6. 8
348 T	Hamilton, Benjn.	Militia Duty	Purvis's Regiment	Anderson's Return	Ninety Six	£ 7. 8. 6¾
352 T	Holloway, Obediah	Militia Duty	Purvis's Regiment	Anderson's Return	Ninety Six	£ 8.17. 1½
357 T	Holsenback, Willm.	Militia Duty	Purvis's Regiment	Anderson's Return	Ninety Six	£ 5.14. 3
360 T	Hatcher, Robert	Militia Duty	Purvis's Regiment	Anderson's Return	Ninety Six	£ 2. 2.10¼
361 T	Hatcher, John	Militia Duty	Purvis's Regiment	Anderson's Return	Ninety Six	£ 2. 2.10¼
365 T	Hammond, Samuel	Militia Duty	Purvis's Regiment	Anderson's Return	Ninety Six	£ 2. 2.10¼
366 T	Hammond, Charles	Militia Duty	Purvis's Regiment	Anderson's Return	Ninety Six	£ 9.12.10¼
374 T	Harvey, Evan	Militia Duty	Purvis's Regiment	Anderson's Return	Ninety Six	£ 1. .
379 T	Harris, Ezekiel	Militia Duty	Purvis's Regiment	Anderson's Return	Ninety Six	£ 1. 2.10¼
387 T	Hargrove, Charles	Militia Duty	Purvis's Regiment	Anderson's Return	Ninety Six	£ 8.17. 1½
389 T	Hill, Isaac	Militia Duty	Purvis's Regiment	Anderson's Return	Ninety Six	£ 5.14. 3¼
402 T	Hog, Thomas	Militia Duty	Purvis's Regiment	Anderson's Return	Ninety Six	£ 1. .
404 T	Hedgewood, James	Militia Duty	Purvis's Regiment	Anderson's Return	Ninety Six	£ 13. 1. 5
408 T	Harling, Samuel	Militia Duty	Purvis's Regiment	Anderson's Return	Ninety Six	£ 19. 2.10¼
409 T	Hunter, Robert	Militia Duty	Purvis's Regiment	Anderson's Return	Ninety Six	£ 8. 2. 6
411 T	Hutson, Samuel	Militia Duty	Purvis's Regiment	Anderson's Return	Ninety Six	£ 1. 8. 6¾

Numb. & Book	To whom Granted	For what Granted			District	Amount Indent
414 T	Jones, Benj[a].	Militia Duty	Anderson's Return	Purvis's Regiment	Ninety Six	£ 2.11. 5
416 T	Jones, Bartley	Militia Duty	Anderson's Return	Purvis's Regiment	Ninety Six	£ 1. 8. 6¾
417 T	Jones, Charles	Militia Duty	Anderson's Return	Purvis's Regiment	Ninety Six	£ 17.17. 1½
432 T	Jones, Matthew	Militia Duty	Anderson's Return	Purvis's Regiment	Ninety Six	£ 23. 5. 8½
433 T	Jonican, Moses	Militia Duty	Anderson's Return	Purvis's Regiment	Ninety Six	£ 3. 2.10¼
434 T	Jonican, Sen. James	Militia Duty	Anderson's Return	Purvis's Regiment	Ninety Six	£ 2. 4. 3¼
439 T	Jenkins, Benj[a].	Militia Duty	Anderson's Return	Purvis's Regiment	Ninety Six	£ 5.14. 3¼
441 T	Jones, Henry	Supplies	Anderson's Return	Purvis's Regiment	Ninety Six	£ 45. .
442 T	Jennings, John	Militia Duty	Anderson's Return	Purvis's Regiment	Ninety Six	£ 2.17. 1½
447 T	Key, Tandy	Militia Duty	Anderson's Return	Purvis's Regiment	Ninety Six	£ 21.15. 8½
457 T	Lee, Robert	Militia Duty	Anderson's Return	Purvis's Regiment	Ninety Six	£ 8.17. 1½
459 T	Loopers, William	Militia Duty	Anderson's Return	Purvis's Regiment	Ninety Six	£ 9.10.
461 T	Lewis, Rosser	Militia Duty	Anderson's Return	Purvis's Regiment	Ninety Six	£ 8.17. 1½
465 T	Lemar, Jun. Thomas	Militia Duty	Anderson's Return	Purvis's Regiment	Ninety Six	£ 5.17. 1½
468 T	Lowry, Matthew	Militia Duty	Anderson's Return	Purvis's Regiment	Ninety Six	£ 3.11. 5
469 T	Lowrey, Sen. Matthew	Militia Duty	Anderson's Return	Purvis's Regiment	Ninety Six	£ 4.15. 8½
472 T	Levingston, Will[m].	Militia Duty	Anderson's Return	Purvis's Regiment	Ninety Six	£ 6.11. 5
473 T	Leach, John	Militia Duty	Anderson's Return	Purvis's Regiment	Ninety Six	£ 6.11. 5
475 T	Lemire, Thomas	Militia Duty & Supplies	Anderson's Return	Purvis's Regiment	Ninety Six	£ 20. 5. 6½
476 T	Lymbike, George	Militia Duty	Anderson's Return	Purvis's Regiment	Ninety Six	£ 26. 5. 8½
480 T	Leathering, James	Militia Duty	Anderson's Return	Purvis's Regiment	Ninety Six	£ 17. 5. 8½
489 T	M[c]Donald, John	Militia Duty	Anderson's Return	Purvis's Regiment	Ninety Six	£ 10. 7. 1½
490 T	M[c]Donald, Jehiel	Militia Duty	Anderson's Return	Purvis's Regiment	Ninety Six	£ 15. .
492 T	M[c]Donald, James	Militia Duty	Anderson's Return	Purvis's Regiment	Ninety Six	£ 19.14. 3¼
493 T	M[c]Donald, Absalom	Militia Duty	Anderson's Return	Purvis's Regiment	Ninety Six	£ 10. 4. 3¼
499 T	Martin, Elijah	Militia Duty	Anderson's Return	Purvis's Regiment	Ninety Six	£ 4. 5. 8½
502 T	Matthews, Isaac	Militia Duty	Anderson's Return	Purvis's Regiment	Ninety Six	£ 3.11. 5
504 T	Matthews, Sen. Daniel	Militia Duty	Anderson's Return	Purvis's Regiment	Ninety Six	£ 2.17. 1½
505 T	Miller, John	Militia Duty	Anderson's Return	Purvis's Regiment	Ninety Six	£ 10.10.
515 T	Mocks, Joseph	Supplies	Anderson's Return	Purvis's Regiment	Ninety Six	£ 3.11. 5
516 T	Mocks, And[w].	Militia Duty	Anderson's Return	Purvis's Regiment	Ninety Six	£ 13.12.10¼
517 T	Mires, Leonard	Militia Duty	Anderson's Return	Purvis's Regiment	Ninety Six	£ 9.19. 3¼

Numb. & Book	To whom Granted	For what Granted			District	Amount Indent
519 T	Melson, Samuel	Militia Duty	Anderson's Return	Purvis's Regiment	Ninety Six	£ 3. 2.10¼
520 T	Melson, David	Militia Duty	Anderson's Return	Purvis's Regiment	Ninety Six	£ 8. 2.10¼
522 T	Morgan, Jesse	Militia Duty	Anderson's Return	Purvis's Regiment	Ninety Six	£ 8. 4. 3¼
523 T	McGee, Thomas	Militia Duty	Anderson's Return	Purvis's Regiment	Ninety Six	£ 4.18. 6¾
524 T	McGee, Thomas	Militia Duty	Anderson's Return	Purvis's Regiment	Ninety Six	£ 2. 2.10¼
526 T	McClendon, Wilson	Militia Duty	Anderson's Return	Purvis's Regiment	Ninety Six	£ 37. .
529 T	McMillen, James	Militia Duty	Anderson's Return	Purvis's Regiment	Ninety Six	£ 2.12.10¼
530 T	McMillen, Bennet	Militia Duty	Anderson's Return	Purvis's Regiment	Ninety Six	£ .11. 5
533 T	Monday, William	Militia Duty	Anderson's Return	Purvis's Regiment	Ninety Six	£ 8.18. 6¾
549 T	Marshal, Daniel	Militia Duty	Anderson's Return	Purvis's Regiment	Ninety Six	£ 8. 8. 6¾
552 T	McGowen, Noble	Militia Duty	Anderson's Return	Purvis's Regiment	Ninety Six	£ 4. .
557 T	Miles, John	Militia Duty	Anderson's Return	Purvis's Regiment	Ninety Six	£ 5.14. 3¼
558 T	Moore, Rich.d	Militia Duty	Anderson's Return	Purvis's Regiment	Ninety Six	£ .11. 5
565 T	Meaners, John	Militia Duty	Anderson's Return	Purvis's Regiment	Ninety Six	£ 5. 2.10¼
576 T	Nichols, Sen.r Will.m	Militia Duty	Anderson's Return	Purvis's Regiment	Ninety Six	£ 8.10.
578 T	Nippers, Benj.n	Militia Duty	Anderson's Return	Purvis's Regiment	Ninety Six	£ 6. 2.10¼
582 T	Norrell, James	Militia Duty & Supplies	Anderson's Return	Purvis's Regiment	Ninety Six	£ 7.15. 4¼
590 T	Offatt, Ezekiel	Militia Duty	Anderson's Return	Purvis's Regiment	Ninety Six	£ 1. 8. 6¾
599 T	Pearce, Sen. John	Militia Duty	Anderson's Return	Purvis's Regiment	Ninety Six	£ 2.17. 1½
610 T	Parnell, Will.m	Militia Duty	Anderson's Return	Purvis's Regiment	Ninety Six	£ 8. 5. 8½
613 T	Palmer, Elijah	Militia Duty	Anderson's Return	Purvis's Regiment	Ninety Six	£ 2.14. 3¼
615 T	Pitman, John	Militia Duty	Anderson's Return	Purvis's Regiment	Ninety Six	£ 5. .
617 T	Pennington, William	Militia Duty	Anderson's Return	Purvis's Regiment	Ninety Six	£ 5. 8. 6¾
620 T	Piles, Samuel	Militia Duty	Anderson's Return	Purvis's Regiment	Ninety Six	£ 3. 8. 6¾
622 T	Rogers, Felix	Militia Duty	Anderson's Return	Purvis's Regiment	Ninety Six	£ 2. 4. 3¼
630 T	Scrimsher, Robert	Militia Duty	Anderson's Return	Purvis's Regiment	Ninety Six	£ 8.18. 6¾
636 T	Seeley, James	Militia Duty	Anderson's Return	Purvis's Regiment	Ninety Six	£ 15.14. 3¼
645 T	Shipman, Edward	Militia Duty	Anderson's Return	Purvis's Regiment	Ninety Six	£ 8.17. 1½
657 T	Singuefield, Est.a. Francis	Militia Duty	Anderson's Return	Purvis's Regiment	Ninety Six	£ 42. 2.10¼
662 T	Smith, Daniel	Militia Duty	Anderson's Return	Purvis's Regiment	Ninety Six	£ 4.14. 3¼
2 U	Smiley, David	Militia Duty	Anderson's Return	Purvis's Regiment	Ninety Six	£ 8. 1. 5
9 U	Stallions, Malachi	Militia Duty	Anderson's Return	Purvis's Regiment	Ninety Six	£ 2. 4. 3¼

Numb. & Book	To whom Granted	For what Granted			District	Amount Indent
11 U	Stevens, Baalam	Militia Duty	Anderson's Return	Purvis's Regiment	Ninety Six	£ 5. 8. 6¾
12 U	Stoker, Robert	Militia Duty	Anderson's Return	Purvis's Regiment	Ninety Six	£ 10.10.
13 U	Stoker, Matthew	Militia Duty Supplies &c.	Anderson's Return	Purvis's Regiment	Ninety Six	£ 13. 2. 6½
14 U	Stoker, John	Militia Duty	Anderson's Return	Purvis's Regiment	Ninety Six	£ 3. 1. 5
17 U	Stringer, William	Militia Duty	Anderson's Return	Purvis's Regiment	Ninety Six	£ 4.17. 1½
18 U	Stawlsworth, Willm.	Militia Duty	Anderson's Return	Purvis's Regiment	Ninety Six	£ 1.10.
22 U	Sullivan, George	Militia Duty	Anderson's Return	Purvis's Regiment	Ninety Six	£ 3. 4. 3¼
26 U	Sullivan, Owen	Militia Duty	Anderson's Return	Purvis's Regiment	Ninety Six	£ 1. 4. 3¼
30 U	Summerlin, James	Militia Duty	Anderson's Return	Purvis's Regiment	Ninety Six	£ 6. 8. 6¾
41 U	Tandy, Achilles	Militia Duty	Anderson's Return	Purvis's Regiment	Ninety Six	£ 23. .
47 U	Thomas, Tarbeyfield	Militia Duty	Anderson's Return	Purvis's Regiment	Ninety Six	£ 9.18. 6¾
48 U	Thomas, Benj^{a}.	Militia Duty	Anderson's Return	Purvis's Regiment	Ninety Six	£ 22.12.10¼
58 U	Todd, John	Militia Duty	Anderson's Return	Purvis's Regiment	Ninety Six	£ 2.12.10¼
70 U	Turner, John	Militia Duty	Anderson's Return	Purvis's Regiment	Ninety Six	£ 19. 8. 6¾
71 U	Turkenot, M^{rs}.	Militia Duty	Anderson's Return	Purvis's Regiment	Ninety Six	£ 4.16. 5
72 U	Tyner, William	Militia Duty	Anderson's Return	Purvis's Regiment	Ninety Six	£ 5. 8. 6¾
79 U	Wallace, James	Militia Duty	Anderson's Return	Purvis's Regiment	Ninety Six	£ 2.17. 1½
80 U	Watts, Jacob	Militia Duty	Anderson's Return	Purvis's Regiment	Ninety Six	£ 4. 5. 8½
82 U	Wasdon, Elijah	Militia Duty	Anderson's Return	Purvis's Regiment	Ninety Six	£ 8.17. 1½
83 U	Warnock, Abraham	Militia Duty	Anderson's Return	Purvis's Regiment	Ninety Six	£ 2. .
86 U	Warren, Reuben	Militia Duty	Anderson's Return	Purvis's Regiment	Ninety Six	£ 2. 4. 3¼
102 U	Wells, Jeremiah	Militia Duty	Anderson's Return	Purvis's Regiment	Ninety Six	£ 10. 8. 6¾
105 U	Weaver, Aaron	Militia Duty	Anderson's Return	Purvis's Regiment	Ninety Six	£ 7.17. 1½
106 U	White, Joseph	Militia Duty	Anderson's Return	Purvis's Regiment	Ninety Six	£ 19.14. 3¼
117 U	Wilson, Jun. James	Militia Duty	Anderson's Return	Purvis's Regiment	Ninety Six	£ 11. .
120 U	Wilson, Thomas	Militia Duty	Anderson's Return	Purvis's Regiment	Ninety Six	£ 1.10.
121 U	Wilcher, Benj^{a}.	Militia Duty	Anderson's Return	Purvis's Regiment	Ninety Six	£ 3. 2.10¼
123 U	Wolton, Moses	Militia Duty	Anderson's Return	Purvis's Regiment	Ninety Six	£ 1. .
124 U	Wood, John	Militia Duty	Anderson's Return	Purvis's Regiment	Ninety Six	£ 6.11. 5
125 U	Wray, Thomas	Militia Duty	Anderson's Return	Purvis's Regiment	Ninety Six	£ 14. 5. 8½
126 U	Wright, Christ^{r}.	Militia Duty	Anderson's Return	Purvis's Regiment	Ninety Six	£ 1. 8. 6¾
135 U	Tin, Willm.	Militia Duty	Anderson's Return	Purvis's Regiment	Ninety Six	£ 4.17. 1½
136 U	Zubly, John	Militia Duty	Anderson's Return	Purvis's Regiment	Ninety Six	£ 6. 2.10¼

Numb. & Book	To whom Granted	For what Granted			District	Amount Indent
140 U	Arnold, Reddock	Militia Duty	Anderson's Return	Purvis's Regiment	Ninety Six	£ 10. .
143 U	Ardist, Jacob	Supplies	Anderson's Return	Purvis's Regiment	Ninety Six	£ 6.15.
145 U	Anderson, Sen. John	Militia Duty	Anderson's Return	Purvis's Regiment	Ninety Six	£ 8. 7. 1½
146 U	Anderson, Jun. John	Militia Duty & Supplies	Anderson's Return	Purvis's Regiment	Ninety Six	£ 20. .
151 U	Adams, Willm.	Militia Duty	Anderson's Return	Purvis's Regiment	Ninety Six	£ 13. 1. 5
152 U	Adams, Willm.	Militia Duty	Anderson's Return	Purvis's Regiment	Ninety Six	£ 6. 8. 6¾
163 U	Allen, James	Militia Duty	Anderson's Return	Purvis's Regiment	Ninety Six	£ 28.15. 8½
165 U	Allen, Robert	Militia Duty	Anderson's Return	Purvis's Regiment	Ninety Six	£ 15. 2.10¼
168 U	Bland, John	Militia Duty	Anderson's Return	Purvis's Regiment	Ninety Six	£ 4. 7. 1½
170 U	Broughton, John	Militia Duty	Anderson's Return	Purvis's Regiment	Ninety Six	£ 2. .
172 U	Bawdy, John	Militia Duty	Anderson's Return	Purvis's Regiment	Ninety Six	£ 26. . 4¼
179 U	Baisden, James	Militia Duty	Anderson's Return	Purvis's Regiment	Ninety Six	£ 8.17. 1½
182 U	Bryant, Willm.	Militia Duty	Anderson's Return	Purvis's Regiment	Ninety Six	£ 5.18. 6¾
183 U	Boone, Fred^{k}.	Militia Duty	Anderson's Return	Purvis's Regiment	Ninety Six	£ 13.15. 8½
186 U	Brooner, Mich^{l}.	Militia Duty	Anderson's Return	Purvis's Regiment	Ninety Six	£ 13.11. 5
190 U	Brooks, Michijah	Militia Duty	Anderson's Return	Purvis's Regiment	Ninety Six	£ 3. 1. 5
192 U	Baker, Nich^{s}.	Militia Duty	Anderson's Return	Purvis's Regiment	Ninety Six	£ 4.12.10¼
193 U	Barratine, James	Militia Duty	Anderson's Return	Purvis's Regiment	Ninety Six	£ 26. .
199 U	Burke, Thomas	Militia Duty	Anderson's Return	Purvis's Regiment	Ninety Six	£ 11.15.
203 U	Brewer, Sen. James	Militia Duty	Anderson's Return	Purvis's Regiment	Ninety Six	£ 7.12.10¼
212 U	Burns, Robert	Militia Duty	Anderson's Return	Purvis's Regiment	Ninety Six	£ 1.10.
216 U	Buckstaner, Daniel	Militia Duty	Anderson's Return	Purvis's Regiment	Ninety Six	£ 3. 4. 3¼
226 U	Britton, Henry	Militia Duty	Anderson's Return	Purvis's Regiment	Ninety Six	£ 5. 1. 9¼
227 U	Coley, John	Militia Duty	Anderson's Return	Purvis's Regiment	Ninety Six	£ 17.10.
229 U	Cauley, George	Militia Duty	Anderson's Return	Purvis's Regiment	Ninety Six	£ 10.14. 3¼
238 U	Castiller, Thos.	Militia Duty	Anderson's Return	Purvis's Regiment	Ninety Six	£ 8. 8. 6¾
239 U	Cockley, Isaac	Militia Duty	Anderson's Return	Purvis's Regiment	Ninety Six	£ 2. 5. 8½
241 U	Chamberlain, John	Militia Duty	Anderson's Return	Purvis's Regiment	Ninety Six	£ 7. 2.10
242 U	Craightington, John	Militia Duty	Anderson's Return	Purvis's Regiment	Ninety Six	£ 4. 5. 8½
243 U	Covington, John	Militia Duty	Anderson's Return	Purvis's Regiment	Ninety Six	£ 4. 5. 8½
245 U	Coleman, Willm.	Militia Duty	Anderson's Return	Purvis's Regiment	Ninety Six	£ 9.17. 1½
258 U	Caughran, Willm.	Militia Duty	Anderson's Return	Purvis's Regiment	Ninety Six	£ 14. 5. 8½
259 U	Crosby, Thomas	Militia Duty	Anderson's Return	Purvis's Regiment	Ninety Six	£ 18. 8. 6¾

Numb. & Book	To whom Granted	For what Granted			District	Amount Indent
264 U	Campbell, Gilbert	Militia Duty	Anderson's Return	Purvis's Regiment	Ninety Six	£ 4.11. 5
265 U	Clay, Nathan	Militia Duty	Anderson's Return	Purvis's Regiment	Ninety Six	£ 12. 2. 6
269 U	Clemons, Zeph	Militia Duty	Anderson's Return	Purvis's Regiment	Ninety Six	£ 2.17. 1½
271 U	Cochran, Willm.	Militia Duty	Anderson's Return	Purvis's Regiment	Ninety Six	£ 2.17. 1½
274 U	Davis, Zach^{h}.	Militia Duty	Anderson's Return	Purvis's Regiment	Ninety Six	£ 11. .
275 U	Davis, Vachel	Militia Duty	Anderson's Return	Purvis's Regiment	Ninety Six	£ 11.10.
276 U	Davis, Ware	Militia Duty	Anderson's Return	Purvis's Regiment	Ninety Six	£ 18. .
277 U	Davis, Scolton	Militia Duty	Anderson's Return	Purvis's Regiment	Ninety Six	£ 3.15. 8½
278 U	Davis, Clemency	Militia Duty	Anderson's Return	Purvis's Regiment	Ninety Six	£ 4. 5. 8½
281 U	Davis, Blandford	Militia Duty	Anderson's Return	Purvis's Regiment	Ninety Six	£ 3. 4. 3¼
282 U	Davis, Isom	Militia Duty	Anderson's Return	Purvis's Regiment	Ninety Six	£ 7.14. 3¼
284 U	Devant, Charles	Militia Duty	Anderson's Return	Purvis's Regiment	Ninety Six	£ 1. 2.10¼
285 U	Deveaus, Francis	Militia Duty	Anderson's Return	Purvis's Regiment	Ninety Six	£ 5.14. 3¼
288 U	Darborough, Hugh	Militia Duty	Anderson's Return	Purvis's Regiment	Ninety Six	£ 2.11. 5
306 U	Dial, Garret	Militia Duty	Anderson's Return	Purvis's Regiment	Ninety Six	£ 4.11. 5
307 U	Dolton, Matthew	Militia Duty	Anderson's Return	Purvis's Regiment	Ninety Six	£ 4. 5. 8½
308 U	Dolton, Thomas	Militia Duty & a Horse	Anderson's Return	Purvis's Regiment	Ninety Six	£ 15. 4. 9½
313 U	Dick, Thomas	Militia Duty	Anderson's Return	Purvis's Regiment	Ninety Six	£ 4.11. 5
319 U	Douglas, Sherrard	Militia Duty	Anderson's Return	Purvis's Regiment	Ninety Six	£ 2. 2.10¼
320 U	Evans, Nathl.	Militia Duty	Anderson's Return	Purvis's Regiment	Ninety Six	£ 4.11. 5
321 U	Evans, Willm.	Militia Duty	Anderson's Return	Purvis's Regiment	Ninety Six	£ 8.17. 1½
323 U	Enoe, Jacob	Militia Duty	Anderson's Return	Purvis's Regiment	Ninety Six	£ 11. 2.10¼
331 U	Foreman, George	Militia Duty	Anderson's Return	Purvis's Regiment	Ninety Six	£ 8. 8. 6¾
336 U	Ripley, Ambrose	Militia Duty	Anderson's Return	Casey's Regiment	Ninety Six	£ 7. 8. 6¾
338 U	Reede, William	Militia Duty	Anderson's Return	Casey's Regiment	Ninety Six	£ 8.11. 5
344 U	Stearns, Aaron	Militia Duty	Anderson's Return	Casey's Regiment	Ninety Six	£ 3. 5. 8½
348 U	Scott, James	Militia Duty	Anderson's Return	Casey's Regiment	Ninety Six	£ 1. 8. 6¾
349 U	Stewart, James	Militia Duty	Anderson's Return	Casey's Regiment	Ninety Six	£ 2. 2.10¼
355 U	Starke, Thomas	Property lost	Anderson's Return	Casey's Regiment	Ninety Six	£ 10.14. 3¼
365 U	Stevens, John	Militia Duty	Anderson's Return	Casey's Regiment	Ninety Six	£ 7. 7.10¼
373 U	Taylor, George	Militia Duty	Anderson's Return	Casey's Regiment	Ninety Six	£ 20.17. 1½
374 U	Thomas, Samuel	Militia Duty	Anderson's Return	Casey's Regiment	Ninety Six	£ 7. 5. 8½
375 U	Trout, Daniel	Militia Duty	Anderson's Return	Casey's Regiment	Ninety Six	£ 3. 2.10¼

Numb. & Book	To whom Granted	For what Granted			District		Amount Indent
376 U	Trout, Adam	Militia Duty	Anderson's Return	Casey's Regiment	Ninety Six	£	6. .
377 U	Trout, George	Militia Duty	Anderson's Return	Casey's Regiment	Ninety Six	£	1.14. 3¼
378 U	Tue, John D.	Militia Duty	Anderson's Return	Casey's Regiment	Ninety Six	£	80.12.10¼
390 U	Williamson, Henry	Militia Duty	Anderson's Return	Casey's Regiment	Ninety Six	£	1. 8. 6¾
391 U	Williams, Joseph	Militia Duty	Anderson's Return	Casey's Regiment	Ninety Six	£	3. 5. 8½
393 U	Williams, Joshua	Militia Duty	Anderson's Return	Casey's Regiment	Ninety Six	£	5.11. 5
397 U	Williams, Daniel	Property lost	Anderson's Return	Casey's Regiment	Ninety Six	£	4. 5. 8½
398 U	Williams, Barwick	Militia Duty	Anderson's Return	Casey's Regiment	Ninety Six	£	7. 8. 6¾
399 U	Welch, William	Militia Duty	Anderson's Return	Casey's Regiment	Ninety Six	£	11. 5. 8½
400 U	Wernald, William	Militia Duty	Anderson's Return	Casey's Regiment	Ninety Six	£	. 8. 6¾
407 U	Whitten, Philip	Militia Duty	Anderson's Return	Casey's Regiment	Ninety Six	£	2. 7. 1½
414 U	White, Samuel	Militia Duty	Anderson's Return	Casey's Regiment	Ninety Six	£	5. 2.10¼
431 U	Adams, Joel	Supplies		Sumter's Brigade	Camden	£	6. 9. 6
433 U	Allston, Est^{a}. Wm Jun.	Supplies			Georgetown	£	45.13. 5½
434 U	Allston, Est^{a}. W^{m}.	Supplies			Georgetown	£	42. 6. 8½
442 U	Brenter, James	Supplies		Marion's Brigade	Camden	£	13. 4.
443 U	Colson, Jacob	Supplies				£	6.10. 9
448 U	Dollard, Pat^{k}.	Supplies		Marion's Brigade	Georgetown	£	4. 7. 1½
453 U	Dingley, Robert	Supplies		Major, Gamball	Camden	£	1.10.
459 U	Davison, Hugh	Militia Duty		Col. Kimball	Camden	£	3.12.10¼
465 U	Foxworth, James	Supplies			Georgetown	£	11.11.
467 U	Gouge, John	Supplies			Georgetown	£	3.17. 1
476 U	Husband, John	Supplies			Cheraw	£	3.11. 6¼
490 U	Lenud, Henry	Sund^{s}.			Georgetown	£	11. 9. 8
494 U	Mathews, Joseph R.	Pay bill for a boat Gun			Georgetown	£	69. .
495 U	Murrell, Willm.	A black Guelding		Marion's Brigade	Georgetown	£	27. 3. 9
501 U	McCaw, Willm.	Supplies		Sumter's Brigade	Camden	£	1. 5. 5
503 U	Martin, Willm.	A bay Horse				£	7. 2.10
505 U	Middleton, Rich^{d}.	Supplies			Georgetown	£	44.18. 4
508 U	McCall, Chas.	Supplies	Powe's Return		Cheraw	£	4.13.10
514 U	Norton, Willm.	Negro hire				£	3.11. 5
520 U	Odam, Benj^{a}.	Supplies			Orangeburgh	£	19.11.
522 U	O'Brian, Willm.	Supplies			Charleston	£	11.11.

Numb. & Book	To whom Granted	For what Granted			District	Amount Indent	
528 U	Penney, Ann	Supplies			Camden	£	16.18. 9
531 U	Pendarvis, Sen. Josiah	Supplies			Beaufort	£	50.12. 2
535 U	Perdriau, John	Supplies & Ferr[a].			Georgetown	£	14.10.11½
536 U	Perdriau, John	Supplies & Ferr[a].			Georgetown	£	2.14. 9
544 U	Rowdus, Eliz[h].	A Horse			Camden	£	7. .
548 U	Reddish, Thomas	Militia Duty	Powe's Return		Cheraw	£	6. 8. 6¾
553 U	Simons, Est[a]. Peter	Supplies			Georgetown	£	8. 3. 4
554 U	Smith, Will[m].	Supplies		Col. Bratton	Camden	£	1. 8. 6
555 U	Sims, Joseph	Supplies		Col. Bratton	Camden	£	1. 8. 6
558 U	Spivey, James	Militia Duty	Powe's Return		Cheraw	£	2.10.
562 U	Teate, Thomas	Supplies		Col. Hill	Camden	£	18.19. 9
569 U	Williams, Thomas	Supplies				£	1.15.
570 U	Williams, Thomas	A Horse				£	6.17. 3
575 U	Witherspoon, Gavin	Supplies	Col. P. Horry		Georgetown	£	24. 7. 8
576 U	Woodard, Sam[l].	Supplies		Col. Middleton	Camden	£	5. 2. 8
595 U	Flake, John	Supplies	Anderson's Return	Purvis's Regiment	Ninety Six	£	4. 5. 8
598 U	Franklin, George	Militia Duty	Anderson's Return	Purvis's Regiment	Ninety Six	£	5.17. 1
600 U	Fender, John	Militia Duty	Anderson's Return	Purvis's Regiment	Ninety Six	£	1. .
601 U	Fender, Will[m]		Anderson's Return	Purvis's Regiment	Ninety Six	£	4.11. 5
602 U	Fitzgerald, Cha[s].	Supplies		Purvis's Regiment	Ninety Six	£	1.14. 3
604 U	Forris, George	Militia Duty	Anderson's Return	Purvis's Regiment	Ninety Six	£	1.14. 3
609 U	Ford, Thomas	Militia Duty	Anderson's Return	Purvis's Regiment	Ninety Six	£	4. 4. 3
612 U	Garbet, George	Militia Duty	Anderson's Return	Purvis's Regiment	Ninety Six	£	8.17. 1
616 U	Gage, Will[m]	Militia Duty	Anderson's Return	Purvis's Regiment	Ninety Six	£	8.17. 1
618 U	Goodby, W[m]	Militia Duty	Anderson's Return	Purvis's Regiment	Ninety Six	£	28.17. 1
622 U	Good, Ernes	A Horse Lost	Anderson's Return	Purvis's Regiment	Ninety Six	£	20. .
626 U	Grimesley, John	Militia Duty	Anderson's Return	Purvis's Regiment	Ninety Six	£	1.10.
631 U	Getty, Henry	Militia Duty	Anderson's Return	Purvis's Regiment	Ninety Six	£	1.10.
632 U	Grigsbey, Enoch	Militia Duty	Anderson's Return	Purvis's Regiment	Ninety Six	£	7.12.10
642 U	Glover, Fred[k].	Militia Duty	Anderson's Return	Purvis's Regiment	Ninety Six	£	2.11. 5
650 U	Gibson, David	Militia Duty	Anderson's Return	Purvis's Regiment	Ninety Six	£	4. 5. 8
652 U	Gough, Francis	Militia Duty	Anderson's Return	Purvis's Regiment	Ninety Six	£	2. 4. 3

Numb. & Book	To whom Granted	For what Granted			District	Amount Indent
2 V	Hood, John	Supplies	Powe's Return		Cheraw	£ 11. 8. 8
3 V	Hatcher, David	Militia Duty	Powe's Return		Cheraw	£ 2.11. 5
4 V	Huse, John	Supplies	Powe's Return		Cheraw	£ .14. 8¾
5 V	Hearrens, Fred^{k}.	Militia Duty	Powe's Return		Cheraw	£ 2.11. 9¼
9 V	Hermon, Ab^{m}.	Supplies	Powe's Return		Cheraw	£ 2.11. 4
11 V	Jackson, Stephen	Supplies & Driv^{g}. Cattle	Powe's Return		Cheraw	£ 3. 7. 6
12 V	Jackson, John	Supplies	Powe's Return		Cheraw	£ 4.17. 6¼
13 V	Irby, Est^{a}. Robt.	Supplies	Powe's Return		Cheraw	£ 7. .
16 V	James, Willm.	Supplies	Powe's Return		Cheraw	£ 1.13. 1
17 V	James, Benjn.	Supplies	Powe's Return		Cheraw	£ 1. 8.
22 V	John, We	Supplies	Powe's Return		Cheraw	£ 1. 7. 9¼
23 V	Jowers, John	Militia Duty	Powe's Return		Cheraw	£ 5.18. 6¾
24 V	Jenkins, John	Militia Duty	Powe's Return		Cheraw	£ 2. 2.10¼
25 V	Kirkling, James	Militia Duty	Powe's Return		Cheraw	£ 2. 8. 6¾
26 V	Kirkland, John	Supplies	Powe's Return		Cheraw	£ 12.15. 5½
32 V	Lewis, Joseph	Militia Duty	Powe's Return		Cheraw	£ 2.10.
36 V	Lunday, James	Supplies	Powe's Return		Cheraw	£ . 4. 8
37 V	Lamar, Lewis	Militia Duty	Powe's Return		Cheraw	£ 2. .
38 V	Lefever, John	Supplies	Powe's Return		Cheraw	£ 19. 8. 4½
42 V	McCall, Henry	Militia Duty	Powe's Return		Cheraw	£ 2.13. 7
47 V	Morgan, Joseph	Militia Duty	Powe's Return		Cheraw	£ 2. 1. 5
51 V	Morison, John	Militia Duty	Powe's Return		Cheraw	£ 2.17. 1½
52 V	McLeland, Stephen	Militia Duty	Powe's Return		Cheraw	£ 2. 5. 8½
53 V	Myles, Willm.	Militia Duty	Powe's Return		Cheraw	£ 1. .
54 V	Neil, Est^{a}. Thomas	Supplies	Powe's Return		Cheraw	£ 26. 1. 9¾
57 V	Outlaw, Edward	Militia Duty	Powe's Return		Cheraw	£ 2. 2.10¼
58 V	Pouncy, Samuel	Supplies	Powe's Return		Cheraw	£ 3. 9. 5¼
64 V	Popwell, William	Supplies	Powe's Return		Cheraw	£ 9. 4. 8
65 V	Pearce, Dixon	Supplies	Powe's Return		Cheraw	£ 5.14. 4
66 V	Quick, Sen. Thomas	Supplies	Powe's Return		Cheraw	£ 7.18.10
67 V	Russell, Willm.	Supplies	Powe's Return		Cheraw	£ 4. 9.10
70 V	Rouse, Deborah	Supplies	Powe's Return		Cheraw	£ 4. 4.11
72 V	Read, James	A grey Horse	Powe's Return		Cheraw	£ 6. 2.10½

Numb. & Book	To whom Granted	For what Granted			District	Amount Indent
73 V	Scott, Francis	Supplies	Powe's Return		Cheraw	£ 1.12. 8
74 V	Scott, Robert	Supplies	Powe's Return		Cheraw	£ 1.15.11
84 V	Skipper, Amos	Supplies	Powe's Return		Cheraw	£ 3. 4. 2
86 V	Thomas, Jun. Willm.	Supplies	Powe's Return		Cheraw	£ 7.14.
88 V	Thomas, Jesse	Militia Duty	Powe's Return		Cheraw	£ 2.18. 6¾
90 V	Todd, Haywood	Militia Duty	Powe's Return		Cheraw	£ 3. 1. 5
92 V	Tomlinson, Willm.	A Horse			Cheraw	£ 14. 5. 8½
94 V	Williamson, J^{r}. Thomas	Militia Duty	Powe's Return		Cheraw	£ 4. 4. 3¼
95 V	Walker, George	A Black Stallion			Cheraw	£ 18.12. 4
100 V	Williams, Jesse	Militia Duty	Powe's Return		Cheraw	£ 2.11. 5
101 V	Williams, Est^{a}. David	Supplies	Powe's Return		Cheraw	£ 67.11. 7¾
102 V	Whittington, Barnett	Militia Duty	Powe's Return		Cheraw	£ 5. 7. 1½
104 V	Wright, Stephen	Militia Duty	Powe's Return		Cheraw	£ 2. 5. 8½
106 V	Windham, Samuel	Supplies	Powe's Return		Cheraw	£ 4. 2. 1½
107 V	Wheeler, John	Militia Duty	Powe's Return		Cheraw	£ 2. 2.10¼
108 V	Wines, Saml.	Supplies	Powe's Return		Cheraw	£ 5. 2. 8
110 V	Warren, Joseph	Militia Duty	Powe's Return		Cheraw	£ 2. 8. 6¾
111 V	Willis, John	Militia Duty	Powe's Return		Cheraw	£ 4.17. 1½
128 V	Johnston, Jacob	Militia Duty		Marion's Brigade	Georgetown	£ 1. 4. 3½
132 V	Johnson, Ja^{s}.	Militia Duty		Marion's Brigade	Georgetown	£ 2.11. 5
135 V	Koker, Thomas	A Gun		Capt. Standard	Cheraw	£ 2. 2.10¼
137 V	Keith, Marg^{t}.	Supplies			Cheraw	£ 3. 4. 2
147 V	Lane, Drury	Militia Duty		Col.		£ 21.17. 1½
170 V	Marlor, Willm.	Militia Duty		Col. Kimball	Camden	£ 9. 1. 5
172 V	Micheau, Jacob	Militia Duty & Supplies			Georgetown	£ 18. 1. 4
173 V	Middleton, Willm.	Supplies			Georgetown	£ 11.11.
176 V	Myrick & Moody	Supplies			Orangeburgh	£ 6.16.
177 V	Major, John	Militia Duty		Capt. Edwd. Martin	Camden	£ 12.15. 8½
182 V	Merrick, Robt.	Supplies		Brandon's Regiment	Ninety Six	£ 4. 7.
204 V	Mattocks, McKenzie	Militia Duty		Col. Taylor	Camden	£ 7. 8. 6¾
205 V	Muckinfus, George	Supplies			Charleston	£ 4. 4.
213 V	McConnell, George	Militia Duty			Georgetown	£ 8.14. 3¼

Numb. & Book	To whom Granted	For what Granted			District	Amount Indent
214 V	McDaniel, Est^a. Jas. & Pearce, John }	Supplies			Cheraw	£ 12.16. 8
218 V	McKensey, Est^a. Alex	Supplies			Orangeburgh	£ 5. 2. 8
231 V	Odam, Danl.	Militia Duty			Orangeburgh	£ 12.11. 5
234 V	Oliver, Peter	Militia Duty			Orangeburgh	£ 13.13. 2½
235 V	O'Neal, Willm	Supplies			Beaufort	£ 3.17.
239 V	Owens, Jun. Benjⁿ.	Militia Duty		Genl. Winn	Camden	£ 4.15. 8½
241 V	Pledger, Philip	Supplies		Col. Benton	Cheraw	£ 5. 2. 8
243 V	Palmer, Thos.	Militia Duty			Charleston	£ 3.11. 5
253 V	Payne, Joseph	Militia Duty		Col. Taylor	Camden	£ 3.14. 3½
274 V	Raymond, Peter	Supplies			Charleston	£ 9.12. 6
278 V	Rogers, John	Supplies		Marion's Brig.	Georgetown	£ 3.17.
312 V	Stafford, Rich^d.	Militia Duty			Beaufort	£ 4. 5. 8½
318 V	Shoemaker, Sampson	Militia Duty			Georgetown	£ 2.17. 1½
332 V	Tanner, Benjⁿ	Militia Duty			Georgetown	£ 2. 7. 1½
334 V	Sausey, David	Supplies	W. Wigg	Genl. Wayne	Beaufort	£ 11.11. 6
335 V	Stoll, David	Supplies	W. Wigg		Beaufort	£ 4. 9.10
337 V	Smith, John	Supplies		Col. Horry	Georgetown	£ 1. 6. 9¾
338 V	Stoutinburgh, Est^a. Willm.	Shoes			Charleston	£ 19. 5.
341 V	Smith, John James	Supplies	W. Wigg	Col. Harden	Beaufort	£ 10.10.10½
346 V	McKelveen, Mary	A Gun			Georgetown	£ 4. .
356 V	McGowen, Ja^s.	Supplies	W. Wigg		Beaufort	£. 18. 8
358 V	Mongin, David	Supplies	W. Wigg		Beaufort	£ 11. 3. 3
361 V	Lawrence, Est^a. Willm.	Supplies	W. Wigg		Beaufort	£. 10. 4
367 V	Winkler, M^{rs}.	Supplies	W. Wigg		Beaufort	£ 21.15. 2
374 V	Page, Thos.	Supplies	W. Wigg		Beaufort	£ 2.11. 4
376 V	Pike, Willm.	Supplies	W. Wigg		Beaufort	£ 5. 9. 3¼
381 V	Volloton, Jerem^h.	Supplies	W. Wigg		Beaufort	£ 3. 1. 9½
383 V	Zimmerman, Mary	Supplies	W. Wigg		Beaufort	£ 4. 2. 1
395 V	Ravenal, Eliz^h.	Supplies			Charleston	£ 25.13. 4
396 V	Green, Isaac	Militia Duty		Capt. W^m. Jenkins	Camden	£ 2.10.

Numb. & Book	To whom Granted	For what Granted		District	Amount Indent
398 V	Howe, Jane	Supplies	Tate's Return	Camden	£ 12. 7.11
403 V	McCleland, David	Militia Duty	Col. Bratton	Camden	£ 13.12.10
406 V	Dover, John	Supplies	Capt. Barber	Camden	£ . 5. 1
407 V	Brunson, Matthew	Supplies	Capt. Warden	Georgetown	£ 2. 2.
408 V	Bradford, Jonᵃ.	Militia Duty			£ 2. 8. 6¾
444 V	Simpson, Willᵐ.	Supplies			£ 3.17. 8¼
453 V	Thomas, Estᵃ. Edwᵈ.	Supplies & Militia Duty	Col. Anderson	Ninety Six	£ 83. 5.
458 V	Tweedy, Robᵗ.	Supplies		Camden	£ 5. 5.
461 V	Twewitts, Elijah	A Horse			£ 28.11. 5
469 V	Wilson, Estᵃ. Jaˢ.	Militia Duty	Col. Anderson	Ninety Six	£ 19. .
473 V	Wallace, Robert	Militia Duty & Supplies	Col. Anderson	Ninety Six	£ 3.12.10¼
488 V	Givens, James	Militia Duty	Capt. Wallace	Camden	£ 9. 5. 8½
490 V	Hamilton, James	Sundries			£ 17. 2. 3
491 V	Hutchinson, Estᵃ. John Elias	Supplies		Charleston	£ 5.13. 0½
505 V	Hopkins, Jesse	Militia Duty	Col. Taylor	Camden	£ 4. 5. 8½
507 V	Humphry, Estᵃ. David	Militia Duty			£ 8. 2.10¼
514 V	Harris, Moses	Militia Duty	Col. Taylor	Camden	£ 7.10.
525 V	Hay, Estᵃ John	Contˡ. Duty			£ 9. 6. 8
528 V	Hicks, John	Supplies		Orangeburgh	£ 2. 4.11
533 V	Hutchinson, Willᵐ.	Supplies	Col. Hayes	Ninety Six	£ 3.18. 6
538 V	Jordan, Robert	Militia Duty		Georgetown	£ 11. 5. 4¼
563 V	Kinesler, Christian	Supplies	Sumter's Brigade	Camden	£ 3. 5.
564 V	Kerby, Archᵈ.	Militia Duty & Suppˢ.	Marion's Brigade	Georgetown	£ 21. 9. 2
592 V	Laycock, Willᵐ.	Mariner's Wages	Frigate Sᵒ. Carᵃ.	Georgetown	£ 22.11. 3
596 V	Leonard, Abel	Militia Duty	Marion's Brigade	Georgetown	£ 3. 1. 5
601 V	Maner, Samˡ.	Militia Duty	Marion's Brigade	Georgetown	£ 1. 4.
602 V	Montgomery, James	Militia Duty	Capt. Pope	Camden	£ 4. 1. 5
605 V	Marion, Gabˡ.	Supplies &c.	Capt. Pope	Camden	£ 29. 7. 8
608 V	Muckleween, Henry	Militia Duty	Col. Marshall	Camden	£ 6.10.
614 V	Minose, Domino	Mariner's Wages	Sᵒ. Carᵃ. Frigate		£ 2.11. 9
634 V	Partin, Robᵗ.	Militia Duty	Marion's Brigade	Georgetown	£ 3. 1. 5
646 V	Rogers, Daniel	Supplies	Col. S. Hammon	Ninety Six	£ 1.18. 6
653 V	Reynolds, Joseph	Supplies	Purvis's Regiment	Ninety Six	£. 10. 8

Numb. & Book	To whom Granted	For what Granted		District	Amount Indent
655 V	Ramsey, James	Militia Duty	Marshal's Regiment	Camden	£ 2.10.
660 V	Rittsendale, Martin	Mariner's Wages	Sº. Carª. Frigate		£ 3. 8. 3
4 W	Todd, Richd.	Contl. Duty			£ 10.10.
9 W	Turner, Amey	Supplies	Marion's Brigade	Georgetown	£ 3. 4. 2
17 W	Ulmer, Jacob	Militia Duty	Marion's Brigade	Orangeburgh	£ 2.13. 6¾
41 W	Weber, Nichs.	Militia Duty	Marion's Brigade	Orangeburgh	£ 2.14. 3¾
68 W	Atkerson, Isaac	Supplies	Marion's Brigade	Georgetown	£ 2. 2.
88 W	Briant, Estª. Willm.	Contl. Duty	Marion's Brigade	Camden	£ 14. .
89 W	Bennett, Saml.	Supplies	Marion's Brigade	Camden	£ 8. 7.
104 W	Brown, Willm.	Militia Duty	Major Crawford	Camden	£ 5.11. 5
107 W	Barnet, Michl.	Militia Duty	Col. Marshal	Camden	£ 2.14. 3½
128 W	Heyward, James	Duty	Charleston Artillery	Charleston	£ 36. 2.10
129 W	Fairchild, Richd.	Duty	Charleston Artillery	Charleston	£ 36. 2.10
135 W	Bayle, Francis	Duty	Charleston Artillery	Charleston	£ 36. 2.10
137 W	Fell, Estª. John	Duty	Charleston Artillery	Charleston	£ 7. 1. 5
159 W	Blunt, Charles	Supplies	Genl. Greene	Orangeburgh	£ 3.17.
162 W	Bell, Willm.	Supplies	Col. Hopkins	Camden	£ 1.19. 3
176 W	Carter, Robt.	Supplies	Col. Singleton	Camden	£ 3. 7. 3½
206 W	Collins, Reuben	Militia Duty	Cols. Kimball & Kershaw	Camden	£ 7. .
223 W	Connor, Thomas	Supplies		Cheraw	£ 3. 4. 2
224 W	Caps, John	Militia Duty	Marion's Brigade	Camden	£ 3.14. 3½
250 W	Deason, Enoch	Militia Duty	Col. Marshal	Camden	£ 15. .
256 W	Duggers, Julius	Supplies	Genl. Marion	Georgetown	£ 12.16. 8
291 W	Griffin, Benjn.	Militia Duty	Col. Marshal	Camden	£ 30.12.10¼
302 W	Gibson, James	Militia Duty	Col. Taylor	Camden	£ 18. .
316 W	Grinet, John	Militia Duty		Camden	£ 23.11. 5
317 W	Gasque, Thos.	Militia Duty		Georgetown	£ 2. 2.10¼
324 W	Gooden or Goodman, Henry	Supplies		Cheraw	£ 3. 4. 2
325 W	Grains, Henry	Militia Duty	Col. Marshal	Camden	£ 2. 8. 6¾
328 W	Glading, James	Supplies	Genl. Marion	Georgetown	£ 4.18.
329 W	Gale, Ransom	Supplies		Camden	£ 5.10. 3

Numb. & Book	To whom Granted	For what Granted			District	Amount Indent
330 W	Garey, William Bayley	Militia Duty	Col. Marshal		Camden	£ 6. 2.10¼
337 W	Austin, Francis	Militia Duty	Casey's Regiment	Anderson's Return	Ninety Six	£ 13. 2.10¼
350 W	Brenan, Estᵃ. Eugene	Ferriages			Beaufort	£ 6. 3.10
363 W	Bryson, James	Supplies	Casey's Regiment	Anderson's Return	Ninety Six	£ 1.12.10¼
380 W	Cooper, Thoˢ.	Supplies			Charleston	£ 8.15.
403 W	Creamor, Willᵐ.	Militia Duty	Col. Marshal		Camden	£ 20. 5. 8½
411 W	Callihan, David	Supplies	Col. Purvis	Anderson's Return	Ninety Six	£ 1. 8. 6¾
417 W	Cockburn, John	Supplies & Militia Duty	Col. Purvis	Anderson's Return	Ninety Six	£ 4. 7. 1½
418 W	Cochran, Phebe	Supplies	Col. Purvis	Anderson's Return	Ninety Six	£. .19. 7
420 W	Cotton, Thomas	Supplies	Casey's Regiment	Anderson's Return	Ninety Six	£ 3.13. 7½
433 W	Duke, Edmᵈ.	Supplies	Casey's Regiment	Anderson's Return	Ninety Six	£ 5.17.10¼
442 W	Davis, John	Supplies	Purvis's Regiment	Anderson's Return	Ninety Six	£ 3. 2.10¼
453 W	Finley, John	Militia Duty	Capt. John Gray		Camden	£ 26. 5. 8
457 W	Ford, Elisha	Supplies	Col. Purvis	Anderson's Return	Ninety Six	£ 5. .
461 W	Guinn, Richᵈ.	Supplies				£. .13. 4
462 W	Greenwood's Wharf	Wharfage			Charleston	£ . 9.5
464 W	Gee, Chaˢ.	Bricklayer's Work			Georgetown	£ 107.10. 9
468 W	Gwen, Willᵐ.	Militia Duty & a Horse	Capt. Killpatrick		Camden	£ 12. 5. 8
469 W	Geary, Thoˢ.	Supplies	Casey's Regiment	Anderson's Return	Ninety Six	£ 8. 9. 8
473 W	Gamble, John	Militia Duty	Casey's Regiment	Anderson's Return	Ninety Six	£ 5.17. 1
486 W	Galton, Sen. John	A Gun	Purvis's Regiment	Anderson's Return	Ninety Six	£ 9. .
489 W	Green, Bryant	Militia Duty	Purvis's Regiment	Anderson's Return	Ninety Six	£ 7.16. 9
497 W	Herring, Willᵐ.	Suppˢ	Marion's Brigade		Georgetown	£ 6. .9
499 W	Houze, James	Supplies & Militia Duty	Sumter's Brigade		Camden	£ 15.11. 5
515 W	Johnston, Charles	A Gelding				£ 15. .
519 W	Irwin, Capt. John	Monˢ. advanced			Ninety Six	£ 18.16.11
535 W	Kennedy, John	Militia Duty			Camden	£ 40. 8. 6
545 W	Lewis, John	Supplies	Capt. Parsons		Ninety Six	£ 7. 1. 9
561 W	Martin, John	Militia Duty & a horse	Anderson's Regiment		Ninety Six	£ 55. 6. 5
564 W	Morris, Burrel	Supplies	Anderson's Regiment		Ninety Six	£ 1.17. 1
588 W	McWharter, Thomas	Supplies			Orangeburgh	£ 6. 8. 4

Numb. & Book	To whom Granted	For what Granted			District	Amount Indent
635 W	Pullam, Robert	Militia Duty		Anderson's Regiment	Ninety Six	£ 14. 5. 8
658 W	River, Willm. S.	A Horse				£ 20. .
5 X	Long, James	Supps. & a Waggon		Winn's Regiment	Camden	£ 1. 1. 5
13 X	Lewis, Esta Willm.	Supplies			Camden	£ 10. 5. 4
16B X	Martin, Robt.	Militia Duty			Camden	£ 5.17. 1½
21 X	Miller, Esta. Phillip	Duty as a Gunner			Camden	£ 33.15.
22 X	Morris, John	Militia Duty		Col. Goodwyn	Camden	£ 4.15. 8½
23 X	Morris, John	Militia Duty		Col. Taylor	Camden	£ 14.15. 8½
39 X	Martin, Esta. Richd.	Militia Duty		Col. Lacey	Camden	£ 19. 2.10¼
44 X	McCall, Henry L.	Contl. Duty				£ 32. 2. 5½
47 X	McCoy, Ruddin	Militia Duty			Camden	£ 5. 4. 3¼
55 X	McDavid, John	Supplies		Capt. Kilgore	Ninety Six	£ 4. 4. 2
63 X	McClaskey, Dennis	Militia Duty		Col. Casey	Ninety Six	£ 33.17. 1½
72 X	McClinton, John	Supps.		Col. Casey	Ninety Six	£ 6.16. 9¾
75 X	Mixson, Michl.	Supps.		Col. Kolb	Cheraw	£ 2.11. 4
77 X	McFaddin, Patk.	Supps.		Capt. Wommock	Orangeburgh	£ 3.10.
90 X	Mills, Henry	Militia Duty		Capt. Wommock	Orangeburgh	£ 23. 5. 8½
91 X	Mellett, Jun. Peter	Militia Duty		Marion's Brigade	Camden	£ 4.14. 3¼
112 X	Pringle, Willm.	Militia Duty		Marion's Brigade	Camden	£ 6. 8. 6¾
113 X	Pearson, Edwd.	Supplies			Camden	£ 18.12.
131 X	Rolleson, Benjn.	Militia Duty		Col. Taylor	Camden	£ 6.12.10¼
145 X	Roger, Meshk.	Militia Duty		Marion's Brigade	Camden	£ 4.17. 1
146 X	Rouse, Debh.	Supplies			Cheraw	£ 15. 8.
151 X	Richardson, Edward	Militia Duty				£ 14. .
161 X	Smith, Simon	Supplies				£ 12.14. 1
166 X	Smith, John of Santee	Militia Duty		Marion's Brigade	Camden	£ 9. 9.10
167 X	Smith, George of Camden	Militia Duty		Col. Taylor	Camden	£ 8.11. 5
169 X	Smith, Susanna	A Mare		Sumter's Brigade	Camden	£ 5. .
187 X	Swinton, Hugh	Pay as Commy. Prisrs.			Charleston	£ 7. .10
190 X	Snelling, John	Militia Duty		Col. Taylor	Camden	£ 2. 2.10
193 X	Skillen, Willm.	Militia Duty			Georgetown	£ 7.15.

Numb. & Book	To whom Granted	For what Granted			District	Amount Indent
201 X	Thomas, Josiah	Supplies	Genˡ. Henderson		Orangeburgh	£ 2.14. 4
206 X	Taylor, Jane	Supplies			Georgetown	£ 9. 6. 1
213 X	Thomson, Nathan	Militia Duty				£ 8.14. 3
215 X	Thomson, Nathan					£ 18.17. 1
216 X	Tollenare, De Charles	Supplies			Charleston	£ 19.13. 5
222 X	Vernidoe, Henry	Supplies	Capt. Rumph		Orangeburgh	£ 2. 3. 6
227 X	Williams, Elizʰ.	Supplies	Col. Davis		Orangeburgh	£ 14.11. 9
228 X	Williams, Robᵗ.	Militia Duty	Col. Marshal		Camden	£ 2. 2.10
231 X	Welch, Willᵐ.	Militia Duty				£ 6. 8. 6
236 X	Wilson, Martha	Supplies	Georgetown Garrison		Georgetown	£ 6.16. 6
242 X	Williamson, Jesse	Militia Duty	Marion's Brigade		Cheraw	£ 2.11. 5
260 X	Wise, Jonathan	Militia Duty	Col. Taylor			£ 2. 4. 3
261 X	Wimberley, James	Militia Duty	Col. Marshal		Camden	£ 5. 8. 6
265 X	Webb, John	Militia Duty				£ 35.14. 3
266 X	Ware, David	Militia Duty	Marion's Brigade		Cheraw	£ 14.11. 5
267 X	Warren, George	A Waggon & Team				£ 6. 5. 8
277 X	Zinn, Horonomas	A Horse				£ 12. .
282 X	Rice, James	Militia Duty & Supplies	Col. Taylor		Camden	£ 10.18. 6
291 X	Stuart, Mary	Supplies		Anderson's Return	Ninety Six	£ 2. 2.10
294 X	Sullivan, John	Militia Duty	Purvis's Regiment	Anderson's Return	Ninety Six	£ 18.14. 7
297 X	Sawyer, John	Supplies	Purvis's Regiment		Ninety Six	£ 5.16.
300 X	Smith, John Jacob M.	Supplies & Militia Duty	Purvis's Regiment		Ninety Six	£ 9. 7. 1
303 X	Sisson, Fredʰ.	Supplies	Third Regiment			£ 15.15.
304 X	Sly, Chaˢ.	Mariners Wages	Brigᵉ. Polly			£ 36. .
307 X	Stobo, Estᵃ. Richᵈ. P.	Negro hire			Charleston	£ 21. 4. 6
308 X	Sanders, Margᵗ.	Supplies				£ 9.19. 3
312 X	Stivener, George	Supplies				£ 6. 8. 4
321 X	Stuart, Isabel	Supplies	Casey's Regiment	Anderson's Return	Ninety Six	£ 7. 2. 5
336 X	Austin, Elizʰ.	Supplies	Capt. Gray		Camden	£ 15. 1. 9
339 X	Atkison, Timothy	Supplies			Ninety Six	£ 26. 8.
355 X	Burnaw, Martin	Mariners Wages				£ 3. 9. 4
357 X	Birch, Joseph	Supplies	Low Craven Co.		Cheraw	£ 8.16.11

Numb. & Book	To whom Granted	For what Granted		Regiment	District	Amount Indent
358 X	Banks, Chas.	Supplies		Capt. Hanna		£ 4.14.6
367 X	Brown, Henry	Militia Duty		Capt. Hanna		£ 8. .
371 X	Bolton, Danl.	Militia Duty				£ 31.19.11
376 X	Bailey, Robert	Supplies	Tate's Return	Col. H^y. Hampton	Camden	£ 2. 2.10¼
378 X	Cousmould, Henry	Cont^l. Duty				£ 6. 4.5
389 X	Creighton, John	Militia Duty		Col. Marshal	Camden	£ 2.17.2
395 X	[blank]	Service on b^d. Eagle Pilot B^t.		Eagle Pilot Boat		£ 25.19.6
400 X	Davis, Hezek^h.	Militia Duty				£ 3. 5.8
408 X	Davis, Nathan	Militia Duty				£ 4. 4.3½
411 X	Dutoutle, John	Mariners Wages		Frigate S^o. Car^a.		£ 6.17.3
413 X	Pearson, Edward	Supplies				£ 18.12.
418 X	Eckles, Willm.	Militia Duty		Marion's Brigade	Georgetown	£ 22. 4.3
420 X	Flowers, Sen. Henry	Supplies		Col. Giles	Georgetown	£ 1. 6.10
428 X	Ford, Hezek^h.	Militia Duty		Col. Taylor		£ 20. 1.5
432 X	Fields, Ab^m.	Cont^l. Duty				£ 10.17.9
436 X	Fitzgerald, Philip	Mariners Wages		Frigate S^o. Car^a.		£ 30. 3. 6¾
438 X	Feigge, Christⁿ.	Mariners Wages		Frigate S^o. Car^a.		£ 4. 3. 1
439 X	Fuller, Est^a. Benjⁿ.	Supplies			Charleston	£ 3.17.
446 X	Gillet, Aaron	Supplies			Charleston	£ 17. 4.9
449 X	Gray, James	Militia Duty				£ 3.11.5
450 X	Goowin, Abel	Militia Duty				£ 4. 8.6
455 X	Griffin, Samuel	Supplies	Tate's Return	Genl. Sumter	Camden	£ .17.10
458 X	Goebel, John	Mariners Wages		Frigate S^o. Car^a.		£ 3.10.
461 X	Hudson, Robt.	Supp^s. & Smiths Work			Beaufort	£ 7. .
468 X	Hodges, Robert	Militia Duty				£ 4. .
476 X	Harkins, John	Supplies	Anderson's Return	Purvis's Regiment	Ninety Six	£ 1. 8.11
483 X	Hatcher, Est^a. Benjⁿ.	A Mare	Anderson's Return	Purvis's Regiment	Ninety Six	£ 15. .
484 X	Huggins, Rebecca	Supplies		Purvis's Regiment	Ninety Six	£ 2. 5.8
500 X	Jordan, Robt.	Militia Duty				£ 6. 7.10
502 X	Jones, Rich^d.	Militia Duty				£ 6. 5.8½
515 X	Knox, Eleanor	Supplies		Col. Kershaw	Camden	£ 19. 3.4
523 X	Kent, Chas.	7 Hhds. Taffia				£ 162.13.1
527 X	Livingston, Willm.	Supplies		Lt. J^{no}. Grimball		£ 5.19.2

48

Numb. & Book	To whom Granted	For what Granted			District	Amount Indent
529 X	Lockhart, Rob.t	Militia Duty		Gen.l Sumter	Camden	£ 8. .
536 X	Lattimore, John	Militia Duty		Col. Neal	Camden	£ 6. 8. 7
546 X	Mc Daniel, Daniel	Militia Duty		Col. H. Hunter	Camden	£ 6.10.
551 X	Morlen, Est.a John	Militia Duty		Col. Hill	Camden	£ 7.11. 5
573 X	Norris, Agathy	Supplies	Anderson's Return	Col. Purvis	Ninety Six	£ . 8.
574 X	Norrell, Mary	Supplies	Anderson's Return	Col. Purvis	Ninety Six	£ 10. 4. 3
577 X	Overstreet, Jethro	Militia Duty			Ninety Six	£ 1.15. 8
586 X	Peek, Tho.s	Militia Duty	Anderson's Return	Col. Purvis	Ninety Six	£ 2. 2.10¼
591 X	Pardue, Joel	Militia Duty	Anderson's Return	Col. Purvis	Ninety Six	£ 2.17. 1
595 X	Rushen, Matthew	Militia Duty				£ 1.10.
605 X	Sutton, Sam.l	Cont.l Duty			Charleston	£ 11. 8.
620 X	Saunders, Will.m	Supplies			Charleston	£ 45.10.
626 X	Tanner, Lynn	Militia Duty			B	£ 2. .
635 X	Walton, Nich.s	A Mare, Saddle, &c			Beaufort	£ 9.10.
636 X	Webster, Jun. Sam.l	Militia Duty				£ 4. .
637 X	Wyn, Will.m	Militia Duty				£ 4.11. 5
639 X	Wilson, Sen.r James	Militia Duty & Supplies		Purvis's Regiment	Ninety Six	£ 5.15. 8
641 X	Yelding, Mary	Supplies			Ninety Six	£ 6. 8. 6
652 X	Trevres, John	Mariner's Wages		Frigate S°. Carolina		£ 3.10.10
653 X	Thomson, Lewis	Supplies				£ 11.13. 4
670 X	Whittles, Burrows	Militia Duty & Supplies		Purvis's Regiment	Ninety Six	£ 10.14. 3
678 X	Wilson, Est.a Rob.t	Supplies			Georgetown	£ 47.10. 4
680 X	White, Allen Will.m	Supplies a Waggon, Horse, &c.			Camden	£ 121. 1. 1
685 X	Wilson, Henry	Supplies	Anderson's Return	Casey's Regiment	Ninety Six	£ 14. .
692 X	Williams, Isaac	Militia Duty	Anderson's Return	Casey's Regiment	Ninety Six	£ 1. 5. 9
702 X	Young, Jun. Robert	Waggon hire &c.		Major Gillam	Ninety Six	£ 58.17. 1
720 X	Bryant, Rich.d	Supplies	Anderson's Return	Brandon's Regiment	Ninety Six	£ 21. 9. 4
721 X	Bryan, Rich.d	Supplies	Anderson's Return	Brandon's Regiment	Ninety Six	£ 4. 7. 1
726 X	Burns, Robert	Shoeing Horses &c.	Anderson's Return	Brandon's Regiment	Ninety Six	£ 5. 3.11

Numb. & Book	To whom Granted	For what Granted			District	Amount Indent
729 X	Coleman, Abner	Supplies	Anderson's Return	Brandon's Regiment	Ninety Six	£ 6.10. 8
733 X	Clayton, Thomas	A Horse	Anderson's Return	Brandon's Regiment	Ninety Six	£ 25.19. 5
742 X	Elder, (Capt.) James	A Horse	Anderson's Return	Roebuck's Regiment	Ninety Six	£ 17. 3. 4
744 X	Eshworth, Benjⁿ.	A Waggon &c, &c.	Anderson's Return	Anderson's Regiment	Ninety Six	£ 33.14. 3
758 X	Forbes, Patrick		Anderson's Return	Anderson's Regiment	Ninety Six	£ . 5. 8
764 X	Guinton, Moses	A Horse	Anderson's Return	Brandon's Regiment	Ninety Six	£ 14. 5. 8
770 X	Grigg, Daniel	Duty as a Spy	Anderson's Return	Col. J. Thomas, Jr.	Ninety Six	£ 43.17. 1
777 X	Hammett, John	A Horse	Anderson's Return	Roebuck's Regiment	Ninety Six	£ 8.11. 5
784 X	Harron, James	Supplies	Anderson's Return	Waters's Regiment	Ninety Six	£ 3. 4. 3
795 X	Jones, Estᵃ. Capt. Thomas	Militia Duty	Anderson's Return	Roebuck's Regiment	Ninety Six	£ 6. .
806 X	Koone, Henry or John	A Horse	Anderson's Return	Waters's Regiment	Ninety Six	£ 12. 2.10
817 X	Little, (Lieut.) John	Riding Express	Anderson's Return	Brandon's Regiment	Ninety Six	£ 2.17. 1
818 X	Lee, Robt.	Supplies	Anderson's Return	Roebuck's Regiment	Ninety Six	£ 1. 8. 6
819 X	Long, Thomas	Supplies	Anderson's Return	Waters's Regiment	Ninety Six	£ 1.18. 6
824 X	McHerd, (decᵈ.) John	Militia Duty	Anderson's Return	Brandon's Regiment	Ninety Six	£ 29.17. 1
831 X	Maynard McDowell, Willᵐ.	Duty as a Spy	Anderson's Return	Anderson's Regiment	Ninety Six	£ 12. 5. 8
833 X	McCall, Estᵃ. Jaˢ.	A Horse	Anderson's Return	Anderson's Regiment	Ninety Six	£ 17. 2.10
834 X	McCall, Thomas	Militia Duty	Anderson's Return	Anderson's Regiment	Ninety Six	£ 7.14. 3

Numb. & Book	To whom Granted	For what Granted			District	Amount Indent
836 X	Martin, Roger	Money p^d. for his Horse	Anderson's Return	Anderson's Regiment	Ninety Six	£ 5.18. 4
844 X	McElworth, John	Supplies	Anderson's Return	Roebuck's Regiment	Ninety Six	£ 1.14. 3
849 X	McGarrity, John	Supplies	Anderson's Return	Roebuck's Regiment	Ninety Six	£ 1. 8. 6
860 X	Neaville, Joseph	Militia Duty	Anderson's Return	Roebuck's Regiment	Ninety Six	£ 7.11. 5
864 X	Putteet, Tobias	A Mare	Anderson's Return	Brandon's Regiment	Ninety Six	£ 8.11. 5
869 X	Putman, Barnet	A Mare	Anderson's Return	Brandon's Regiment	Ninety Six	£ 5.14. 3
872 X	Pucket, Julany	A Horse	Anderson's Return	Brandon's Regiment	Ninety Six	£ 14. 5. 8
884 X	Russel, Willm.	A Horse	Anderson's Return	Waters's Regiment	Ninety Six	£ 14. 5. 8
896 X	Simpson, John	Waggon hire	Anderson's Return		Ninety Six	£ 12. .
915 X	Thomason, Turner Willm.	Supplies	Anderson's Return	Roebuck's Regiment	Ninety Six	£ 4.11. 8
918 X	Thacker, Isaac	A Mare	Anderson's Return		Ninety Six	£ 5. .
938 X	Booth, Est^a. John	Cont^l. Duty				£ 8.17.11
954 X	Black, Alex^r.	Militia Duty	Tate's Return	Col. Bratton	Camden	£ 6. 1. 5
972 X	Carsan, Saml.	Militia Duty	Tate's Return	Col. Bratton	Camden	£ 17. 1. 5
1000 X	Gardiner, John	Sundries	Tate's Return		Camden	£ 18. 5. 8
1007 X	Hatcher, Willm.	Militia Duty	Tate's Return	Col. Taylor	Camden	£ 8.18. 6
1051 X	Sords, John	Militia Duty	Tate's Return	Col. Bratton	Camden	£ 3. 5. 8
1055 X	Tison, John	Militia Duty		Col. Bourquin	Beaufort	£ 6.17. 1
1064 X	Wallace, James	Supplies	Tate's Return	Col. Bratton	Camden	£ 13. 5. 4
1073 X	Akin, Arch^d.	Militia Duty	Anderson's Return	Roebuck's Regiment	Ninety Six	£ 9.11. 5
1074 X	Akin, Ezekiel	Militia Duty	Anderson's Return	Roebuck's Regiment	Ninety Six	£ 5.17. 1½
1075 X	Abbett, Solomon	Militia Duty	Anderson's Return	Roebuck's Regiment	Ninety Six	£ 9. 8. 6¾

Numb. & Book	To whom Granted	For what Granted			District	Amount Indent
1076 X	Ashley, John	Militia Duty	Anderson's Return	Roebuck's Regiment	Ninety Six	£ 3. 5. 8½
1078 X	Averet, Elijah	Militia Duty	Anderson's Return	Roebuck's Regiment	Ninety Six	£ 1. 8. 6¾
1082 X	Burchfield, Adam	Militia Duty	Anderson's Return	Roebuck's Regiment	Ninety Six	£ 1. 2.10¼
1098 X	Gibbs, James	Militia Duty	Anderson's Return	Roebuck's Regiment	Ninety Six	£ .14. 3¼
1099 X	Gentry, Rich.d	Militia Duty	Anderson's Return	Roebuck's Regiment	Ninety Six	£ 3. .
1107 X	Hughes, Sam.l	Militia Duty	Anderson's Return	Roebuck's Regiment	Ninety Six	£ 6.11. 5
1109 X	Hammett, John	Militia Duty	Anderson's Return	Roebuck's Regiment	Ninety Six	£ 11.11. 5
1110 X	Jones, Hiram	Militia Duty	Anderson's Return	Roebuck's Regiment	Ninety Six	£ 3. .
1111 X	Jordan, Tho.s	Militia Duty	Anderson's Return	Roebuck's Regiment	Ninety Six	£ 6. .
1120 X	M.cBee, Mathias	Militia Duty	Anderson's Return	Roebuck's Regiment	Ninety Six	£ 3.15. 8½
1122 X	Neil, Moses	Militia Duty	Anderson's Return	Roebuck's Regiment	Ninety Six	£ 5.11. 5
1123 X	Neil, Aaron	Militia Duty	Anderson's Return	Roebuck's Regiment	Ninety Six	£ 6. 2.10¼
1125 X	O'Benian, Ben	Militia Duty	Anderson's Return	Roebuck's Regiment	Ninety Six	£ 3.11. 5
1126 X	Oliphant, Obediah	Militia Duty	Anderson's Return	Roebuck's Regiment	Ninety Six	£ .17.10¼
1128 X	Pierce, Hugh	Militia Duty	Anderson's Return	Roebuck's Regiment	Ninety Six	£ 3. .
1131 X	Robinson, Isaac	Militia Duty	Anderson's Return	Roebuck's Regiment	Ninety Six	£ 7. 2.10

Numb. & Book	To whom Granted	For what Granted			District	Amount Indent
1136 X	Saunders, Sen. Willm.	Militia Duty	Anderson's Return	Roebuck's Regiment	Ninety Six	£ 1. 5. 8
1137 X	Saunders, Jun. Willm.	Militia Duty	Anderson's Return	Roebuck's Regiment	Ninety Six	£ 6.10.
1138 X	Saunders, Corn^s.	Militia Duty	Anderson's Return	Roebuck's Regiment	Ninety Six	£ 3.17. 1
1143 X	Shippy, Saml.	Militia Duty	Anderson's Return	Roebuck's Regiment	Ninety Six	£ 8. .
1144 X	Stone, Cathbert	Militia Duty	Anderson's Return	Roebuck's Regiment	Ninety Six	£ 6.11. 5
1146 X	Thompson, Swan	Militia Duty	Anderson's Return	Roebuck's Regiment	Ninety Six	£ 3. 1.5
1147 X	Thompson, Theophilus	Militia Duty	Anderson's Return	Roebuck's Regiment	Ninety Six	£ 1. 8. 6
1152 X	Underwood, Geo^e.	Militia Duty	Anderson's Return	Roebuck's Regiment	Ninety Six	£ 1. 8. 6
1154 X	Whitter, Fendol	Militia Duty	Anderson's Return	Roebuck's Regiment	Ninety Six	£ 3. 1.5
1155-A X	Young, Edward	Militia Duty	Anderson's Return	Roebuck's Regiment	Ninety Six	£ 6.19. 4
1164 X	Broom, James	Militia Duty	Anderson's Return	Waters's Regiment	Ninety Six	£ 7. 2.10
1169 X	Bundrick, Chas.	Militia Duty	Anderson's Return	Waters's Regiment	Ninety Six	£ 2. 2.10
1177 X	Davis, Francis	Militia Duty	Anderson's Return	Roebuck's Regiment	Ninety Six	£ 16.17. 1½
1183 X	Eargle, John	Militia Duty	Anderson's Return	Waters's Regiment	Ninety Six	£ 7. 2.10¼
1185 X	French, Mich^l.	Militia Duty	Anderson's Return	Roebuck's Regiment	Ninety Six	£ 23.11. 5
1193 X	Gortman, John	Militia Duty	Anderson's Return	Waters's Regiment	Ninety Six	£ 1.14. 3¼
1197 X	Grim, John	Militia Duty	Anderson's Return	Waters's Regiment	Ninety Six	£ 1.14. 3¼
1205 X	Haulman, George	Militia Duty	Anderson's Return	Waters's Regiment	Ninety Six	£ 7. 2.10¼
1210 X	Knox, James	Militia Duty	Anderson's Return	Roebuck's Regiment	Ninety Six	£ 15. .

Numb. & Book	To whom Granted	For what Granted			District	Amount Indent	
1225 X	Massingal, Joseph	Militia Duty	Anderson's Return	Roebuck's Regiment	Ninety Six	£	8.11. 5
1324 X	Atkins, Francis	Supplies	Anderson's Return	Waters's	Ninety Six	£	5. 3. 2½
1326 X	Adkinson, Timothy	Supplies	Anderson's Return	Purvis's	Ninety Six	£	1.12. 1½
1336 X	Benson, James	Militia Duty &c.	Anderson's Return	Brandon	Ninety Six	£	14.10. 8½
1338 X	Bind, Daniel	Supplies	Anderson's Return	Purvis's Regiment	Ninety Six	£	6. 8. 4
1339 X	Bisber, Casper	Supplies	Anderson's Return	Waters's	Ninety Six	£	.18. 2½
1353 X	Bradshaw, Will[m].	Supplies	Anderson's Return	Col. Thomas	Ninety Six	£	.18. 1
1357 X	Brookes, Dudley	Supplies	Anderson's Return	Casey's Regiment	Ninety Six	£	5.14. 3¼
1363 X	Buchanan, Will[m].	A Horse & Gun	Anderson's Return	Brandon's Regiment	Ninety Six	£	14. 5. 8½
1369 X	Bayley, Lucy	Supplies	Anderson's Return	Brandon's Regiment	Ninety Six	£	1.15. 8½
1376 X	Barnett, Joseph	Supplies	Anderson's Return	Roebuck's Regiment	Ninety Six	£	2. 2.10¼
1378 X	Curenton, Will[m].	Supplies	Anderson's Return	Waters's Regiment	Ninety Six	£	1.15. 8½
1383 X	Clarke, Benj[a].	Supplies	Anderson's Return	Brandon's Regiment	Ninety Six	£	3. 4. 3¼
1385 X	Cannady, John	Supplies	Anderson's Return	Brandon's Regiment	Ninety Six	£	.14. 3¼
1388 X	Celley, Joseph	Supplies	Anderson's Return		Ninety Six	£	2. 5.
1392 X	Campbell, David	Supplies	Anderson's Return		Ninety Six	£	2. 2.10¼
1394 X	Conner, John	Supplies	Anderson's Return	Roebuck's Regiment	Ninety Six	£	.19. 2¼
1395 X	Commins, James	Supplies	Anderson's Return	Casey's Regiment	Ninety Six	£	.11. 8¾
1396 X	Crow, Thomas	Supplies	Anderson's Return	Roebuck's Regiment	Ninety Six	£	2. 2.10¼
1401 X	Dial, Nath[l].	Militia Duty	Anderson's Return	Brandon's Regiment	Ninety Six	£	2.17. 1½
1403 X	Dottey, Sarah	Supplies	Anderson's Return	Brandon's Regiment	Ninety Six	£	3. 5. 4
1404 X	Dottey, Jerem[h].	Supplies	Anderson's Return	Roebuck's Regiment	Ninety Six	£	5.12. 2½

Numb. & Book	To whom Granted	For what Granted		Regiment	District	Amount Indent
1405 X	Douglas, John	Supplies	Anderson's Return	Col. Hammond	Ninety Six	£ . 9. 7½
1406 X	Dawkins, Chloe	Supplies	Anderson's Return	Col. Beard	Ninety Six	£ 2.12.10¼
1410 X	Davis, Claman	Supplies	Anderson's Return		Ninety Six	£ .12.10¼
1411 X	Davidson, Sarah	Supplies	Anderson's Return	Brandon's Regiment	Ninety Six	£ 1.14. 5
1413 X	Drake, John	Negro hire on the lines			Charleston	£ 14.10.
1415 X	Every, James	Supplies	Anderson's Return	Brandon's Regiment	Ninety Six	£ 2. 2.10
1419 X	Edmanson, Isaac	Supplies	Anderson's Return	Brandon's Regiment	Ninety Six	£ 1.14. 3¼
1430 X	Forr, George	Supplies	Anderson's Return	Waters's Regiment	Orangeburgh	£ 2.13. 2½
1434 X	Gearry, Jun. Thoˢ.	Supplies	Anderson's Return	Casey's Regiment	Ninety Six	£ .16. 6
1435 X	Gore, John	Supplies	Anderson's Return	Brandon's Regiment	Ninety Six	£ 1. 8. 6¾
1436 X	Griffith, Willᵐ.	Supplies	Anderson's Return	Roebuck's Regiment	Ninety Six	£ .19. 7
1437 X	Green, Peter	Supplies				£ 20. .
1447 X	Gexson, Samuel	Supplies	Anderson's Return	Cols. Brandon, Waters, & Roebuck	Ninety Six	£ 1.13. 4
1452 X	Hooker, Edward	A Saddle	Anderson's Return	Cols. Brandon, Waters, & Roebuck	Ninety Six	£ 2. 2.10¼
1453 X	Horsekead, John	A Saddle	Anderson's Return	Cols. Brandon, Waters, & Roebuck	Ninety Six	£ 2. 2.10¼
1458 X	Hackins, Francis	Supplies	Anderson's Return	Cols. Brandon, Waters, & Roebuck	Ninety Six	£ 10. 3. 6¾
1459 X	Hawkins, Francis	Supplies	Anderson's Return	Cols. Brandon, Waters, & Roebuck	Ninety Six	£ .10.
1462 X	Jant, John	Supplies	Anderson's Return	Cols. Brandon, Waters, & Roebuck	Ninety Six	£ 2.17. 1½
1471 X	Johnston, Thoˢ.	Supplies	Anderson's Return	Roebuck's Regiment	Ninety Six	£ 1. 3. 2
1473 X	Jenkins, John	Supplies	Anderson's Return	Brandon's	Ninety Six	£ .13. 6¾
1479 X	Jordan, Adam	Duty as a Spy	Anderson's Return	Col. Beard	Ninety Six	£ 7. 8. 6¾

Numb. & Book	To whom Granted	For what Granted			District	Amount Indent
1485 X	Hatton, James	Supplies	Anderson's Return	Col. Beard	Ninety Six	£ 1. 8. 6¾
1486 X	Kinnard, Martin	Supplies	Anderson's Return	Brandon's	Ninety Six	£ .18. 9
1488 X	Kennedy, John	Supplies	Anderson's Return	Brandon's	Ninety Six	£ 2.14. 6
1492 X	Loper, David	Militia Duty	Anderson's Return	Capt. Garvin	Ninety Six	£ 2. 2.10
1493 X	Leavell, Robert	Supplies	Anderson's Return		Ninety Six	£ 4.12. 6
1499 X	Lawson, Benjamin	Supplies	Anderson's Return		Ninety Six	£ 5. 5. 8
1503 X	Littleton, Chas.	Ferriage	Anderson's Return		Ninety Six	£ 1. 8. 6
1513 X	McLemore, Esta. Wright	Militia Duty	Anderson's Return	Capt. Garvin	Ninety Six	£ 3. 2.10¼
1517 X	Mellon, Nechanya	Supplies	Anderson's		Ninety Six	£ . 3. 6
1518 X	Montgomery, George	Supplies	Anderson's	Waters's Regiment	Ninety Six	£ 4. 5. 4
1522 X	Menuare, Willm.	Supplies	Anderson's	Col. Glyn	Ninety Six	£ 1.11. 5
1526 X	Maliel, Robert	Supplies	Anderson's	Col. Brandon	Ninety Six	£ 2. 2.10
1533 X	McDougall, Alexr.	Supplies	Anderson's		Ninety Six	£ 8.13. 11
1534 X	McDugan, Alexr.	Supplies	Anderson's		Ninety Six	£ .12.
1535 X	Matley, John	Militia Duty	Anderson's	Col. Elijah Clark	Ninety Six	£ 2. 2.10
1538 X	Mayfield, Robt.	Supplies	Anderson's	Cols. Thomas } Bramdon}	Ninety Six	£ 6. 7. 6
1540 X	McKendrick, Cathl.	Supplies	Anderson's Return	Brandon's Regiment	Ninety Six	£ 3.14. 3
1545 X	Neal, Hugh	Supplies	Anderson's Return	Col. Twigg	Ninety Six	£ . 9.
1546 X	Nesbit, Jun. Robert	Supplies	Anderson's Return	Col. Twigg	Ninety Six	£ 2.14. 6
1564 X	Perry, Thos.	Supplies	Anderson's Return	Col. [Illegible]	Ninety Six	£ .14. 3
1577 X	Plunket, James	Supplies	Anderson's Return	Col. Casey	Ninety Six	£ 2.18.11
1578 X	Plunket, Robert	Supplies	Anderson's Return		Ninety Six	£ 1.12. 1
1579 X	Pearson, Enoch	Supplies	Anderson's Return		Ninety Six	£ 1. 1. 5
1589 X	Rogers, Willm.	Supplies	Anderson's Return	Brandon's Regiment	Ninety Six	£ 17.18.11
1593 X	Recker, Geoe.	Supplies	Anderson's Return	Waters's	Ninety Six	£ 1.13.11
1612 X	Smith, Christr.	A Saddle			Ninety Six	£ 1.15. 8
1614 X	Sinkfield, Esta. Francis	Supplies			Ninety Six	£ 1. 2.10
1623 X	Stock, Willm. Clerk	Supplies			Ninety Six	£ 19. 2.10
1626 X	Singley, Rachel	Supplies			Ninety Six	£ 1. 6. 8
1632 X	Thomas, Willm.	Supplies	Powe		Cheraw	£ 8.19. 8

Numb. & Book	To whom Granted	For what Granted		District	Amount Indent		
1633 X	Thomas, Willm.	Militia Duty	Powe	Cheraw	£	3.	1. 5
1635 X	Thompson, Elizabeth	Supplies	Anderson's Return	Ninety Six	£	2.	5. 8
1636 X	Towsen, John	Supplies	Anderson's Return	Ninety Six	£	1.15.	8
1639 X	Thorn, Eliz^h.	Supplies	Anderson's Return	Ninety Six	£	3.10.	4
1641 X	Tyet, Mary	Supplies	Anderson's Return	Ninety Six	£	1.	4. 3
1643 X	Taylor, John	Supplies	Anderson's Return	Ninety Six	£	.	8. 6
1644 X	Tayley, John	Supplies	Anderson's Return	Ninety Six	£	.11.	5
1649 X	Vessels, Mich^l.	Supplies	Anderson's Return	Ninety Six	£	8.11.	5
1658 X	White, Joseph	Supplies	Anderson's Return	Ninety Six	£	4.	5. 8
1668 X	Wood, Willm.	Waggon hire	Anderson's Return	Ninety Six	£	5.	2.10
1669 X	Witherton, John	Supplies	Anderson's Return	Ninety Six	£.		17. 1
1692-A X	Crawford, Est^a. Joseph	Militia Duty	Maj. Crawford	Camden	£	25.	8. 6
1711 X	Gilmore, James	Supplies	Tate	Camden	£	4.16.	1
1738 X	Smiley, Willm.	Supplies	Tate	Camden	£	4.19.	3
1751 X	Hemphill, Alex^r.	Bal. Acco^t.	Tate	Camden	£	8.11.	5
1815 X	Hazelheart, John	Militia Duty	Waters's Regiment	Ninety Six	£	5.14.	3
1844 X	Nelson, Robert	Militia Duty	Roebuck's Regiment	Ninety Six	£	2.	4. 3
1848 X	Potcher, Peter	Militia Duty	Waters's Regiment	Ninety Six	£	5.14.	3
1856 X	Rash, Adam	Militia Duty	Waters's Regiment	Ninety Six	£	8.	7. 1
1914 X	Kennedy, Thos.	Militia Duty	Brandon	Ninety Six	£	1.18.	6¾
1922 X	Reisinger, Thos.	Militia Duty	Waters	Ninety Six	£	3.	. .
1935 X	~~Bennett~~ Barnett, John	Militia Duty	Capt. J. Hampton		£	3.	2.10¼
1936 X	Buchannon, Robt.	Militia Duty	Capt. J. Hampton		£	3.18.	6¾
1937 X	Billing, Jasper	Militia Duty	Capt. J. Hampton		£	1.	2.10¼
1938 X	Corbett, Danl.	Militia Duty	Capt. J. Hampton		£	2.10.	
1940 X	Felistion, John	Militia Duty	Capt. J. Hampton		£	3.	2.10¼
1941 X	Hollingsworth, Zebulon	Militia Duty	Capt. J. Hampton		£	1.	4. 3¼
1942 X	Hollingsworth, Jun. Zebulon	Militia Duty	Capt. J. Hampton		£	1.10.	
1943 X	Jones, John	Militia Duty	Capt. J. Hampton		£	3.	2.10¼
1944 X	Jones, Thos.	Militia Duty	Capt. J. Hampton		£	3.	2.10¼
1945 X	Phillips, Stephen	Militia Duty	Capt. J. Hampton		£	2.14.	3¼
1946 X	Rice, Thos.	Militia Duty	Capt. J. Hampton		£	3.	2.10¼

Numb. & Book	To whom Granted	For what Granted			District	Amount Indent
1947 X	Sap, John	Militia Duty	Capt. J. Hampton			£ 1. 5. 8½
1948 X	Sap, Caleb	Militia Duty	Capt. J. Hampton			£ 1. 5. 8½
1949 X	Sap, Shadk.	Militia Duty	J. Hampton's Comp			£ 1. 5. 8½
1950 X	Sap, Henry	Militia Duty	J. Hampton's Comp			£ 1. 8. 6¾
1951 X	Wood, Alexr.	Militia Duty	J. Hampton's Comp			£ 3. 2.10¼
1952 X	Wood, Jun. Alexr.	Militia Duty	J. Hampton's Comp			£ 3. 2.10¼
1953 X	Wiggins, Willm.	Militia Duty	J. Hampton's Comp			£ 3. 2.10¼
1954 X	Wallace, Josiah	Militia Duty	J. Hampton's Comp			£ 1. 8. 6¾
2164 X	Rogers, Alexr.	Arrears of Clothing	Sumter's Brigade			£ 4.13. 8
2165 X	Hager, Simon	Arrears of Clothing	Sumter's Brigade		Camden	£ 5.12. 4
2166 X	Gray, John	Arrears of Clothing	Sumter's Brigade		Camden	£ 7. . 4
2346 X	Cooke, P. Wanmuck	Militia Duty	Brandon's Regiment	Anderson's Return	Ninety Six	£ 8.12.10¼
2349 X	Earle, Samuel	Militia Duty	Brandon's Regiment	Anderson's Return	Ninety Six	£ 9.14. 3¼
2351 X	Gregory, John	Militia Duty	Brandon's Regiment	Anderson's Return	Ninety Six	£ 5. 5. 8½
2374 X	Johnson, Thos.	Militia Duty	Brandon's Regiment	Anderson's Return	Ninety Six	£ 2. 4. 3¾
2430 X	Tankesley, Chas.	Militia Duty	Brandon's Regiment	Anderson's Return	Ninety Six	£ 4. 8. 6¾
2434 X	Word, Thos.	Militia Duty	Brandon's Regiment	Anderson's Return	Ninety Six	£ 4. 5. 8½
2446 X	Buchannon, Jun. John	Militia Duty	Waters's Regiment	Anderson's Return	Ninety Six	£ 3. .
2449 X	Boyd, John	Militia Duty	Waters's Regiment	Anderson's Return	Ninety Six	£ 4. 8. 6¾
2450 X	Brown, Sims	Militia Duty	Waters's Regiment	Anderson's Return	Ninety Six	£ 4. 8. 6¾
2454 X	Bunderick, Chas.	Militia Duty	Waters's Regiment	Anderson's Return	Ninety Six	£ 5. .
2455 X	Buntrick, Chas.	Militia Duty	Waters's Regiment	Anderson's Return	Ninety Six	£ 2. 2.10¼
2457 X	Broom, Jas.	Militia Duty	Waters's Regiment	Anderson's Return	Ninety Six	£ 1.14. 3¼
2458 X	Black, Adam	Militia Duty	Waters's Regiment	Anderson's Return	Ninety Six	£ 9. 7. 1½
2476 X	Caldwell, Sen. Joseph	Militia Duty	Waters's Regiment	Anderson's Return	Ninety Six	£ 1. 8. 6¾
2477 X	Caldwell, Jun. Joseph	Militia Duty	Waters's Regiment	Anderson's Return	Ninety Six	£ 2.11. 5
2488 X	Crookes, Samuel	Militia Duty	Waters's Regiment	Anderson's Return	Ninety Six	£ 6.18. 6¾

Numb. & Book	To whom Granted	For what Granted			District	Amount Indent			
2492 X	Dunkin, Jun. John	Militia Duty		Anderson's Return	Waters's Regiment	Ninety Six	£	1.11.	5
2494 X	Dobbins, Jaˢ.	Militia Duty		Anderson's Return	Waters's Regiment	Ninety Six	£	2. 4.	3¼
2500 X	Dougharty, Jaˢ.	Militia Duty		Anderson's Return	Waters's Regiment	Ninety Six	£	4.15.	8½
2504 X	Evans, Nathan	Militia Duty		Anderson's Return	Waters's Regiment	Ninety Six	£	4. 5.	8½
2513 X	Furr, John	Militia Duty		Anderson's Return	Waters's Regiment	Ninety Six	£	5. 1.	5
2519 X	Fritts, Henry	Militia Duty		Anderson's Return	Waters's Regiment	Ninety Six	£	5.	.
2522 X	Footrice, John	Militia Duty		Anderson's Return	Waters's Regiment	Ninety Six	£	19.10.	
2532 X	Grad, Willᵐ.	Militia Duty		Anderson's Return	Waters's Regiment	Ninety Six	£	8.14.	3¼
2534 X	Goulding, Willᵐ.	Militia Duty		Anderson's Return	Waters's Regiment	Ninety Six	£	6. 8.	6¾
2545 X	Harrol, Jonathan	Militia Duty		Anderson's Return	Waters's Regiment	Ninety Six	£	2. 4.	3¼
2551 X	Hearne, Willᵐ.	Militia Duty		Anderson's Return	Waters's Regiment	Ninety Six	£	1.11.	5
2554 X	Hay, James	Militia Duty		Anderson's Return	Waters's Regiment	Ninety Six	£	2. 2.10¼
2557 X	Harbison, Willˡ.	Militia Duty		Anderson's Return	Waters's Regiment	Ninety Six	£	9. 5.	8½
2560 X	Jacobs, Shadᵏ.	Militia Duty		Anderson's Return	Waters's Regiment	Ninety Six	£	1. 1.	5
2561 X	Jacob, Joshua	Militia Duty		Anderson's Return	Waters's Regiment	Ninety Six	£	1. 1.	5
2568 X	Jackson, Willᵐ.	Militia Duty		Anderson's Return	Waters's Regiment	Ninety Six	£	4. 5.	8½
2569 X	Kalts, Michˡ.	Militia Duty		Anderson's Return	Waters's Regiment	Ninety Six	£	9. 1.	5
2570 X	Kalts, Martin	Militia Duty		Anderson's Return	Waters's Regiment	Ninety Six	£	6.15.	8½
2588 X	Leavolt, John	Militia Duty		Anderson's Return	Waters's Regiment	Ninety Six	£	6. 1.	5
2593 X	Livingston, Michˡ.	Militia Duty		Anderson's Return	Waters's Regiment	Ninety Six	£	2. 4.	3¼
2600 X	Martin, Peter	Militia Duty		Anderson's Return	Waters's Regiment	Ninety Six	£	2.17.	1½
2605 X	McCoy, John	Militia Duty		Anderson's Return	Waters's Regiment	Ninety Six	£	2.17.	1½
2615 X	Oriack, James	Militia Duty		Anderson's Return	Waters's Regiment	Ninety Six	£	2. 4.	3¼
2618 X	Pister, Gasper	Militia Duty		Anderson's Return	Waters's Regiment	Ninety Six	£	2.12.10¼
2630 X	Russell, Andrew	Militia Duty		Anderson's Return	Waters's Regiment	Ninety Six	£	4. 8.	6¾
2632 X	Russell, Willᵐ.	Militia Duty		Anderson's Return	Waters's Regiment	Ninety Six	£	5. 8.11
2633 X	Ruff, Geoᵉ.	Militia Duty		Anderson's Return	Waters's Regiment	Ninety Six	£	4. 8.	6¾
2639 X	Sleigh, Geoᵉ.	Militia Duty		Anderson's Return	Waters's Regiment	Ninety Six	£	5.	.
2640 X	Sleigh, Jacob	Militia Duty		Anderson's Return	Waters's Regiment	Ninety Six	£	5.	.
2641 X	Smith, Enoch	Militia Duty		Anderson's Return	Waters's Regiment	Ninety Six	£	4.10.	
2650 X	Shierer, Jacob	Militia Duty		Anderson's Return	Waters's Regiment	Ninety Six	£	4. 5.	8½
2651 X	Sowers, Willᵐ.	Militia Duty		Anderson's Return	Waters's Regiment	Ninety Six	£	1.18.	6¾
2657 X	Stockman, Stoffle	Militia Duty		Anderson's Return	Waters's Regiment	Ninety Six	£	2. 4.	3¼

Numb. & Book	To whom Granted	For what Granted			District	Amount Indent
2660 X	Stucker, Jacob	Militia Duty	Anderson's Return	Waters's Regiment	Ninety Six	£ 19. .
2674 X	Valentine, Nich^s.	Militia Duty	Anderson's Return	Waters's Regiment	Ninety Six	£ 1.11. 5
2683 X	Wells, John	Militia Duty	Anderson's Return	Waters's Regiment	Ninety Six	£ 5. .
2684 X	Wells, Willm.	Militia Duty	Anderson's Return	Waters's Regiment	Ninety Six	£ 5. .
2685 X	Wells, Serg^t. Willm.	Militia Duty	Anderson's Return	Waters's Regiment	Ninety Six	£ 2. 2.10¼
2691 X	Whicker, Henry	Militia Duty	Anderson's Return	Waters's Regiment	Ninety Six	£ 2. 4. 3¼
2692 X	Willson, Hugh	Militia Duty	Anderson's Return	Waters's Regiment	Ninety Six	£ 6.18. 6¾
2693 X	Wilson, Hughey	Militia Duty	Anderson's Return	Waters's Regiment	Ninety Six	£ 1.11. 5
2698 X	Wood, John	Militia Duty	Anderson's Return	Waters's Regiment	Ninety Six	£ 2.17. 1½
2699 X	Wood, Serg^t. Hickebud	Militia Duty	Anderson's Return	Waters's Regiment	Ninety Six	£ 2.15. 4¼
2704 X	Young, Matthew	Militia Duty	Anderson's Return	Waters's Regiment	Ninety Six	£ 2.12.10¼
2711 X	Adams, Howel	Militia Duty	Anderson's Return	Brandon's Regiment	Ninety Six	£ 7.17. 1½
2723 X	Bevins, James	Militia Duty	Anderson's Return	Brandon's Regiment	Ninety Six	£ 6. 8. 6¾
2730 X	Burges, Rich^d.	Militia Duty	Anderson's Return	Brandon's Regiment	Ninety Six	£ 1. .
2748 X	Bagley, James	Militia Duty	Anderson's Return	Brandon's Regiment	Ninety Six	£ 6.17. 1½
2749 X	Brooks, John	Militia Duty	Anderson's Return	Brandon's Regiment	Ninety Six	£ 5. 7. 1½
2753 X	Bowbo, Sampson	Militia Duty	Anderson's Return	Brandon's Regiment	Ninety Six	£ 4.14. 3¼
2755 X	Bearden, Absalom	Militia Duty	Anderson's Return	Brandon's Regiment	Ninety Six	£ 4.17. 1½
2759 X	Barnet, Hump^y.	Militia Duty	Anderson's Return	Brandon's Regiment	Ninety Six	£ 1.18. 6¾
2760 X	Barns, Willm.	Militia Duty	Anderson's Return	Brandon's Regiment	Ninety Six	£ 2. .
2762 X	Barnet, Jacob	Militia Duty	Anderson's Return	Brandon's Regiment	Ninety Six	£ 1.18. 6¾
2766 X	Coiler, Moses	Militia Duty	Anderson's Return	Brandon's Regiment	Ninety Six	£ 4.17. 1½

Numb. & Book	To whom Granted	For what Granted			District	Amount Indent
2770 X	Cooke, Willm.	Militia Duty	Anderson's Return	Brandon's Regiment	Ninety Six	£ 2. 5. 8½
2773 X	Clifton, Willm.	Militia Duty	Anderson's Return	Brandon's Regiment	Ninety Six	£ 1. 1. 5
2787 X	Cowley, Willm.	Militia Duty	Anderson's Return	Brandon's Regiment	Ninety Six	£ 8.11. 5
2792 X	Davison, Joseph	Militia Duty	Anderson's Return	Brandon's Regiment	Ninety Six	£ 5.17. 1½
2798 X	Davis, Simon	Militia Duty	Anderson's Return	Brandon's Regiment	Ninety Six	£ 4. .
2804 X	Dodd, Willm.	Militia Duty	Anderson's Return	Brandon's Regiment	Ninety Six	£ 1. 8. 6¾
2805 X	Dodd, John	Militia Duty	Anderson's Return	Brandon's Regiment	Ninety Six	£ 2. 2.10¼
2806 X	Dixon, Willm.	Militia Duty	Anderson's Return	Brandon's Regiment	Ninety Six	£ 10. .
2809 X	Dawson, Larkin	Militia Duty	Anderson's Return	Brandon's Regiment	Ninety Six	£ 2.17. 1½
2811 X	Endsworth, Willm.	Militia Duty	Anderson's Return	Brandon's Regiment	Ninety Six	£ 2.12.10¼
2812 X	Ewbanks, John	Militia Duty	Anderson's Return	Brandon's Regiment	Ninety Six	£ 3. 5. 8½
2826 X	Garman, James	Militia Duty	Anderson's Return	Brandon's Regiment	Ninety Six	£ 6. 8. 6¾
2847 X	Goodwin, Willm.	Militia Duty	Anderson's Return	Brandon's Regiment	Ninety Six	£ 5. .
2849 X	Geeseling, Willm.	Militia Duty	Anderson's Return	Brandon's Regiment	Ninety Six	£ 4. 5. 8½
2861 X	Holcum, Elisha	Militia Duty	Anderson's Return	Brandon's Regiment	Ninety Six	£ 5. .
2863 X	Holcum, Elisha	Militia Duty	Anderson's Return	Brandon's Regiment	Ninety Six	£ 8.11. 5

Numb. & Book	To whom Granted	For what Granted			District	Amount Indent
2872 X	Henry, James	Militia Duty	Anderson's Return	Brandon's Regiment	Ninety Six	£ 5.16. ¾
2874 X	Hainey, Robt.	Militia Duty	Anderson's Return	Brandon's Regiment	Ninety Six	£ 6.17. 1½
2876 X	Heaton, Salathiel	Militia Duty	Anderson's Return	Brandon's Regiment	Ninety Six	£ 4. 5. 8½
2894 X	Hayse, Jacob	Militia Duty	Anderson's Return	Brandon's Regiment	Ninety Six	£ 6. 5. 8½
2896 X	Hughes, Matthew	Militia Duty	Anderson's Return	Brandon's Regiment	Ninety Six	£ 10.14. 3¾
2898 X	Haild, Capt. James	Militia Duty	Anderson's Return	Brandon's Regiment	Ninety Six	£ 25.15. 4¾
2902 X	Howard, Thomas	Militia Duty	Anderson's Return	Brandon's Regiment	Ninety Six	£ 3. 1. 5
2905 X	Howard, James	Militia Duty	Anderson's Return	Brandon's Regiment	Ninety Six	£ 2. 2.10½
2913 X	Ham, Littleton	Militia Duty	Anderson's Return	Brandon's Regiment	Ninety Six	£ 2.18. 6¾
2914 X	Ham, Mc'Ilberry	Militia Duty	Anderson's Return	Brandon's Regiment	Ninety Six	£ 3. 5. 8½
2927 X	Littlejohn, Thomas	Militia Duty	Anderson's Return	Brandon's Regiment	Ninety Six	£ 3.11. 5
2942 X	Jackson, Jordan	Militia Duty	Anderson's Return	Brandon's Regiment	Ninety Six	£ 2.17. 1½
2943 X	Jackson, John	Militia Duty	Anderson's Return	Brandon's Regiment	Ninety Six	£ 2. 2.10½
2945 X	Jetter, Corn^s.	Militia Duty	Anderson's Return	Brandon's Regiment	Ninety Six	£ 26.10.
2954 X	Kindrick, Palmer	Militia Duty	Anderson's Return	Brandon's Regiment	Ninety Six	£ 4. 8. 6¾
2957 X	Knave, Willm.	Militia Duty	Anderson's Return	Brandon's Regiment	Ninety Six	£ 5. .

Numb. & Book	To whom Granted	For what Granted			District	Amount Indent
2964 X	Lenier, Clemwood	Militia Duty	Anderson's Return	Brandon's Regiment	Ninety Six	£ 12.17. 1½
2971 X	Lee, Elliot	Militia Duty	Anderson's Return	Brandon's Regiment	Ninety Six	£ 14.17. 1½
2984 X	Miller, Rob.t	Militia Duty	Anderson's Return	Brandon's Regiment	Ninety Six	£ 11. .
2985 X	McNamar, Jesse	Militia Duty	Anderson's Return	Brandon's Regiment	Ninety Six	£ 7. 2.10¼
2992 X	Michael, Will.m	Militia Duty	Anderson's Return	Brandon's Regiment	Ninety Six	£ 12. 8. 6¾
3033 X	McGowen, James	Militia Duty	Anderson's Return	Brandon's Regiment	Ninety Six	£ 4. 5. 8½
3057 X	Osburn, Will.m	Militia Duty	Anderson's Return	Brandon's Regiment	Ninety Six	£ 4. 8. 6¾
3065 X	Patton, John	Militia Duty	Anderson's Return	Brandon's Regiment	Ninety Six	£ 2. 1. 5
3066 X	Patton, Will.m	Militia Duty	Anderson's Return	Brandon's Regiment	Ninety Six	£ 7. 2.10¼
3070 X	Pinion, Lewis	Militia Duty	Anderson's Return	Brandon's Regiment	Ninety Six	£ 2. .
3095 X	Rogers, Rich.d	Militia Duty	Anderson's Return	Brandon's Regiment	Ninety Six	£ 2. .
3099 X	Rush, Benj.n	Militia Duty	Anderson's Return	Brandon's Regiment	Ninety Six	£ 4. 5. 8½
3101 X	Savage, Jun. Benj.n	Militia Duty	Anderson's Return	Brandon's Regiment	Ninety Six	£ .14. 3¼
3102 X	Savage, Rob.t	Militia Duty	Anderson's Return	Brandon's Regiment	Ninety Six	£ 5. .
3105 X	Saunders, Joshua	Militia Duty	Anderson's Return	Brandon's Regiment	Ninety Six	£ . 5. 8½
3108 X	Scism, David	Militia Duty	Anderson's Return	Brandon's Regiment	Ninety Six	£ 4. 5. 8½

Numb. & Book	To whom Granted	For what Granted			District	Amount Indent
3109 X	Seelton, Rob[t].	Militia Duty	Anderson's Return	Brandon's Regiment	Ninety Six	£ 12.17. 1½
3118 X	Shockley, John	Militia Duty	Anderson's Return	Brandon's Regiment	Ninety Six	£ 1. .
3134 X	Steel, Will[m].	Militia Duty	Anderson's Return	Brandon's Regiment	Ninety Six	£ 9.17. 1½
3135 X	Story, Anth[y].	Militia Duty	Anderson's Return	Brandon's Regiment	Ninety Six	£ 1. 1. 5
3136 X	Storey, George	Militia Duty	Anderson's Return	Brandon's Regiment	Ninety Six	£ 4.19. 3¾
3140 X	Sweetingburg, Aberhart	Militia Duty	Anderson's Return	Waters's Regiment	Ninety Six	£ 5.14. 3¾
3143 X	Tankinsley, Will[m].	Militia Duty	Anderson's Return	Brandon's Regiment	Ninety Six	£ 4.14. 3¾
3144 X	Taylor, Lewis	Militia Duty	Anderson's Return	Brandon's Regiment	Ninety Six	£ 4. 1. 5
3150 X	Thompson, Est[a]. John	Militia Duty	Anderson's Return	Brandon's Regiment	Ninety Six	£ 7.14. 3¾
3176 X	Weeks, Jun. Joseph	Militia Duty	Anderson's Return	Brandon's Regiment	Ninety Six	£ 2. 5. 8½
3177 X	Welch, Nich[s].	Militia Duty	Anderson's Return	Brandon's Regiment	Ninety Six	£ 2. 2.10¼
3181 X	Wells, Lewis	Militia Duty	Anderson's Return	Brandon's Regiment	Ninety Six	£ 6.17. 1½
3184 X	Wheeler, Will[m].	Militia Duty	Anderson's Return	Brandon's Regiment	Ninety Six	£ 4. 5. 8½
3185 X	Whitaker, James	Militia Duty	Anderson's Return	Brandon's Regiment	Ninety Six	£ 2.14. 3¾
3192 X	Whitmire, Fred[k].	Militia Duty	Anderson's Return	Brandon's Regiment	Ninety Six	£ 5. .
3193 X	Willard, John	Militia Duty	Anderson's Return	Brandon's Regiment	Ninety Six	£ 2. 5. 8½
3203 X	Woolbank, Rich[d].	Militia Duty	Anderson's Return	Brandon's Regiment	Ninety Six	£ 6. 2.10¼

Numb. & Book	To whom Granted	For what Granted			District	Amount Indent
3205 X	Yarborough, Ambrose	Militia Duty	Anderson's Return	Brandon's Regiment	Ninety Six	£ 6.12.10¼
3206 X	Young, Danl.	Militia Duty	Anderson's Return	Brandon's Regiment	Ninety Six	£ 2. 2.10¼
3207 X	Young, Jesse	Militia Duty	Anderson's Return	Brandon's Regiment	Ninety Six	£ 2. 5. 8½
3209 X	Young, Isaac	Militia Duty	Anderson's Return	Brandon's Regiment	Ninety Six	£ 5.15. 8½
3210 X	Young, Rich^d.	Militia Duty	Anderson's Return	Brandon's Regiment	Ninety Six	£ 4.14. 3¼
3228 X	Neilson, Willm.	Militia Duty	Anderson's Return	Roebuck's Regiment	Ninety Six	£ 6. . .
3240 X	Steen, Willm.	Militia Duty	Anderson's Return	Waters's Regiment	Ninety Six	£ 4. 6. 9¼
3244 X	Thompson, Chas.	Militia Duty	Anderson's Return	Brandon's Regiment	Ninety Six	£ 2.18. 6¾
3246 X	Wallen, Mich^l.	Militia Duty	Anderson's Return	Roebuck's Regiment	Ninety Six	£ 4. 5. 8½
3253 X	Young, Levi	Militia Duty	Anderson's Return	Brandon's Regiment	Ninety Six	£ 2.12.10¼
3260 X	Barlow, John	Supplies		Waters	Ninety Six	£ 3. 7. 1½
3280 X	Goodwin, John	Supplies			Ninety Six	£ 8. 2. 1
3282 X	Gartman, John	Supplies			Ninety Six	£ 5. 6.
3289 X	Hallman, John	Supplies		Waters	Ninety Six	£ 3. 8. 6¾
3294 X	Hill, Willm.	Supplies		Waters	Ninety Six	£ 3. .10
3295 X	Hill, Willm.	Supplies		Brandon	Ninety Six	£ 5. 5. 3
3307 X	Jay, John	Supplies		Waters	Ninety Six	£ 6.18. 9
3310 X	Johnston, Alex^r.	Supplies		Waters	Ninety Six	£ 4. 4. 3
3321 X	Lutis, John	Supplies		Waters	G.T.	£ 3. 6.11
3323 X	Martin, Zach^h.	Supplies	Horry		Georgetown	£ 15. 5. 8
3329 X	McKenney, Geo^e.	Supplies		Waters	Ninety Six	£ 1. 6. 9
3331 X	Malone, Willm.	Supplies			Ninety Six	£ 1. 8. 6
3345 X	Arundel, Reddock	Militia Duty		Roebuck's Regiment	Ninety Six	£ 3. 1. 5

Numb. & Book	To whom Granted	For what Granted			District	Amount Indent
3346 X	Austin, Jesse	Militia Duty		Roebuck's Regiment	Ninety Six	£ 2. 8. 6¾
3347 X	Barnet, John	Militia Duty	Anderson's Return	Roebuck's Regiment	Ninety Six	£ 6.17. 1½
3360 X	Bearden, Thomas	Militia Duty	Anderson's Return	Brandon's Regiment	Ninety Six	£ 15.11. 5
3362 X	Belien, David	Militia Duty	Anderson's Return	Roebuck's Regiment	Ninety Six	£ 2.18. 6¾
3363 X	Bennett, John	Militia Duty	Anderson's Return	Waters's Regiment	Ninety Six	£ 2. 1. 5
3368 X	Bond, John	Militia Duty	Anderson's Return	Brandon's Regiment	Ninety Six	£ 1. 2.10¼
3369 X	Bonner, Thos.	Militia Duty	Anderson's Return	Roebuck's Regiment	Ninety Six	£ 4. .
3371 X	Brandon, Edwd.	Militia Duty	Anderson's Return	Brandon's Regiment	Ninety Six	£ 10. 2.10¼
3373 X	McCleur, Jas.	Bala. Accot.	Capt. Tate		Camden	£ 4. 5. 8
3388 X	Seales, George	Supplies	Col. Anderson		Ninety Six	£ 3. 8. 6
3400 X	Weeks, Willm.	Supplies	Col. Anderson		Ninety Six	£ 12. 9. 9
3401 X	Wilhelm, Peter	Supplies	Col. Anderson		Ninety Six	£ 1.11. 5
3408 X	Brock, Isaac	Militia Duty	Col. Anderson	Roebuck's Regiment	Ninety Six	£ 2. 1. 5
3416 X	Buffington, Joseph	Militia Duty	Col. Anderson	Roebuck's Regiment	Ninety Six	£ 38.17. 1½
3417 X	Buise, John	Militia Duty	Col. Anderson	Roebuck's Regiment	Ninety Six	£ 5. .
3419 X	Bullian, Thos.	Militia Duty	Col. Anderson	Roebuck's Regiment	Ninety Six	£ 2.17. 1½
3420 X	Bussy, Benjn.	Militia Duty	Col. Anderson	Roebuck's Regiment	Ninety Six	£ 1.11. 5
3424 X	Camp, John	Militia Duty	Col. Anderson	Roebuck's Regiment	Ninety Six	£ 2. 1. 5
3426 X	Calhoun, Thos.	Militia Duty	Col. Anderson	Roebuck's Regiment	Ninety Six	£ 5.17. 1½

Numb. & Book	To whom Granted	For what Granted		District	Amount Indent
3430 X	Champaign, Gibson	Militia Duty	Col. Anderson	Roebuck's Regiment	Ninety Six	£ 7.17. 1½
3441 X	Cotter, Anth^y.	Militia Duty	Col. Anderson	Roebuck's Regiment	Ninety Six	£ 4.15.
3445 X	Conner, John	Militia Duty	Col. Anderson	Roebuck's Regiment	Ninety Six	£ 12.17. 1½
3446 X	Connaway, Jerry	Militia Duty	Col. Anderson	Roebuck's Regiment	Ninety Six	£ .14. 3¾
3460 X	Cron, Thomas	Militia Duty	Col. Anderson	Roebuck's Regiment	Ninety Six	£ 7.14. 3¼
3463 X	Curry, Thomas	Militia Duty	Col. Anderson	Roebuck's Regiment	Ninety Six	£ 3. 5. 8½
3467 X	Delough, Willm.	Militia Duty	Col. Anderson	Roebuck's Regiment	Ninety Six	£ 5.11. 5
3469 X	Dixon, James	Militia Duty	Col. Anderson	Roebuck's Regiment	Ninety Six	£ 2.17. 1½
3473 X	Doeck, Thos.	Militia Duty	Col. Anderson	Roebuck's Regiment	Ninety Six	£ 1.18. 6¾
3490 X	Finnell, Est^a. Ambrose	Militia Duty	Col. Anderson	Roebuck's Regiment	Ninety Six	£ 15. 4. 3¼
3505 X	Fynch, Daniel	Militia Duty	Col. Anderson	Roebuck's Regiment	Ninety Six	£ 3.11. 5
3506 X	Gage, James	Militia Duty	Col. Anderson	Roebuck's Regiment	Ninety Six	£ 3.14. 3¼
3509 X	Gillaspie, James	Militia Duty	Col. Anderson	Roebuck's Regiment	Ninety Six	£ 57.11. 5
3520 X	Gowen, Est^a. David	Militia Duty	Col. Anderson	Roebuck's Regiment	Ninety Six	£ 12. 4. 3¼
3524 X	Griggs, Daniel	Militia Duty	Col. Anderson	Roebuck's Regiment	Ninety Six	£ 15. 5. 4¼
3533 X	Harris, Thomas	Militia Duty	Col. Anderson	Roebuck's Regiment	Ninety Six	£ 2. 1. 5

Numb. & Book	To whom Granted	For what Granted			District	Amount Indent
3534 X	Harris, West	Militia Duty	Col. Anderson	Roebuck's Regiment	Ninety Six	£ 1. 2.10¼
3541 X	Hem, James	Militia Duty	Col. Anderson	Roebuck's Regiment	Ninety Six	£ 4. 4. 3¾
3542 X	Hambrey, Drury	Militia Duty	Col. Anderson	Roebuck's Regiment	Ninety Six	£ 8.12.10¼
3545-A X	Hightower, Thos.	Militia Duty	Col. Anderson	Roebuck's Regiment	Ninety Six	£ 2. 8. 6¾
3547 X	Holcom, Esta. John	Militia Duty	Col. Anderson	Roebuck's Regiment	Ninety Six	£ 4.12.10¼
3548 X	Holcom, Joseph	Militia Duty	Col. Anderson	Roebuck's Regiment	Ninety Six	£ 13. 5. 8½
3554 X	Hooker, Edward	Militia Duty	Col. Anderson	Roebuck's Regiment	Ninety Six	£ 4. 8. 6¾
3556 X	Howard, Thomas	Militia Duty	Col. Anderson	Roebuck's Regiment	Ninety Six	£ 6. .
3557 X	Howell, Jospeh	Militia Duty	Col. Anderson	Roebuck's Regiment	Ninety Six	£ 14.16. 9¼
3559 X	Hulsey, James	Militia Duty	Col. Anderson	Roebuck's Regiment	Ninety Six	£ 3.15.
3565 X	Jones, Benja.	Militia Duty	Col. Anderson	Roebuck's Regiment	Ninety Six	£ 1. 5. 8½
3567 X	Jones, Matthew	Militia Duty	Col. Anderson	Roebuck's Regiment	Ninety Six	£ 2.14. 3¼
3568 X	Johnston, Jas.	Militia Duty	Col. Anderson	Roebuck's Regiment	Ninety Six	£ 3.14. 3¼
3573 X	Kearsey, Levi	Militia Duty	Col. Anderson	Roebuck's Regiment	Ninety Six	£ 23.11. 5
3574 X	Kearsey, Randolph	Militia Duty	Col. Anderson	Roebuck's Regiment	Ninety Six	£ 23.11. 5
3575 X	Keville, Benjn.	Militia Duty	Col. Anderson	Roebuck's Regiment	Ninety Six	£ 7. 2. 6

Numb. & Book	To whom Granted	For what Granted		District	Amount Indent
3580 X	Kithcart, Saml.	Militia Duty	Col. Anderson	Roebuck's Regiment	Ninety Six	£ 3. .
3586 X	Lee, James	Militia Duty	Col. Anderson	Roebuck's Regiment	Ninety Six	£ 24. 5. 8½
3590 X	Leech, David	Militia Duty	Col. Anderson	Roebuck's Regiment	Ninety Six	£ 2.17. 1½
3593 X	Lucas, John	Militia Duty	Col. Anderson	Roebuck's Regiment	Ninety Six	£ 2.17. 1½
3599 X	McCarty, Est^a. Martha	Indigo Impressed			Beaufort	£ 46.15. 4¼
3600 X	McKee, Thos.	Militia Duty	Col. Anderson	Roebuck's Regiment	Ninety Six	£ 5. .
3605 X	McBee, Mathias	Militia Duty	Col. Anderson	Roebuck's Regiment	Ninety Six	£ 6. 4. 3¼
3616 X	McHaffey, Ja^s.	Militia Duty	Col. Anderson	Roebuck's Regiment	Ninety Six	£ 1. 2.10¼
3620 X	McKee, Thos.	Militia Duty	Col. Anderson	Roebuck's Regiment	Ninety Six	£ 3. 2.10¼
3628 X	Miller, John	Militia Duty	Col. Anderson	Roebuck's Regiment	Ninety Six	£ 27.15. 8½
3632 X	Moeboy, Matthew	Militia Duty	Col. Anderson	Roebuck's Regiment	Ninety Six	£ 2. .
3647 X	Morrow, Robt.	Militia Duty	Col. Anderson	Roebuck's Regiment	Ninety Six	£ 3. 7. 1½
3652 X	Navill, Joseph	Militia Duty	Col. Anderson	Roebuck's Regiment	Ninety Six	£ 51.14. 3¾
3664 X	Owens, Thos.	Militia Duty	Col. Anderson	Roebuck's Regiment	Ninety Six	£ 2.14. 3¼
3671 X	Pettit, Est^a. Joshua	Militia Duty	Col. Anderson	Roebuck's Regiment	Ninety Six	£ 3. 5. 8½
3676 X	Powers, Francis	Militia Duty	Col. Anderson	Roebuck's Regiment	Ninety Six	£ 1. 2.10¼
3679 X	Randals, Saml.	Militia Duty	Col. Anderson	Roebuck's Regiment	Ninety Six	£ 5.11. 5

Numb. & Book	To whom Granted	For what Granted			District	Amount Indent
3685 X	Rhodes, James	Militia Duty	Col. Anderson	Roebuck's Regiment	Ninety Six	£ 3. .
3693 X	Roebuck, John	Militia Duty	Col. Anderson	Roebuck's Regiment	Ninety Six	£ 3. 4. 3¾
3702 X	Simmons, Will[m].	Militia Duty	Col. Anderson	Roebuck's Regiment	Ninety Six	£ 6.17. 1½
3703 X	Smith, Aaron	Militia Duty	Col. Anderson	Col. Roebuck	Ninety Six	£ 4. 2.10¼
3707 X	Smith, Giles	Militia Duty	Col. Anderson	Roebuck's Regiment	Ninety Six	£ 1. 7. 1½
3722 X	Stone, Benj[n].	Militia Duty	Col. Anderson	Roebuck's Regiment	Ninety Six	£ 5.11. 5
3723 X	Stevens, Daniel	Militia Duty	Col. Anderson	Roebuck's Regiment	Ninety Six	£ 3. 8. 6¾
3726 X	Sullivan, Pat[k].	Militia Duty	Col. Anderson	Roebuck's Regiment	Ninety Six	£ 5. .
3727 X	Taylor, Drury	Militia Duty	Col. Anderson	Roebuck's Regiment	Ninety Six	£ .14. 3¾
3728 X	Taylor, John	Militia Duty	Col. Anderson	Roebuck's Regiment	Ninety Six	£ 4. 5. 8½
3732 X	Temple, Jesse	Militia Duty	Col. Anderson	Roebuck's Regiment	Ninety Six	£ 1. 5. 8½
3738 X	Thompson, Moses	Militia Duty	Col. Anderson	Roebuck's Regiment	Ninety Six	£ 5.11. 5
3742 X	Tippings, Philip	Militia Duty	Col. Anderson	Roebuck's Regiment	Ninety Six	£ 8. 2.10¼
3748 X	Turner, John	Militia Duty	Col. Anderson	Roebuck's Regiment	Ninety Six	£ 5. 1. 5
3749 X	Turner, Jon[a].	Militia Duty	Col. Anderson	Roebuck's Regiment	Ninety Six	£ 5. .
3756 X	Wakefield, Cha[s].	Militia Duty	Col. Anderson	Roebuck's Regiment	Ninety Six	£ 8.11. 5
3758 X	Walker, Geo[e].	Militia Duty	Col. Anderson	Roebuck's Regiment	Ninety Six	£ 5. 8. 6¾

Numb. & Book	To whom Granted	For what Granted			District	Amount Indent
3763 X	Wareing, Willm.	Militia Duty	Col. Anderson	Roebuck's Regiment	Ninety Six	£ 1. 2.10¼
3768 X	Watts, Jacob	Militia Duty	Col. Anderson	Roebuck's Regiment	Ninety Six	£ 3. 1. 5
3769 X	Watson, Willm.	Militia Duty	Col. Anderson	Roebuck's Regiment	Ninety Six	£ 3. .
3773 X	White, Ja^s.	Militia Duty	Col. Anderson	Roebuck's Regiment	Ninety Six	£ 1.13. 2½
3774 X	White, Joseph	Militia Duty	Col. Anderson	Roebuck's Regiment	Ninety Six	£ 2. .
3775 X	Whitsworth, Fendol	Militia Duty	Col. Anderson	Roebuck's Regiment	Ninety Six	£ 1. 8. 6¾
3783 X	Wood, Capt. Willm.	Militia Duty	Col. Anderson	Roebuck's Regiment	Ninety Six	£ 37. .
3789 X	Young, Willm.	Militia Duty	Col. Anderson	Roebuck's Regiment	Ninety Six	£ 1. 2.10¼
3800 X	Colhoun, Alex^r.		Capt. Tate		Camden	£ 5. .
3812 X	Hannah, Jun. Robt.	Militia Duty	~~Tate~~	Col. Kilgore	Ninety Six	£ 5. .
3826 X	McWilliams, Ja^s.	Militia Duty		Col. Kilgore	Ninety Six	£ 14. 5. 8
3844 X	Richardson, John	Apprehend^g a Deserter		Col. Thompson	Orangeburgh	£ 7. 2.10
3845 X	Rogers, Willm.	Militia Duty		Col. Kilgow	Ninety Six	£ 5. .
3876 X	Anderson, Joseph	Militia Duty		Col^s. Garden & Harden	Beaufort	£ 2. 1. 5
3883 X	Burkett, John	Militia Duty		Col^s. Garden & Harden	Beaufort	£ 2. 8. 8
3884 X	Burkett, Thomas	Militia Duty		Col^s. Garden & Harden	Beaufort	£. 2.10
3885 X	Bryan, Lewis	Militia Duty		Col^s. Garden & Harden	Beaufort	£ 1.15.10
3886 X	Bryan, Joseph	Militia Duty		Col^s. Garden & Harden	Beaufort	£. 17. 1
3887 X	Bryan, Willm.	Militia Duty		Col^s. Garden & Harden	Beaufort	£ 1.12.10

Numb. & Book	To whom Granted	For what Granted			District	Amount Indent
3888 X	Bryan, Simon	Militia Duty		Col.ˢ Garden & Harden	Beaufort	£ 9. 2.10
3892 X	Brown, Tarlton	Militia Duty		Col.ˢ Garden & Harden	Beaufort	£ 2.10.
3894 X	Brown, Sen. Bartlet	Militia Duty		Col.ˢ Garden & Harden	Beaufort	£ .14. 3
3896 X	Brown, Willᵐ.	Militia Duty		Col.ˢ Garden & Harden	Beaufort	£ .17. 1
3897 X	Brown, Benjⁿ.	Militia Duty		Col.ˢ Garden & Harden	Beaufort	£ 2.14. 3
3898 X	Blount, James	Militia Duty		Col.ˢ Garden & Harden	Beaufort	£ 7.12.10
3899 X	Barber, James	Militia Duty		Col.ˢ Garden & Harden	Beaufort	£ 6. 1. 5
3900 X	Belcher, Dennis	Militia Duty		Col.ˢ Garden & Harden	Beaufort	£ 3. 7. 1
3901 X	Brewer, Willᵐ.	Militia Duty		Col.ˢ Garden & Harden	Beaufort	£ 1. 1. 5
3908 X	Carroll, Estᵃ. John	Balᵃ. Accoᵗ. A Mare	Capt. Tate		Camden	£ 13. 7. 1
3910 X	Colden, John	Militia Duty		Col.ˢ Garden & Harden	Beaufort	£ 2 2.10
3911 X	Colden, Samˡ.	Militia Duty		Col.ˢ Garden & Harden	Beaufort	£ 3. 1. 5
3912 X	Colden, Blanchᵈ.	Militia Duty		Col.ˢ Garden & Harden	Beaufort	£ 3. 2.10
3913 X	Cary, Thomas	Militia Duty		Col.ˢ Garden & Harden	Beaufort	£ 4.12.10
3914 X	Connoway, Philip	Militia Duty		Col.ˢ Garden & Harden	Beaufort	£ 1. 5. 8
3915 X	Dobbs, John	Militia Duty		Col.ˢ Garden & Harden	Beaufort	£ .17. 1
3916 X	Deloach, Michˡ.	Militia Duty		Col.ˢ Garden & Harden	Beaufort	£ 2. 1. 5

Numb. & Book	To whom Granted	For what Granted			District	Amount Indent
3917 X	Deloach, Will[m].	Militia Duty		Col[s]. Garden & Harden	Beaufort	£ .10.
3918 X	Deloach, Hardy	Militia Duty		Col[s]. Garden & Harden	Beaufort	£ 2. 1. 5
3919 X	Davis, David	Militia Duty		Col[s]. Garden & Harden	Beaufort	£ 1. 8. 8
3920 X	Day, Josiah	Militia Duty		Col[s]. Garden & Harden	Beaufort	£ 3. .
3921 X	David, Will[m].	Militia Duty		Col[s]. Garden & Harden	Beaufort	£ 2.15. 8
3922 X	Dewees, John	Militia Duty		Col[s]. Garden & Harden	Beaufort	£ 11. 2.10
3923 X	Eagle, Arch[d].	Militia Duty		Col[s]. Garden & Harden	Beaufort	£ 2.17. 1
3926 X	Freeman, John	Militia Duty		Col[s]. Garden & Harden	Beaufort	£ 2.15. 8
3928 X	Fulton, Est[a]. Tho[s].	A Horse/ bal. Acco[t].	Capt. Tate			£ 34. 5. 8
3929 X	Gambell, Will[m].	Militia Duty		Col[s]. Garden & Harden	Beaufort	£ .12.10
3930 X	Garnett, Joseph	Militia Duty		Col[s]. Garden & Harden	Beaufort	£ 1. .
3931 X	Ginn, Madric	Militia Duty		Col[s]. Garden & Harden	Beaufort	£ 2.11. 5
3933 X	Hodge, David	Militia Duty		Col[s]. Garden & Harden	Beaufort	£ 2. 1. 5
3934 X	Joice, John	Militia Duty		Col[s]. Garden & Harden	Beaufort	£ .8. 6
3936 X	Joice, Will[m].	Militia Duty		Col[s]. Garden & Harden	Beaufort	£ 3.12.10
3937 X	Kirkland, Reuben	Militia Duty		Col[s]. Garden & Harden	Beaufort	£ 5. 2.10
3938 X	Kirkland, Rich[d].	Militia Duty		Col[s]. Garden & Harden	Beaufort	£ 5. 7. 1

Numb. & Book	To whom Granted	For what Granted			District	Amount Indent
3939 X	Kirkland, John	Militia Duty		Col^s. Garden & Harden	Beaufort	£ .10.
3940 X	Kirk, Willm.	Militia Duty		Col^s. Garden & Harden	Beaufort	£ 4.15. 8
3941 X	Kirk, Gideon	Militia Duty		Col^s. Garden & Harden	Beaufort	£ 2.14. 3
3942 X	Knight, Ja^s.	Militia Duty		Col^s. Garden & Harden	Beaufort	£ 2.12.10
3943 X	Kelly, Joseph	Militia Duty		Col^s. Garden & Harden	Beaufort	£ 1. 8. 8
3945 X	Larriey, John	Militia Duty		Col^s. Garden & Harden	Beaufort	£ 4.10.
3946 X	Lewis, Lanty	Militia Duty		Col^s. Garden & Harden	Beaufort	£ 4.12.10
3949 X	Long, Thos.	Militia Duty		Col^s. Garden & Harden	Beaufort	£ 9.14. 3
3950 X	Moore, Lieut. Ja^s.	Militia Duty		Col^s. Garden & Harden	Beaufort	£ 3. 5.
3952 X	Moore, Sen. John	Militia Duty		Col^s. Garden & Harden	Beaufort	£ 3. 2.10
3953 X	Moore, Jun. John	Militia Duty		Col^s. Garden & Harden	Beaufort	£ .10.
3954 X	~~Lewis~~ Moore, Lewis	Militia Duty		Col^s. Garden & Harden	Beaufort	£ 1. .
3955 X	Maner, Willm.	Militia Duty		Col^s. Garden & Harden	Beaufort	£ .18. 6
3956 X	Maner, Samuel	Militia Duty		Col^s. Garden & Harden	Beaufort	£ 1.11. 5
3958 X	McClendon, John	Militia Duty		Col^s. Garden & Harden	Beaufort	£ 3. 7. 1
3959 X	Miller, Willm.	Militia Duty		Col^s. Garden & Harden	Beaufort	£ . 8. 6

Numb. & Book	To whom Granted	For what Granted			District	Amount Indent
3960 X	McCay, Ja^{s}.	Militia Duty		Col^{s}. Garden & Harden	Beaufort	£ 2.15. 8
3962 X	McClelland, Robt.	Militia Duty	Capt. Tate	Col. Bratton	Camden	£ 16. .
3964 X	Owens, Thos.	Militia Duty		Col^{s}. Garden & Harden	Beaufort	£ 3.10.
3965 X	Ogelvie, Elijah	Militia Duty		Col^{s}. Garden & Harden	Beaufort	£ . 4. 3
3966 X	Pelham, Edwd.	Militia Duty		Col^{s}. Garden & Harden	Beaufort	£ 3. 2.10
3968 X	Powell, John	Militia Duty		Col^{s}. Garden & Harden	Beaufort	£ .15. 8
3970 X	Popewell, Paul	Militia Duty		Col^{s}. Garden & Harden	Beaufort	£ 1. 8. 6
3971 X	Richardson, Ja^{s}.	Militia Duty		Col^{s}. Garden & Harden		£ .10.
3972 X	Roberts, George	Militia Duty		Col^{s}. Garden & Harden	Beaufort	£ .10.
3976 X	Smith, Ab^{m}.	Militia Duty		Col^{s}. Garden & Harden	Beaufort	£ 1. 8. 6
3977 X	Richardson, Ja^{s}.	Militia Duty		Col^{s}. Garden & Harden	Beaufort	£ 1. 8. 6
3978 X	Stafford, Eleazer	Militia Duty		Col^{s}. Garden & Harden	Beaufort	£ .12.10
3982 X	Sharber, Arthur	Militia Duty		Col^{s}. Garden & Harden	Beaufort	£ .10.
3983 X	Sterling, Isaac	Militia Duty		Col^{s}. Garden & Harden	Beaufort	£ 8. .
3985 X	Steel, Joseph	A Horse		Col. Bratton	Camden	£ 13. 8. 6
3988 X	Thomas, Gilshot	Militia Duty		Col^{s}. Garden & Harden	Beaufort	£ 2.15. 8
3989 X	Thomas, Ja^{s}.	Militia Duty		Col^{s}. Garden & Harden	Beaufort	£ 4.14. 3

Numb. & Book	To whom Granted	For what Granted			District	Amount Indent
3990 X	Taylor, James	Militia Duty	Col^s. Garden & Harden		Beaufort	£ 4. 8. 6
3991 X	Thompson, Willm.	Militia Duty	Col^s. Garden & Harden		Beaufort	£ 4. .
3992 X	Tuctrel, Thos.	Militia Duty	Col^s. Garden & Harden		Beaufort	£ 6. 8. 6
3995 X	Williams, Samuel	Militia Duty	Col^s. Garden & Harden		Beaufort	£ 2.15. 8
3997 X	Wise, Willm.	Militia Duty	Col^s. Garden & Harden		Beaufort	£ 1. 8. 6
3998 X	Wilkins, Alex^r.	Militia Duty	Col^s. Garden & Harden		Beaufort	£ . 8. 6
2 Y	Adams, Thos.	Supplies		Capt. J. Carter	Ninety Six	£ 2.18. 4
25 Y	Johnston (Waxhaw) James	Supplies			Camden	£ 2.11. 7¼
26 Y	Lee, Nich^s.	Surgeon's Pay			Camden	£ 38.11. 5
27 Y	Logue, Saml.	Militia Duty		Col. Taylor	Camden	£ 23. 5. 8½
32 Y	McDow, John	A Horse			Camden	£ 14. 5. 8½
47 Y	Baker, Alex^r.	Militia Duty		Capt. A. Thomas	Camden	£ 34. 7. 1
48 Y	Buxton, Saml.	Militia Duty			Camden	£ 8. 5. 8½
50 Y	Beem, Jesse	Militia Duty		Capt. A. Thomas	Camden	£ 34. 7. 1½
53 Y	Barton, Thomas	Supplies		Genl. Marion	Chas.ton	£ 2.18. 9½
56 Y	Bolton, Agnes	Supplies				£ 21.17. 6
64 Y	Campbell, Eliz^h.	Supplies		Col. Harden	Orangeburgh	£ 3.16. 1½
76 Y	Davis, Mary	Supplies			Beaufort	£ 21.18.10
77 Y	Davis, Jun. John	Constable's Fees			Camden	£ 1. 3. 8
79 Y	Dougherty, Est. John	Militia Duty			Camden	£ 27.11. 1½
81 Y	Eddingfield, Willm.	Supplies		G^l. Greene	Orangeburgh	£ 2. 3. 6
83 Y	Beckom, Russel	Militia Duty		Col. S. Hammond	Ninety Six	£ 4. 2.10
84 Y	Beckom, Reuben	Militia Duty		Col. S. Hammond	Ninety Six	£ 4. 2.10
88 Y	Carter, Ja^s.	Supplies			Camden	£ 2.11. 4
89 Y	Davis, Isham	Militia Duty		Col. S. Hammond	Ninety Six	£ 4. 2.10
104 Y	Hillery, Est^d. John	Cont^l. Duty				£ 18.13. 4

Numb. & Book	To whom Granted	For what Granted			District	Amount Indent
107 Y	Harlen, Eliz.ʰ	A Flatt			Ninety Six	£ 35.14. 3
108 Y	Harley, Joseph	Militia Duty				£ 24.10.
110 Y	James, /Major/ John	Supplies			Georgetown	£ 4. 9.10
113 Y	Kean, John	Supplies			Beaufort	£ 21. .
115 Y	Ladson, /Major/ Thoˢ.	Militia Duty	Colleton Co. Regiment		Charleston	£ 33. 8. 7
119 Y	Love, John	Militia Duty	Col. Marshal		Camden	£ 9.10.
126 Y	Mitchell, John	Supplies	Col. Harden		Charleston	£ 5.12. 9
130 Y	Mackie, John	Supplies			C̶a̶r̶	£ 12. 3. 1½
132 Y	MᶜCain, Alex.ʳ	A Mare				£ 25. .
137 Y	Mobley, Micaijah	Militia Duty	Col. Winn		Camden	£ 3. 8. 6
144 Y	Nelson, Sam.ˡ	Militia Duty	Col. S. Hammond		Ninety Six	£ 4. 2.10
145 Y	Nelson, David	Militia Duty	Col. S. Hammond		Ninety Six	£ 4. 2.10
151 Y	Perry, Thoˢ.	Contˡ. Duty				£ 9. 6. 8
153 Y	Pickett, Estᵃ. Thoˢ.	A Horse			Ninety Six	£ 15. .
154 Y	Pawley, Percival	Indigo Impressed				£ 127.13.11
162 Y	Roachell, John	Militia Duty	Col. Winn		Camden	£ 6.15. 8
184 Y	Varnon, John	Waggon Team &c.				£ 12.11. 5
187 Y	Woodward, John	Militia Duty	Col. Hopkins		Camden	£ 4. 8. 6
188 Y	Welcher, Benjⁿ.	Militia Duty	Col. S. Hammond		Ninety Six	£ 4. 2.10
190 Y	Williams, John	Militia Duty	Col. S. Hammond		Ninety Six	£ 4.13. 2
197 Y	Bowers, Benjⁿ.	A Horse	1ˢᵗ Regiment St. Troops			£ 11. 8. 4
205 Y	Blackwell, Jun. Estᵃ. Daniel	Militia Duty	An Indepᵗ. Compʸ.			£ 9. 4. 3
216 Y	Gray, James	Supplies			Ninety Six	£ 10. 4. 3
217 Y	Gore, Margᵗ.	Supplies	Col. Lacey		Ninety Six	£ 28. 2. 8
226 Y	Heyward, Jun. Thoˢ.	Supplies			Charleston	£ 6. 5.11
229 Y	James, Alex.ʳ	A Horse				£ 9. 8.10
233 Y	Meisereau, Joshua	Carpenter's Wages	Frigᶜᵉ. Sᵒ. Carᵃ.			£ 48. 6. 8
239 Y	Price, (96) Willᵐ.	A Horse, Saddle, &c.			Ninety Six	£ 9.15.10
246 Y	Singleton, John	Supplies				£ 8.16. 5
247 Y	Seabrook, Joseph	Indigo Impressed			Beaufort	£ 173.15.10
251 Y	Tillman, Estᵃ. Willᵐ.	Supplies	Gˡ. Sumter		Camden	£ 9.11.

Numb. & Book	To whom Granted	For what Granted			District	Amount Indent
255 Y	Adams, And^w	Cont^l. Duty				£ 66. .
288 Y	Heyward, Sen. Thos.	Supp^s.			Chas. ton	£ 2.12. 3
293 Y	Laboyteaux, John	Midshipman's Pay	Frig^e. S^o. Car^a.		Camden	£ 45. .
296 Y	Lany, John	Militia Duty	Marshall's Regiment		Camden	£ 2.17. 1
310 Y	Pouncy, Roger	A Horse				£ 22. 2. 3
319 Y	Ulmer, Est^a. John	Supplies			Orangeburgh	£ 12.16. 8
321 Y	Williams, Joseph	Supplies			Charleston	£ 3. 4. 2
332 Y	Brown, Willm.	Supplies & Militia Duty	Maj. Thomson		Camden	£ 14. 8. 7
338 Y	Bigem, John	Militia Duty	Marion's Bridg^e.			£ 5.14. 3
344 Y	Caborne, Robt.	Supplies	Legislature		Charleston	£ 5. 2. 8
349 Y	Digmon, John	Militia Duty	Marion's Bridg^e			£ 5.14. 3
354 Y	Freeman, James	Militia Duty	Marion's Bridg^e			£ 13. 6. 5
357 Y	Ginn, Gootsberry	Militia Duty	J^no. Moore's Indp^t. Co.			£ 18. .
360 Y	Green, Drury	Militia Duty	Sumter's Brigade			£ 6. .
362 Y	Harris, Timothy	Militia Duty	Marion's Bridg^e.			£ 2. 2.10
364 Y	Harris, James	Militia Duty	Colleton Co. Regiment			£ 14. 4. 3
372 Y	Johnston, Lewis	Militia Duty	Marion's Bridg^e.			£ 5. 1. 5
376 Y	Kuhn, Henry	Militia Duty	Marion's Bridg^e.			£ 9.15.
380 Y	Miles, Est^a. Ja^s	Supplies			Charleston	£ 15.13.
384 Y	McKelduff, Adam	Supplies	G^l. Henderson	Horry	Georgetown	£ . 7.
386 Y	Marshall, Adam	Supplies	1st & 3rd Regiment			£ 3.10.11
392 Y	McCulloch, Saml.	Cont^l. Duty				£ 7.15. 6
402 Y	Roberts, Willm.	Supplies	Marion's Bridg^e.		Georgetown	£ 43.11. 6
403 Y	Roberts, Zeph^h.	Militia Duty			Ninety Six	£ 7.14. 3
412 Y	Thomson, Alex^r.	Supplies			Georgetown	£ 12.10. 3
414 Y	Tyler, Samuel	Militia Duty	Marion's Bridg^e.			£ 3. 4. 3
417 Y	Veitch, John	Supplies	Wiltown Comp^y.		Charleston	£ 1.10.
420 Y	Ward, Dickey	Militia Duty	Col. Taylor		Camden	£ 6.11. 5
432 Y	Dudley, Thos.	Militia Duty	Granville Co. Regiment			£ 3. 2. 4

Numb. & Book	To whom Granted	For what Granted		District	Amount Indent
443 Y	Gray, Ja⁵.	Militia Duty	Granville Co. Regiment		£ 3. 2. 4
446 Y	Gotee, Henry	Militia Duty	Granville Co. Regiment		£ 3. 2. 4
447 Y	Garven, John	Militia Duty	Granville Co. Regiment		£ 3. 2. 4
454 Y	Hawkins, Estᵃ. Philip	Suppˢ. & Waggon Duty		Charleston J.L.G.	£ 31.12. 6½
455 Y	Hawkins, James	A Horse	Col. Farr	Ninety Six	£ 1. 7.10¼
456 Y	Hodges, Robert	Militia Duty	Granville Co. Regiment		£ 3. 2. 4
459 Y	Jones, Robᵗ.	Militia Duty	Granville Co. Regiment		£ .17. 1½
462 Y	Jones, Willᵐ.	Militia Duty	Granville Co. Regiment		£ 1.11. 5
463 Y	Jones, Richᵈ.	Militia Duty	Granville Co. Regiment		£ 3. 2.10¼
464 Y	Jackson, Jaˢ.	Militia Duty	Col. Grassett	Orangeburgh	£ 7.10.
465 Y	Johnston, Nathan	Militia Duty	Granville Co. Regiment		£ 3. 2.10¼
468 Y	Kirkwood, Est. Hugh	A Mare	Gˡ. Williamson		£ 8.11. 5
470 Y	Lowther, George	Supplies	Col. Roebuck	Ninety Six	£ 7. .
476 Y	McCay, Randal	Militia Duty	Granville Co. Regiment		£ 2. 5. 8½
480 Y	Mathews, Sergᵗ. James	Militia Duty			£ 15.16. ¾
482 Y	Moore, Willᵐ.	Militia Duty	Col. Bratton	Camden	£ 8.17. 1½
488 Y	Overstreet, Jethro	Militia Duty	Granville Co. Regiment	Beaufort	£ 3. 2. 4
493 Y	Peek, Thoˢ.	Militia Duty	Granville Co. Regiment	Beaufort	£ 1.14.
495 Y	Ross, Jun. Isaac	Supplies		Camden	£ 5. 5.
497 Y	Rosell, Estᵃ. Geoᵉ.	Militia Duty	Granville Co. Regiment	Beaufort	£ 3. 2. 4

Numb. & Book	To whom Granted	For what Granted			District	Amount Indent
500 Y	Ratcliff, Elisha	Militia Duty		Granville Co. Regiment	Beaufort	£ 1.11. 2
501 Y	Russell, James	Militia Duty		Col. Marshall	Camden	£ 6. .
503 Y	Saunders, John	Militia Duty		Thomas's Regiment	Ninety Six	£ 65. 4. 3
507 Y	Smith, George	Militia Duty		Granville Co. Regiment	Beaufort	£ 3. 2.10
509 Y	Tanner, Esta. Lynn	Militia Duty		Granville Co. Regiment	Beaufort	£ 3. 2.10
511 Y	Tison, John	Militia Duty		Granville Co. Regiment	Beaufort	£ 3. 2.10
513 Y	Williams, John	Militia Duty		Granville Co. Regiment	Beaufort	£ 1.15. 5
515 Y	Webster, Saml.	Militia Duty		Granville Co. Regiment	Beaufort	£ 3. 2. 4
522 Y	Bean, Jas	Supplies		Capt. John Moore	Ninety Six	£ 3.11. 5
523 Y	Bennett, Saml.	Militia Duty		Marion's Brigade	Cheraw	£ 2. 4. 3
524 Y	Bennett, George	Militia Duty		Marion's Brigade	Cheraw	£ 2. 8. 6
526 Y	Barnett, Esta. Alexr.	Militia Duty		Capt. Joseph Vince	Cheraw	£ 8.11. 5
536 Y	Cartledge, Edmd.	Sunds.		Col. S. Hammond	Ninety Six	£ 66.14. 8
546 Y	Forness, Willm.	Supplies			Cheraw	£ 5.10.11
555 Y	Hesse, Geoe.	Supplies			Orangeburgh	£ 3.18.
557 Y	Huey, Jas.	Militia Duty		Capts. Frost & Thomas	Camden	£ 15.14. 3
558 Y	Hunter, Andw.	Supplies		Gl. Greene	Cheraw	£ 10. 6. 6
564 Y	Jones, James	Supplies				£ 9.16. 3
575 Y	McMahon, Patk.	Contl. Duty				£ 14. .
586 Y	Newman, Thos.	Militia Duty		Marion's Brigade	Cheraw	£ 6. .
588 Y	Price, Henry	Supplies		Gl. Greene	Georgetown	£ 13. 1. 4
602 Y	Ross, Andw.	Supplies at 96		Col. S. Hammond	Ninety Six	£ 5.
603 Y	Rose, John	Supplies			Charleston	£ 18.16. 4
606 Y	Scriven, Elisha	A Horse		Col. Washington		£ 26.10. 9
634 Y	Woodward, Burbage	Militia Duty		Majr. Pearson	Camden	£ 6. 7. 1
641 Y	Mayfield, Saml.	Militia Duty		Col. Bratton	Camden	£ 5. 2. 1

Numb. & Book	To whom Granted	For what Granted			District	Amount Indent	
642 Y	McLewrath, Robert	Gunsmiths Tools				£	31. 4. 1
649 Y	Pickett, Jon^{a}.	Militia Duty & Supp^{s}.		Col. Williams	Ninety Six	£	5. 2.11
652 Y	Rusk, David	Pails & Tubs				£	2. 9. 5
656 Y	Sumers, John	Supplies			Orangeburgh	£	7. .
667 Y	Adams, Willm.	A Horse		Maj^{r}. Postell	Cheraw	£	16. .
677 Y	Baker, John	Militia Duty		Col. Kimball	Camden	£	19.12.10¼
686 Y	Bartley, Robt.	Militia Duty		Col. Marshall	Camden	£	6. 5. 8½
691 Y	Bowler, Est^{a}.Thos.	Supplies		G^{l}. Gist		£	3.17.
698 Y	Bradley, Arthur	Militia Duty		Capt. McCauley	Camden	£	3.12.10¼
701 Y	Conn, Thos.	Militia Duty		Col. Benton	Cheraw	£	2. 2.10¼
732 Y	Dewitt, Est^{a}.Reuben	Cont^{l}. Duty				£	17.10.
743 Y	Drose, Mary	Supplies		G^{l}. Greene	Cheraw	£	. 7.
744 Y	Davis, Henry	Supplies		G^{l}. Greene	Cheraw	£	4. 9.10
754 Y	Field, Thos.	Supplies		~~G^{l}. Greene~~	~~Cheraw~~ Camden	£	5.15. 6
755 Y	Ferry, Willm.	Militia Duty		Col. Lacey	Camden	£	6. .
769 Y	Glyn, Thos.	Supplies		Col. Brandon	Ninety Six	£	8.10.
777 Y	Hodges, James	Militia Duty		Marion's Brigade	Cheraw	£	2. 5. 8½
778 Y	Hagin, David	Militia Duty		Col. Benton	Cheraw	£	4. 5. 8½
786 Y	Hudgins, Ambrose	Supplies		Maj. Millwee	Ninety Six	£	2. 2.
789 Y	Hudson, Willm.	Militia Duty		Round O Comp^{y}.		£	24. .
790 Y	Hindley, Edward	Militia Duty		Col. Benton	Cheraw	£	3.11. 5
791 Y	Herrin, Willm.	Supplies		G^{l}. Greene	Cheraw	£	6. 8. 4
793 Y	Hadger, Charles	Militia Duty		Marion's Bridg^{e}.	Georgetown	£	11.17. 1½
796 Y	Howard, John	Militia Duty		Marion's Bridg^{e}.		£	22.10.
799 Y	Jones,Simeon	Militia Duty		Capt. Lewis	Camden	£	2. 2.10¼
805 Y	Johnston, Martha	Supplies			Charleston	£	3.11.10¼
808 Y	Johnston, Barnet	Militia Duty		Col. Marshal	Camden	£	13. 4. 3¼
826 Y	Burns, Laird	A Mare		G^{l}. Sumter	Camden	£	5. .
837 Y	Commander, Thomas	Supplies & Ferriage				£	45.15. 1½
840 Y	Clark, Willm.	Constable Fees			Camden	£	2. 1.9
841 Y	Dumpard, John	Militia Duty		Capt. A. Thomas	Camden	£	34. 7. 1½
842 Y	Dickson, James	Militia Duty		Capt. A. Thomas	Camden	£	34. 7. 1½
843 Y	Dickson, Joel	Militia Duty		Capt. A. Thomas	Camden	£	34. 7. 1½

Numb. & Book	To whom Granted	For what Granted		District	Amount Indent
844 Y	Dove, Alexr.	Militia Duty	Capt. A. Thomas	Camden	£ 34.7. 1½
857 Y	Wright, John	Contl. Duty			£ 28. . .
858 Y	Waters, Charles	A Horse			£ 2.13. 7½
863 Y	Kays, Michl.	Supplies	Capts. Towles & Linquefield	Ninety Six	£ 7. . .
866 Y	Cassells, Jun. Henry	Militia Duty	Marion's Bridge.	Georgetown	£ 2.14. 3¾
872 Y	Lucas, John	Driving Cattle	Marion's Bridge.	G-Town Cheraw	£ 6. .
877 Y	Mucklewain, Mary	Supplies	Gl. Greene	Cheraw	£ 1. 8.
878 Y	Montgomery, Nathl.	Militia Duty	Col. McDonald	Cheraw	£ 4.14. 3¾
879 Y	Montgomery, Henry	Militia Duty	Col. Richison	Cheraw	£ 42.17. 1½
885 Y	Murphye, Ruduff	Supplies	Gl. Greene	Cheraw	£ 7.14.
886 Y	Murfee, Malachi	Supplies	Gl. Marion	Georgetown	£ 11.11.
890 Y	Mason, Thos.	Contl. Duty	Gl. Marion	Cheraw	£ 7. .
892 Y	Martin, Robert	Supplies	Col. Benton Winn	Cheraw Camden	£ 2. 3. 6
893 Y	Marsh, Sen. John	Militia Duty	Col. Benton	Cheraw	£ 4.14. 3¾
903 Y	McCay, Mrs Cabton	Supplies	Maj. Postell	Cheraw	£ 5.11. 7
910 Y	Newman, Thos.	Militia Duty	Col. Richardson	Cheraw	£ 5. 1. 5
915 Y	Neil, Thos.	Supplies	Waxhaw Station	Camden	£ 1.18. 6
917 Y	Pickett, Micaijah	Supplies & a Mare	Col. H. Hampton	Camden	£ 23.15. 2¾
923 Y	Parson, Willm.	Militia Duty	Col. McDonald		£ 23.15. 8½
933 Y	Reiley, Esta. David	Contl. as a Matross			£ 11. 4. 7
937 Y	Roach, James	Militia Duty	Col. Giles		£ 5. 1. 5
940 Y	Rawlinson, John	Militia Duty	Col. Benton	Cheraw	£ 2. 7. 1½
942 Y	Richardson, Willm.	Horses	Marion's Bridge.	Georgetown	£ 31.19. 4
943 Y	Richey, Jas.	Militia Duty & a Gun	Col. Marshel	Camden	£ 7. 2.10½
946 Y	Roberts, Abraham	Care of a Negro (Hesick)		Georgetown	£ 1. 1. 9
947 Y	Roberts, Zach.	Supplies	Gl. Greene		£ 3.17.
949 Y	Russell, Michl.	Militia Duty	Col. Baxter	Georgetown	£ 8.12.10¼
958 Y	Smith, Robert	Supplies		Orangeburgh	£ 2. 4.11
959 Y	Smith, Esta. John	Contl. Duty			£ 12. 8.10½
963 Y	Simmons, Vincen	Militia Duty	Marion's Bridge.	Cheraw	£ 2. 4. 3¾
969 Y	Scott, Thos.	Supplies	Gl. Greene	Beaufort	£ 3.17.
995 Y	Wilburn, Richd.	Militia Duty	Gl. Marion	Not to be delivd.	£ 42.17. 1½

Numb. & Book	To whom Granted	For what Granted		District	Amount Indent
999 Y	Welch, Rich^d.	Militia Duty	G^l. Marion	Cheraw	£ 2.11.5
1003 Y	Bee, Joseph	Hire of Carpenters		Charleston	£ 19.16.7¾
1004 Y	Brown, Est^a. Bartlet	Supplies	Garden's Regiment	Beaufort	£ 1.4.3¾
1005 Y	Brown, John	Militia Duty	G^l. Marion Capt. Odam	Orangeburgh	£ 20.8.6¾
1007 Y	Chester, David	Waggon hire &c.	G^l. Marion		£ 17.11.
1011 Y	Dennis, Rich^d.	Militia Duty	G^l. Marion		£ 2.12.10¼
1016 Y	Goan, Gideon	Militia Duty	G^l. Marion		£ 4.7.1½
1019 Y	Hope, Geo^e.	Militia Duty	Col. Hopkins	Camden	£ 38.1.5
1032 Y	Smith, Ja^s. High	Militia Duty	Capt. B. Odam	Orangeburgh	£ 20.8.6¾
1051 Y	Daniel, Oliver	Freight of Indigo			£ 66.1.
1071 Y	Waters, Est^a. Bordwine	A Mare		Ninety Six	£ 8.12.2
1099 Y	Brown, Willm.	Supplies	Sumter's Bridg^e.	Camden	£ 10.14.3¼
1106 Y	Crawford, John	Supplies		Sta. N^o. Carolina	£ 3.4.2
1111 Y	Davis, Est^a. John	Supplies	Col. Lacey	Camden	£ 1.15.5½
1124 Y	Hilton, Amey	Supplies		Camden	£ 7.1.2
1126 Y	Jones, L. Willm.	Supplies		Camden	£ 32.13.4
1130 Y	Pennington, Jacob	Militia Duty	Roebuck's Regiment	Ninety Six	£ 12.8.6¾
1131 Y	Prince, Isam	Supplies	Brandon's Regiment	Ninety Six	£ 12.8.
1139 Y	Buxton, Jacob	Supplies		Beaufort	£ 18.12.4½
1142 Y	Bowler, Willm.	Supplies	Sumter's Brigade	Camden	£ 5.2.8
1148 Y	Faulkner, Thos.	Supplies		Camden	£ 4.11.
1151 Y	Harvey, Thos.	A Horse	Seige of Augusta		£ 15. .
1155 Y	Mitchell, Stephen	Supplies	G^l. Marion	Sta. Georgia	£ 5.1.3
1163 Y	Snipes & Ford	Supplies	Colleton Co. Regiment	Charleston	£ 5.8.9
1164 Y	Schad, Abraham	Supplies	Geotown Hosp^l.	Georgetown	£ 7.18.8
1167 Y	Williams, Michijah	Supplies		Georgetown	£ 12.7.6
1168 Y	White, Thomas	Supplies	Hilton Head Co.	Beaufort	£ 3.17.
1169 Y	Anderson, Hugh	A Mare & Saddle	Col. Maham	Beaufort	£ 6.10.6
1179 Y	Bearden, Edm^d.	Militia Duty	Col. White	Ninety Six	£ 11.14.3

Numb. & Book	To whom Granted	For what Granted		District	Amount Indent
1180 Y	Boyd, Willm.	Militia Duty & Supp^s.	Col. Williams	Ninety Six	£ 39. 2. 6
1185 Y	Boykin, Saml.	Supplies			£ 9.19. 6
1187 Y	Baker, Est^a. Benj^m.	Scantling			£ 23. 9. 8
1195 Y	Carrol, Est^a. John	A bay Mare	G^l. Sumter		£ 8.11. 4
1198 Y	Duncan, Ja^s.	Constable's Fees		Camden	£ 6.16. 2
1202 Y	Dick, Robert	A Horse	Col. Horry	Georgetown	£ 21.15.
1204 Y	Doyal, John	Supplies	Camden Station	Cheraw	£ 4.18.
1206 Y	Elliott, Est^a. Chas.	Rice		Chas. ton	£ 136.10.
1210 Y	Goodwin, Lewis	Cont^l. Duty			£ 29. 8.
1212 Y	Gaddis, Christiana	Supplies		Ninety Six	£ .16.11
1214 Y	Grimes, James	Militia Duty	Col. Hicks	Cheraw	£ 7. 2.10
1216 Y	Gray, John	Supplies	Capt. J. Bell	Ninety Six	£ 4. 6.10
1225 Y	Hicklin, Arthur	Duty	Col^s. Winn & Postele	Camden	£ 8.11. 5
1229 Y	Hadger, Chas.	A Negro executed		Georgetown	£ 100. .
1231 Y	Howard, Jun. Edwd.	Militia Duty	Marion's Bridg^e.	Georgetown	£ 27.17. 1
1232 Y	Henley, Est^a. Saml.	Militia Duty	Col. Casey	Ninety Six	£ 52. 2.10
1236 Y	Jolly, Joseph	Supplies	G^l. Greene	Georgetown	£ 19. 5.
1241 Y	Keating, John	Supplies			£ 16.12. 6
1246 Y	~~Jolly~~ Lee, Lewis	Militia Duty	Capt. Odam	Orangeburgh	£ 16. 2.10
1248 Y	McTeer, John	Supplies	Col. Horry	Beaufort	£ 35. 7.
1250 Y	Mannon, Beasley	Supplies & Militia Duty	Marion's Brigade	Georgetown	£ 7. 1. 3
1252 Y	McCants, Thomas	Militia Duty	Ponpon Co.		£ 8. 2.10
1253 Y	McCay, Joseph	Militia Duty & Supp^s.	Genl. Marion	Camden	£ 3.12. 9
1258 Y	Rainey, Benjn.	Supp^s.	Genl. Greene	Ninety Six	£ 36. 2. 4
1263 Y	Singleton, John	Supp^s.	Col^s. White & Horry	Georgetown	£ 26. 2. 8
1265 Y	Taggart, John	A Horse & Militia Duty	Neil's Regiment	Camden	£ 14. 8. 6
1272 Y	Walker, Elijah	Militia Duty	Winn's Regiment	Camden	£ 15.11. 5
1273 Y	Walker, Jerem^h.	Militia Duty	Winn's Regiment	Camden	£ 6.15. 8
1277 Y	McDonald, Martin	Militia Duty	Marion's Brigade	Camden	£ 2. 7. 1
1282 Y	Strobhar, John	Supplies	Low Granville Co. Regiment	Beaufort	£ 7.14.

Numb. & Book	To whom Granted	For what Granted			District	Amount Indent
1283 Y	Spence, Ja^s.	Duty	Hampton's Regiment		Ninety Six	£ 5. .
1289 Y	Brunson, Josiah	Supplies			Beaufort	£ 3.17.
1292 Y	Con, George	Militia Duty	Col. Hopkins		Camden	£ 26. 5. 8½
1304 Y	McMullen, David	A Horse	G^l. Sumter		Camden	£ 15. .
1305 Y	McCluney, Willm.	Militia Duty	Hopkin's Regiment		Camden	£ 17.17. 1½
1306 Y	McCrea, Joseph	Militia Duty	Marion's Bridg^e.		Georgetown	£ 8.10.
1312 Y	Robins, Est^a. Willm.	Militia Duty	Lacey's Regiment		Camden	£ 27.14. 3¼
1323 Y	Cheesborough, John Junr.	Supplies	Col. M. Simons		Chas. ton	£ 14. 1. 6
1325 Y	Fanny, John	Cont^l. Duty				£ 63.15. 6
1328 Y	Lupton, Mary	Supplies				£ 14. 3. 2
1329 Y	Linam, George	Militia Duty	Col. Brandon		Ninety Six	£ 33.19. 7
1330 Y	Linn, John	A Mare			Camden	£ 14. 5. 8
1331 Y	Montgomery, Willm.	Militia Duty	Kershaw's & Marshall's Regiment		Camden	£ 10. 7. 1
1333 Y	Martin, Edwd.	Negro & Boat hire				£ 32. 9.11
1334 Y	Marsh, Jun. John	Militia Duty	Benton's Regiment		Cheraw	£ 6.11. 5
1336 Y	Marsh, Joshua	A Gun	Capt. Standard		Cheraw	£ 1.10.
1340 Y	McMichael, Willm.	A Horse		Battle Fishdam	Camden	£ 9. 6.
1342 Y	Miller, Est^a. Adam	Cont^l. Duty				£ 63.15. 6
1348 Y	Punch, Mary	Supplies	Genl. Greene			£ 4. 9.10
1357 Y	Saltzer, Jacob	Militia Duty	Marion's Bridg^e.		Orangeburgh	£ 8. . 4
1363 Y	Shockley, Thos.	Supplies			Camden	£ 2.16.10
1373 Y	Woodberry, Rich^d.	Supplies	Genl. Greene		Camden	£ 5. 2. 8
1374 Y	Williams, Edwd.	Duty & Rid^g. Express	Kershaw & Kimball's Regiment		Camden	£ 7.10.
1388 Y	Dehay, Est^a.	Saddle Trees & Pill^ns.	Col. P. Horry		Georgetown	£ 25.18.
1397 Y	Griffies, Est^a. Edwd.	Rice				£ 10.10.
1400 Y	Hicklin, Isaac	Supplies	Station at Camden		Camden	£ 4. 5. 8
1406 Y	Kelly, Joseph	A Horse & Mare	Col. Casey		Ninety Six	£ 28.11. 5
1410 Y	Moss, Stephen	Supplies	St. Comm^y.			£ 3.16. 1
1415 Y	Ravo, Ab^m.	Supplies	G^l. Wayme		Beaufort	£ 3.11.10

Numb. & Book	To whom Granted	For what Granted		District	Amount Indent
1421 Y	Wall, James	Sunds.			£ 70. 4.
1423 Y	Alcorn, Esta. Jas.	A Horse			£ 12.
1426 Y	Baillie, Esta. Robt. Carnibe	Contl. Duty			£ 102.14.
1435 Y	Latta, Willm.	Militia Duty	Capt. Mills	Camden	£ 3. 9. 7
1439 Y	Burch, Joseph	A Boat	Col. Lee		£ 20.
1441 Y	Bell, John N.	Militia Duty	Winn's Regiment	Camden	£ 4.
1445 Y	Founton, Zouston	Supplies	Edisto Compy.		£ .11.
1446 Y	Gardon, Capt. Joseph	Duty			£ 38.11. 5
1450 Y	Philips, James	Supplies	Col. Roebuck	Ninety Six	£ 1. 4. 8
1460 Y	Bruce, Mrs.	Supplies		Orangeburgh	£ 2. 3. 6
1466 Y	Impfinger, John	Supplies	Col. Washington		£ 2. 3. 3
1469 Y	Noveltown, Mrs.	Supplies	Sumter's Brigade		£ .9. 4
1478 Y	Conneley, Patrick	A Horse	Sumter's Brigade		£ 6. 8. 6
1480 Y	Gibbs, Robt.	Supplies		Charleston	£ 65. 9.
1481 Y	Gibbs, Robt.	Supplies		Charleston	£ 181. 6. 3
1524 Y	Davis, Mary	Supplies		Beaufort	£ 4. 9.10
1529 Y	Rapley, Rich.d And.w.			Ninety Six	£ 42. 8. 3
1540 Y	Atkins, Elisha	Supplies	Col. Winn	Camden	£ 3. 5. 5
1541 Y	Ackor, Willm.	Militia Duty		Beaufort	£ 3. 3.
1550 Y	Crawford, Robt.	Militia Duty	Col. Richardson	Camden	£ 8.17.10
1552 Y	Davis, John	Militia Duty	Col. Marshal	Camden	£ 5.18. 6
1553 Y	Dubose, Elias & others	Militia Duty &c.		Cheraw	£ 6. 4. 1
1555 Y	Fear, Isham	Militia Duty	Cols. Taylor & Hopkins	Camden	£ 7. 2.10
1558 Y	Griffiths, Esta. Edward	Supplies		Beaufort	£ 41.10. 8
1562 Y	Hinclin, Willm.	Duty	Gl. Sumter & Co. Marshall	Camden	£ 5. 8. 7
1563 Y	Johnston, James	Supps.	Army at Monks Corner	Charleston	£ 41. 3. 2
1567 Y	Knox, Isaac	Militia Duty	Col. Marshal	Camden	£ 5.14. 3
1568 Y	Keath, Sarian	Supplies		Georgetown	£ .18.11
1578 Y	Thomson, Alexr.	Militia Duty	Marion's Bride.	Georgetown	£ 8.11. 5
1581 Y	Wood, (Corpl.) Thos.	Militia Duty	Col. Beekman	Georgetown	£ 9. 4. 9

Numb. & Book	To whom Granted	For what Granted			District	Amount Indent
1588 Y	Baker, Nich^s.	Militia Duty		Col. S. Hammond	Ninety Six	£ 22.17. 1
1590 Y	Dickey, John	Militia Duty		Col. Niel	Camden	£ 7.17. 1
1592 Y	Falker, Jacob	Militia Duty		Col. Bean	Ninety Six	£ 11. .
1598 Y	Leeper, Jun. Robt.	Militia Duty		Col. Bratton	Camden	£ 4. 1. 5
1603 Y	Flowers, John	Hogs Impressed		Claud^s. Pegues, Jr.	Cheraw	£ 3. 3. 8
1604 Y	Flowers, John	Hogs Impressed		Claud^s. Pegues, Jr.	Cheraw	£ 8.12. 6
1606 Y	Hodge, Henry	Hogs Impressed		Claud^s. Pegues, Jr.	Cheraw	£ 1. 1. 2
1607 Y	Keightley, Peter	Hogs Impressed		Claud^s. Pegues, Jr.	Cheraw	£ 37.16. 5
1611 Y	Murfee, Moses	Hogs Impressed		Claud^s. Pegues, Jr.	Cheraw	£ 8. 4. 6
1612 Y	Murfee, Morris	Hogs Impressed		Claud^s. Pegues, Jr.	Cheraw	£ 20.11. 4
1614 Y	McCall, John	Hogs Impressed		Claud^s. Pegues, Jr.	Cheraw	£ 9.19.
1615 Y	McIntosh, Alex^r.	Supplies Impressed		Claud^s. Pegues, Jr.	Cheraw	£ 8.10.10
1616 Y	Neal, Thos.	Supplies Impressed		Claud^s. Pegues, Jr.	Cheraw	£ 7.19. 3
1619 Y	Pouncey, Roger	Supplies Impressed		Claud^s. Pegues, Jr.		£ 46.11. 5
1622 Y	Tyrrel, Willm.	Supplies Impressed		Claud^s. Pegues, Jr.		£ 11.19. 1
1623 Y	Whitefield, Rodia	Supplies Impressed		Claud^s. Pegues, Jr.		£ 3.19. 7
1624 Y	Williamson, Thos.	Supplies Impressed		Claud^s. Pegues, Jr.		£ 20. 2. 6
1625 Y	Wright, Geo^e.	Supplies Impressed		Claud^s. Pegues, Jr.		£ 5. 6.
1626 Y	Freeman, Est^a. Henry	Cont^l. Duty	G^l. Huger's Regiment	5th Regt^t.		£ 26. 8.10
1627 Y	Gorman, Est^a. John	Cont^l. Duty		1st Regt^t.		£ 26. 8.10
1632 Y	Steward, Hardy	Cont^l. Duty		3rd Regt^t.		£ 26. 8.10
10 Z	Holcum, Moses	Duty	Col. Anderson	Col. Roebuck	Ninety Six	£ 13. 5. 8
15-A Z	Turner, John	Militia Duty			Georgetown	£ 2.17. 1½
53 Z	Jenkins, Reuben	Militia Duty		Col. Hicks	Georgetown [Cheraw]	£ 6. .
59 Z	Mobley, Benj^a...	Militia Duty		G^l. Winn	Camden	£ 5.10.
62 Z	Naramore, Edwd.	Militia Duty Indorses (J. ???)		Col. Marshal	Camden	£ 20.14. 3¼
75 Z	Spears, Willm.	A Horse lost	Col. Anderson	Cherokee Exped^n.	Ninety Six	£ 11. 8. 6¾
76 Z	Strange, John	A Horse lost	Col. Anderson	Cherokee Exped^n.	Ninety Six	£ 8.18. 6¾
77 Z	Williams, Thos.	A Horse lost	Col. Anderson	Cherokee Exped^n.	Ninety Six	£ 11. 8. 6¾
110 Z	Stringer, John	A Horse lost & Supp^s.	Col. Anderson	Col. Anderson	Ninety Six	£ 10. 9.

Numb. & Book	To whom Granted	For what Granted			District	Amount Indent
161 Z	Bogan, James	Waggon hire	Col. Anderson	Brandon's Regiment	Ninety Six	£ 7. 8. 6
164 Z	Clark, Redias	Supplies	Col. Anderson	Brandon's Regiment	Ninety Six	£ 2. 2.10
165 Z	Chesney, Willm.	A Horse lost		Cherokee Expedn.	Ninety Six	£ 3.12.10
174 Z	Grant, Willm.	A Horse lost			Ninety Six	£ 12.17. 1½
180 Z	Hill, Willm.	A Horse lost		Col. Brandon	Ninety Six	£ 8.11. 5
186 Z	Jolley, Esta. Benjn.	Waggon hire &c.		Col. Brandon	Ninety Six	£ 20.11. 5
241 Z	Dunn, Jas.	Militia Duty Tate	Capt. Tate	Col. Patton	Camden	£ 6.15.
244 Z	Price, Henry	Militia Duty			Ninety Six	£ 3.10. 8
245 Z	Philips, Jas.	Militia Duty	Col. Anderson	Col. Roebuck	Ninety Six	£ 14. 2.10
248 Z	Ash, Willm.	Militia Duty	Capt. Tate	Col. Bratton	Camden	£ 10. .
251 Z	Ash, Robert		Capt. Tate	Col. Bratton	Camden	£ 10. .
261 Z	Howe, Willm.		Capt. Tate	Col. Bratton	Camden	£ 5.14. 8
262 Z	Hembree, Joel	A Horse	Col. Anderson	Col. Roebuck	Ninety Six	£ 7.10. 4
269 Z	Muldoon, Jas.		Capt. Tate		Camden	£ 14. 2. 8
274 Z	Peninton, Henry	Militia Duty		Col. Roebuck	Ninety Six	£ 31. 8. 7
276 Z	Robison, Basdale		Anderson's	Col. Casey	Ninety Six	£ 14. 5. 8
279 Z	Smith, Ralph	Supplies	Col. Anderson	Roebuck	Ninety Six	£ 3. 5.10
282 Z	Winkler, Lewis	Rice		Col. Garden	Beaufort	£ 35. .
284 Z	Copeland, John	Militia Duty		Col. Bratton	Camden	£ 2.10.
285 Z	Parker, John	Militia Duty		Bratton's Regiment	Camden	£ 4.18. 6
286 Z	Wood, Lazarus	Militia Duty		Bratton's Regiment	Camden	£ 4.11. 5
303 Z	McClinton, Robert	Taylor's Work	Col. Anderson	Col. Anderson	Ninety Six	£ 17. 7. 4
347 Z	Gaston, Thos.	Militia Duty		Col. Marshal	Camden	£ 7. 4. 3
355 Z	Willson, Esta. Jas.	Loses at Brier Creek		Col. Bratton	Camden	£ 10.11.
361 Z	Bedshaw, Thos.	A Gun	Col. P. Horry		Georgetown	£ 1. 8. 6
362 Z	Berry, Thos.	Supplies			Ninety Six	£ 2.13. 8
364 Z	Boone, Thos.	Militia Duty		Col. Casey	Ninety Six	£ 6. 8. 6
365 Z	Breler, Abm.	Militia Duty			Ninety Six	£ 4. 8. 6
378 Z	Oates, Martin	Militia Duty		Col. Roebuck	Ninety Six	£ 1.11. 5
385 Z	Douglass, Jas.	Supplies		Col. Waters	Ninety Six	£ 5.12.10
386 Z	Dobbin, Thos.	Supps.	Col. P. Horry	Gl. Greene	Georgetown	£ 15. 8.

Numb. & Book	To whom Granted	For what Granted			District	Amount Indent
387 Z	Dudley, Thos.	Militia Duty				£ 2. .
388 Z	Dunlap, Ja^s.	Militia Duty		Col. Kershaw	Camden	£ 1. 8. 6
389 Z	Darby, Asa	Militia Duty		Capt^s. Frost & Gore	Camden	£ 5. .
391 Z	Eady, Henry	Militia Duty		Col. E. Kershaw & Marshal	Camden	£ 8.11. 5
395 Z	Dottey, Jerem^h.	A Horse lost		Cherokee Exped^n.	Ninety Six	£ 5.14. 3
397 Z	Henderson, Joseph	Riding Express		Col. Hill	Camden	£ .7.
398 Z	Harris, Robert	Wheat	Col. Anderson	B.W.R.	Ninety Six	£ 5. 8. 6
399 Z	Hill, Thos.		Col. Anderson	Col. Brandon	Ninety Six	£ 5. 7. 2
400 Z	Hodges, John	Supplies	Powe		Cheraw	£ 1. 3.
402 Z	King, Thos.	Supplies	Capt. Tate		Camden	£ 5. 3. 2
404 Z	Leverett, Robt.		Col. Anderson	Col. Brandon	Ninety Six	£ 26.13. 6
413 Z	Owners of the Ship Columbia	Sund^s.				£ 277.14.10
418 Z	Smith, Benj^a.	Supplies	Col. Anderson	Col. Purvis	Ninety Six	£ 4. 3. 6
419 Z	Screven, Benjn.	Supplies	Col. P. Horry	G^l. Greene	Georgetown	£ 5. 2. 8
421 Z	Tucker, Willm.	Supplies		Col. Brandon	Camden	£ 3.17.
422 Z	Turner, John	Supplies	Col. Anderson	Col. Waters	Ninety Six	£ 5.10. 8
423 Z	Towles, Jane	Supplies	Col. Anderson	Col. Casey	Ninety Six	£ 4. 5. 8
424 Z	Varcene, Willm.	A Horse		Capt. S. Price		£ 14. 5. 8
426 Z	Wooters Philip	Supplies		G^l. Greene		£ 19.12.
429 Z	Cocker, Joseph	A Waggon &c.	Col. Anderson	B.W. & R.	Ninety Six	£ 41.14. 2
469 Z	Bigger, John		Capt. Tate		Camden	£ 9. 5. 8
477 Z	Kennedy, Sen. Willm.	Militia Duty	Col. Anderson	Col. Brandon	Ninety Six	£ 10. 5. 8
478 Z	Linam, George	A Horse	Col. Anderson	B.W. & R.	Ninety Six	£ 8.11. 5
514 Z	Fuller, Mess.	Militia Duty		Col. Hicks	Cheraw	£ 6. .
515 Z	Hanna, Ja^s	Militia Duty	Tate	Col. Lacey	Camden	£ 6.11. 5
523 Z	Massey, Willm.	Supplies		Col. Lacey	Camden	£ 2.17. 4
526 Z	Wilson, James	Militia Duty		Col. Lacey	Camden	£ 59.17. 1
538 Z	Brebner, Willm.	Duty		Bowie's Comp^y.	Ninety Six	£ 5.10. 4
539 Z	Bradley, Ja^s.	Duty		Bowie's Comp^y.		£ 16.18. 6
540 Z	Berrier, Ja^s.	Duty		Bowie's Comp^y.		£ 16.10. 6
545 Z	Cousart, Nathan	Militia Duty		Col. Kershaw	Camden	£ 11.11. 5
547 Z	Depree, Saml.	Duty		Bowie's Comp^y.		£ 3.15.

Numb. & Book	To whom Granted	For what Granted			District	Amount Indent
549 Z	Gaillard, John	Negroes		Sta. Cavalry	Georgetown [Charleston]	£ 926.11.
550 Z	Haik, John	Duty		Bowie's Comp^y.		£ 16.18. 6
555 Z	Wood, John	Militia Duty		Col. Hicks	Cheraw	£ 6. . .
556 Z	Jones, Vincen	Militia Duty		Col. Taylor	Camden	£ 6.14. 3
557 Z	Lang, Willis	Militia Duty		Col. Hicks	Cheraw	£ 6. . .
558 Z	Laremore, Ja^s.	Duty		Bowie's Comp^y.	Ninety Six	£ 2. 7. 1
559 Z	Martin, Benjn	Duty		Bowie's Comp^y.		£ 13.10.
560 Z	Neel, Willm.	Duty		Bowie's Comp^y.		£ 16.18. 6
561 Z	Neel, Ja^s.	Duty		Bowie's Comp^y.		£ 16.18. 6
562 Z	Pouncey, Anth^y.	Duty		Col. Hicks	Cheraw	£ 7.10.
564 Z	Rowland, David	Duty		Bowie's Comp^y.		£ 16.18. 6
565 Z	Veatch, James	Duty		Taylor's Regiment		£ 8.17. 1
567 Z	Waterfield, Ja^s.	Duty		Bowie's Comp^y.		£ 2.11. 5
569 Z	Ayres, Hartwell	Duty		Col. Hicks	Cheraw	£ 6. . .
570 Z	Brannam, James	Duty		Col. Hicks	Cheraw	£ 6. . .
571 Z	Cox, Saml.	Duty		Col. Hicks	Cheraw	£ 6. . .
573 Z	Davis, Thos.	Duty		Col. Hicks	Cheraw	£ 6. . .
574 Z	Keel, Willm.	Duty		Col. Hicks	Cheraw	£ 6. . .
575 Z	Levens, Rich^d.	Duty		Col. Hicks	Cheraw	£ 6. . .
576 Z	McNeal, Alex^r.	Duty		Col. Hicks	Cheraw	£ 6. . .
577 Z	Mixon, Mich^l.	Duty		Col. Hicks	Cheraw	£ 6. . .
578 Z	Owens, Joshua	Duty		Col. Hicks	Cheraw	£ 6. . .
579 Z	Wood, Benj^a.	Duty		Col. Hicks	Cheraw	£ 6. . .
581 Z	Ross, Robt.	Duty	Anderson's	Col. Casey	Ninety Six	£ 7.17.1
583 Z	Ledger, John	Supplies			Georgetown	£ 2.11.4
19 AA	Leacraft	Bal^a. another Ind^t.				£ 4.10.8
21 AA	Waller, Benjn.	Bal^a. another Ind^t.				£ 11. 9.6
27 AA	Russell, Nathl.	Bal^a. another Ind^t.				£ 3. 9.8½
16 FEC	Est^a Wm Gibbes	Claim ag^t. Forf^d. Est^a.				£ 90. 7. 8

Numb. & Book	To whom Granted	For what Granted			District		Amount Indent
	Perry, Estᵃ. John	Supplies			Georgetown	£	33.10.10½
	Kennedy, John	Militia Duty			Camden	£	40. 8. 6
	Green, Peter	Corn				£	20. .

[Page 15]

Aggregate of the foregoing Schedule.

Amounts	Page		
		1	£ 1,775.12. 9¼
		2	£ 782.19. 4
		3	£ 611. 1.11¼
		4	£ 1,527.11. 7¾
		5	£ 941. 8. 0¼
		6	£ 1,054.12.10¼
		7	£ 687.15. 2
		8	£ 640.13. 9½
		9	£ 677. 7. 9¼
		10	£ 229.11. 7
		11	£ 805.16. 1
		12	£ 502. 1. 3¾
		13	£ 1,249.12. 0¼
		14	£ 1,786. 2. 0½

£12,672. 6. 4

Deduct the following Indents entered in the ~~follow~~ foregoing Schedule and not delivered   Vizt.

Nº.	108	Book	E	John Hustess	£	5. 5.
	32	"	O	Robert Martin		84. .
	503	"	P	Jacob Swicard		11.14.
	709	"	T	James Snow		33. 7. 4
	586	"	X	Thomas Peek		2. 2.10¼
	885	"	Y	Ruduffe Murfee		7.14.

£ 144. 3. 2¼

£12,528. 3. 1¾

Add the following Indents not entered in the foregoing Schedule, Vizt.

Nº.	614	Book	C	John Scrimsler	£	12. 6.	
	134	"	dº.	Chaˢ. McGinney		5. 0. 3	Sent by T.N. to Colm. p recᵗ. on other side
	81	"	F	Estª. Philip Britton		6. 8. 4	
	96	"	dº.	Estª. Martha Chisham		7.14.	
	133	"	G	James Frasher		24. 2. 2	
	106	"	L	Zilpha Lowder		3. 5.	
	164	"	dº.	Jesse Demsey & Willis Purkins		118. 4. 3	
	217	"	dº.	Robert Warren		20. 4. 5½	
	3	"	O	John Jennings		2. 6. 9	
	287	"	dº.	William Carter		6.13.10½	
	81	"	P	John Miller		23.10. 4¼	
	491	"	dº.	Abraham Richardson		5. .	Sent by T.N. to Col. p recᵗ. on other side
	555	"	U	Joseph Sims		1. 8. 6	Ditto
	302	"	W	James Gibson		18. .	Ditto
	236	"	X	~~Joel~~ Martha Wilson		6.16. 6	

591	"	dº	Joel Pardue	2.17. 1		
3599	"	dº	Estª. Martha McCarty	46.15. 4¼		
332	"	Y	William Brown	14. 8. 7		
937	"	dº	James Roach	5. 1. 5	[Illegible]
963	"	dº	Vincen Simmons	2. 4. 3¼	Ditto
16	"	FEC	Estª. Wᵐ Gibbes	90. 7. 8	
19	"	AA	Leecraft	4.10. 8	
21	"	dº.	Benjamin Waller	11. 9. 6	
27	"	dº.	Nathaniel Russell	3. 9. 8½	£ 442. 4. 8¼

Errors Excepted }
23 June 1791   }   Tho' Nicholls   ??? £12,970. 7.10

[Page 16]

Received this 1ˢᵗ day of July 1791 from William Hort Esq. Treasurer in Charleston the following Indents Vizᵗ.

No. 491	Book	P	to	Abᵐ Richardson	for	£	5. 0. 0
555	"	U	to	Joseph Sims	for		1. 8. 6
963	"	Y	to	Vincen Simmons	for		2. 4. 3¼
591	"	X	to	Joel Pardue	for		2.17. 1
302	"	W	to	James Gibson	for		18. .
134	"	Dº	to	Chˢ McGinney	for		5. 0. 3

34.10. 1¼

amounting to Thirty four pounds Ten shillings & One Penny farthing which I am to forward to Benjamin Waringᵉʳ Esqʳ. Treasurer at Columbia.

Thoˢ. Nicholls

The following three Indents are not included in the foregoing Schedule Vizᵗ·

231	H	Estª. John Perry Provisⁿˢ. & Forage £	33. 1.10½
535	W	John Kennedy Militia Duty Camden	40. 8. 6
1437	X	Peter Green Corn	20. .

£ 93.10. 4½

Amounting to Ninety three Pounds, ten Shillings & four pence half penny/

Thoˢ. Nicholls
6 July 1791

Page	Number of Indents	Amount	Page	Number of Indents	Amount
1	50	£ 306. 3. 1½	17	53	£ 511.11.11½
2	53	£ 399. 1. 4½	18	53	£ 505.11.10¼
3	52	£ 386.12. 9¼	19	54	£ 636. 1. 5¾
4	52	£ 264.16. 1¾	20	56	£ 482.11. 8
5	51	£ 459. 3. ¼	21	56	£ 237. 1.11½
6	51	£ 430. . 4	22	57	£ 238. 1.11¾
7	51	£ 436.16.10¾	23	57	£ 238. 5.10½
8	49	£ 273. 3. 3¾	24	59	£ 287. 9. 7
9	49	£ 489. 1. 3¾	25	59	£ 306.17.10½
10	52	£ 391.15.10¼	26	58	£ 444.19. 5
11	51	£ 346. . 2¼	27	58	£ 508. 9.11¾
12	52	£ 462. 2. 9½	28	53	£ 566.13.10
13	51	£ 397.14. ½	29	51	£ 563.11. 6
14	54	£ 498. 1. 4½	30	55	£ 639. 5. 3¼
15	54	£ 405. 4. 9¼	31	54	£ 505. 7. 4½
16	54	£ 304.11. ½	32	39	£ 402.11. 5
	827	£ 6250. 8. 4¼		872	£ 7074.13. ¼
				827	£ 6250. 8. 4¼
			Indents 1699		£13325. 1. 4

Deduct the follow^g. Indents left by mistake in Charleston vizt.

N°. 134	Book D	Charles McGinney	£ 5. 0. 3	}
N°. 491	"	P Abrah^m Richardson	£ 5. .	} Rec^d. from Charleston July 4th, 1791
N°. 555	"	S Joseph Sims	£ 1. 8. 6	}
N°. 302	"	W Ja^s. Gibson	£ 18. .	} £ 29. 8. 9

1699 Indents, deduct^g. 4 remains 1695 Indents amo^{tg}. to £13295.12. 7

| 591 | Book X | Joel Pardue | £ 2.17. 1 |
| 963 | " Y | Vincen Simmons | £ 2. 4. 3¼ |

1st Regiment	78, 87	Arthur	22, 26
1st Regiment State Troops	77	Arthur, W.	7, 8
3rd Regiment	47	Arundel, Reddock	65
5th Regiment	87	Ash, Robert	88
Abbett, Solomon	51	Ash, William	88
Ackor, William	86	Ashley, John	52
Adair, Sarah	28	Askew, Thomas	9
Adams, Andrew	78	Atkerson, Isaac	44
Adams, David	18	Atkins, Elisha	86
Adams, David & Co.	1	Atkins, Francis	54
Adams, Howel	60	Atkins, Joseph	28
Adams, James	4	Atkison, Timothy	47
Adams, Joel	38	Audey, Christopher	14
Adams, John	4	Augusta, Georgia	83
Adams, Thomas	9, 76	Austin, Elizabeth	47
Adams, William	36	Austin, Francis	45
Adams, William	81	Austin, Jesse	66
Addis, Richard	14	Averet, Elijah	52
Adkinson, James	3	Ayres, Hartwell	90
Adkinson, Timothy	54	B.W. & R.	89
Akin, Archibald	51	B.W.R.	89
Akin, Ezekiel	51	Babilitman, Zora	24
Alcorn, James	86	Bacon, Thomas	14
Alison, James H.	24	Baggs, John	9
Allen, Benjamin	12	Bagley, James	60
Allen, James	36	Bailey, Robert	48
Allen, Joel	28	Baillie, Robert Carnibe	86
Allen, Robert	36	Baisden, James	36
Allen, Sallathiel	24	Baker, Alexander	76
Allergottie, Anthony	9	Baker, Benjamin	84
Allison, Dorothea	3	Baker, John	81
Allison, James	28	Baker, Nicholas	36, 87
Allston, Peter	12	Baldwin, Isaac	25
Allston, William	38	Ball, William	13
Allston, William, Jr.	38	Banks, Charles	48
Altman, Sarah	10, 22	Bar, Christopher	20
Anderson	15 – 19, 22, 26 – 39, 43, 45, 47 – 66, 88, 90	Barber, Captain	43
		Barber, James	72
		Barber, Mary	7
Anderson, Captain	16	Barksdale, Hickison	9
Anderson, Colonel	9, 10, 12, 18, 22, 43, 66 – 71, 87 – 89	Barlain, Babister	28
		Barlow, John	65
		Barnet, Captain	12
Anderson, Henry	3	Barnet, Humphrey	60
Anderson, Hugh	83	Barnet, Jacob	60
Anderson, John	3	Barnet, John	66
Anderson, John, Jr.	36	Barnet, Joseph	14
Anderson, John, Sr.	36	Barnet, Michael	44
Anderson, Joseph	71	Barnett, Alexander	80
Anderson, Robert	3	Barnett, John	57
Anderson's Regiment	16, 17, 27, 28, 45, 46, 50	Barnett, Joseph	54
		Barns, William	60
Andress, Israel	18	Baron, William	25
Ardist, Jacob	36	Barratine, James	36
Arnold, Reddock	36	Barrett, Nathaniel	28
Arnold, William	25	Barron, Thomas	6

Bartley, Robert	81	Bevins, James	60
Barton, Thomas	76	Beyer, Hans Peter	1
Barton, William	20	Bigem, John	78
Baskins, Captain	16	Bigger, John	89
Bates, Thomas	19	Billing, Jasper	57
Battle of Fishdam	84	Bind, Daniel	54
Baucart, Mary	1	Birch, Joseph	47
Bawdy, John	36	Bisber, Casper	54
Baxter, Colonel	82	Bishop, Samuel	28
Baxter, James	3	Black, Adam	58
Baxter, John	3	Black, Alexander	51
Baxter, Robert	3, 28	Black, Captain	10
Bayle, Francis	44	Black, William	28
Bayley, Lucy	54	Blackmond, Thomas	3
Bean, Colonel	87	Blackwell, Abraham	25
Bean, James	80	Blackwell, Daniel, Jr.	77
Bean, Thomas	21	Blair, James	18, 21
Bean, William, Jr.	28	Blakely, John	28
Beard, Colonel	55, 56	Bland, John	36
Bearden, Absalom	60	Blount, James	72
Bearden, Edmumd	83	Blunt, Charles	44
Bearden, Thomas	66	Blythe, Samuel	9
Beaseley, Henry	29	Bogan, James	88
Beckom, Reuben	76	Bolton, Agnes	76
Beckom, Russel	76	Bolton, Daniel	48
Bedshaw, Thomas	88	Bolton, John	25
Bee, Joseph	83	Bolton, Spencer	25
Beekes, Samuel	28	Bond, John	66
Beekman, Colonel	86	Bonds, Elisha	29
Beem, Jesse	76	Bone, James	3
Belcher, Dennis	72	Bonner, James	9
Belien, David	66	Bonner, Thomas	66
Bell, Captain	12	Boone, Fredrick	36
Bell, J. Captain	84	Boone, Thomas	21, 88
Bell, John	6	Booth, John	51
Bell, John N.	86	Booth, Joseph	6
Bell, Robert	9	Botsford	25
Bell, Thomas	6	Bouchillon, Captain	16
Bell, William	44	Boughman, Joseph	24
Bellinger, Edmund, Jr.	9	Boull, William	22
Bellinger, John	2	Bourline, Joseph	5
Bellinger, William	2, 18	Bourquin, Colonel	51
Bellune, Francis	3	Bowbo, Sampson	60
Benbow, Martha	18	Bowers, Benjamin	77
Bennet, Hugh	18	Bowers, Mrs.	2
Bennett, George	80	Bowers, Sylvan	22
Bennett, John	57, 66	Bowie's Company	89, 90
Bennett, Samuel	44, 80	Bowler, Thomas	81
Benson, Andrew	22	Bowler, William	83
Benson, James	54	Bowman, Thomas	24
Benthen, Samuel	25	Boyd, Hardy	22
Benton, Colonel	25, 42, 81, 82	Boyd, John	58
Benton's Regiment	85	Boyd, William	84
Berrier, James	89	Boyes, Charles	9
Berry, Richard	6	Boykin, Samuel	84
Berry, Thomas	88	Bradford, Jonathan	43

Bradford, Richard	26	Brown, Sims	58
Bradley, Arthur	81	Brown, Tarlton	72
Bradley, James	89	Brown, William	44, 72, 78, 83,
Bradley, John	3		93
Bradshaw, William	54	Bruce, Caleb	13
Brailsford, Joseph	21	Bruce, Mrs.	86
Branden, John	4	Brumfield, Elizabeth	14
Brandon	54, 56, 57, 65	Brunson, David	3
Brandon, Colonel	4, 23, 39, 43,	Brunson, Josiah	85
	55, 56, 79 – 81,	Brunson, Matthew	43
	85	Bryan, Joseph	71
Brandon, Edward	66	Bryan, Lewis	71
Brandon's Regiment	22, 41, 49 – 51,	Bryan, Richard	49
	54, 55, 58, 60 –	Bryan, Simon	72
	66, 83, 88, 89	Bryan, William	71
Brannam, James	90	Bryant, Richard	49
Bratton, Captain	11	Bryant, Thomas	25
Bratton, Colonel	7, 10 – 14, 21,	Bryant, William	36
	23, 25, 51, 57,	Bryson, James	45
	87, 88	Buchanan, John, Doctor	20
Bratton's Regiment	88	Buchanan, Thomas	25
Brazell, James	24	Buchanan, William	54
Braziel, Wood	9	Buchannon, John, Jr.	58
Bready, William	9	Buchannon, Robert	57
Brebner, William	89	Buckholts, Peter	24
Breler, Ab^m.	88	Buckstaner, Daniel	36
Brenan, Eugene	45	Buffington, Joseph	66
Brenter, James	38	Buise, John	66
Brewer, James, Sr.	36	Bullian, Thomas	66
Brewer, William	72	Bunderick, Charles	58
Brewton, George	25	Bundrick, Charles	53
Briant, William	44	Buntrick, Charles	58
Bridges, John	13	Burch, Charles	4
Bridges, Joseph	11	Burch, Joseph	86
Bridges, Mary	13	Burchfield, Adam	52
Brier Creek	10, 88	Burdel, William	9
Brig *Polly*	47	Burdit, Fredrick	28
Briggs, John	28	Burges, Richard	60
Britton, Henry	36	Burgess, William	21
Britton, Philip	92	Burke, Thomas	36
Brock, Isaac	66	Burkett, John	25, 71
Brookes, Bartlett	28	Burkett, Thomas	71
Brookes, Dudley	54	Burnaw, Martin	47
Brooks, John	60	Burns, Laird	81
Brooks, Michijah	36	Burns, Robert	36, 49
Broom, James	53, 58	Burquett, Ephraim	12
Brooner, Michael	36	Burrows, Joseph	3
Broughton, John	36	Burrows, Samuel, Jr.	3
Brown, Bartlet	83	Bush, John	7, 25
Brown, Bartlet, Sr.	72	Bussy, Benjamin	66
Brown, Benjamin	12, 72	Butler, Pierce	10
Brown, Burrell	14	Butler, Thomas	3
Brown, Henry	48	Buxton, Jacob	83
Brown, James	10	Buxton, Samuel	76
Brown, John	9, 83	Caborne, Robert	78
Brown, Samuel	21	Cain, James	10

Caldwell, Joseph, Jr.	58	Cheesborough, John, Jr.	85
Caldwell, Joseph, Sr.	58	Cherokee Expedition	87 – 89
Calhoun, Captain	15 –17, 19	Cherrey, William	13
Calhoun, John	10	Chesney, William	88
Calhoun, Thomas	66	Chester, David	83
Callihan, David	45	Childs, John	13
Camden Station	84, 85	Chisham, Martha	92
Camp, John	66	Chisham, Mary	3
Campbell, Alexander	5	Christian, Philip	26
Campbell, Andrew	6	Citts, George	2
Campbell, David	54	Clanton, David	2
Campbell, Elizabeth	76	Clanton, Richard, Sr.	21
Campbell, Gilbert	37	Clark, Alexander, Sr.	10
Campbell, Henry	10	Clark, Elijah, Colonel	56
Campbell, Patrick	10	Clark, James	7
Campbell, Thomas	6	Clark, Redias	88
Campbell, William	20	Clark, William	2, 81
Cane, Richard	13	Clarke, Bartly	18
Cannady, John	54	Clarke, Benjamin	54
Cannon, Robert	29	Clarke, Harman	13
Cannon, Samuel	28	Clay, Nathan	37
Cannon, William	29	Clayter, Laurence	13
Cantey, William	4	Clayton, Abraham	20
Caps, John	44	Clayton, Isaac	14
Carr, John	4	Clayton, Isham	26
Carrithers, Captain	19	Clayton, Thomas	50
Carrol, John	84	Clements, Joseph	25
Carroll, John	72	Clemons, Zeph	37
Carsan, James	6	Clifford, Elizabeth	2
Carsan, Samuel	51	Clifton, William	61
Carter, J., Captain	76	Cloud, James	7
Carter, James	76	Cobia, Nicholas	2
Carter, John	7	Cochran, Phebe	45
Carter, Robert	18, 29, 44	Cochran, William	37
Carter, William	15, 92	Cockburn, John	45
Cartledge, Edmund	80	Cocker, Joseph	89
Cary, Thomas	72	Cockfield, James	22
Casettee, William	25	Cockfield, Joseph	22
Casey, Colonel	46, 56, 84, 85, 88 – 90	Cockley, Isaac	36
		Coiler, Moses	60
Casey, Elizabeth	4	Coker, Nathan	13
Casey's Regiment	28, 29, 31, 32, 37, 38, 45, 47, 49, 54, 55	Colden, Blanch[d].	72
		Colden, John	72
		Colden, Samuel	72
Cassells, Henry, Jr.	82	Cole, Daniel	13
Castellaw, William	7	Cole, David	13
Castiller, Thomas	36	Coleman, Abner	50
Caughran, William	36	Coleman, William	36
Cauley, George	36	Coley, John	36
Celley, Joseph	54	Colhoun, Alexander	71
Chalmers, Martha	1	Colleton County Regiment	77, 78, 83
Chamberlain, John	36	Collier, John	25
Chambers, John	7	Collins, Cary	13
Champaign, Gibson	67	Collins, Harakin John	1
Charleston Artillery	44	Collins, Reuben	44
Cheat, Ellice	29	Collins, Samuel	21

Colson, Jacob	38	Creamor, William	45
Columbia	89	Creath, William, Jr.	7
Commander, Samuel	4	Creighton, John	48
Commander, Thomas	81	Crofts, Edward	4
Commins, James	54	Cron, Thomas	67
Con, George	85	Crookes, Samuel	58
Cone, Matthew	13	Crosby, James	10
Conn, Thomas	81	Crosby, Thomas	36
Connaway, Jerry	67	Crossley, Jarmon	26
Conneley, Patrick	86	Crow, Thomas	54
Conner, John	54, 67	Crumley, Martin	21
Connor, Jonathan	3	Crummy, Stephen	13
Connor, Thomas	44	Crusie, Jesse	1
Connoway, Philip	72	Cullreaker, Joseph	8
Continental Duty	10, 11, 14, 15,	Cummins, William	29
	22, 23, 43, 44,	Cunningham, James	4
	46, 48, 49, 51,	Curenton, William	54
	76 – 78, 80 – 82,	Curry, Thomas	67
	84 – 87	Cuyler, Abraham	1
Cook, John	8	Damewood, Henry	15
Cooke, John	4	Danel, Thomas	10
Cooke, P. Wanmuck	58	Daniel, Oliver	83
Cooke, William	61	Danseller, Henry	8
Cooley, John	26	Danseller, Henry John	8
Cooper, Captain	10	Darborough, Hugh	37
Cooper, Ezekiel	22	Darby, Asa	89
Cooper, Thomas	45	Darby, Jacob	17
Copacke, Joseph	10	Dardon, George	15
Copeland, John	88	Dardon, John	15
Copelin, John	9	Darling, Ephraim	15
Corbett, Daniel	57	Darrington, Thomas	2
Corbett, James	26	Dasher, Christian	26
Corkshadden, Robert	7	David, William	73
Cotter, Anthony	67	David, Zekiel	13
Cotton, Thomas	45	Davidson, Sarah	55
Couch, Millington	29	Davis, Blandford	37
Coughran, Robert	10	Davis, Claman	55
Cousart, James	4	Davis, Clemency	37
Cousart, Nathan	89	Davis, Colonel	47
Cousmould, Henry	48	Davis, David	73
Covington, John	36	Davis, Edward	21
Cowan, Captain	15, 17	Davis, Francis	53
Cowan, John	10	Davis, Gardner	15
Cowley, William	61	Davis, Henry	81
Cowsant, James	5	Davis, Henry, Jr.	24
Cox, James	10	Davis, Hezekiah	48
Cox, Josiah	13	Davis, Isham	76
Cox, Samuel	90	Davis, Isom	37
Cox, William	13	Davis, James, Jr.	15
Craightington, John	36	Davis, Jesse	26
Crawford, Gilbert	10	Davis, John	21, 45, 83, 86
Crawford, John	83	Davis, John, Jr.	76
Crawford, Joseph	57	Davis, Joseph	15
Crawford, Major	13, 21, 44, 57	Davis, Major	4
Crawford, Nathaniel	7	Davis, Mary	76, 86
Crawford, Robert	86	Davis, Nathan	48

Davis, Scolton	37	Doharty, James	24
Davis, Simon	61	Dollard, Patrick	38
Davis, Thomas	15, 21, 90	Dolton, Matthew	37
Davis, Vachel	37	Dolton, Thomas	37
Davis, Ware	37	Donald, John	18
Davis, William	22	Donaldson, Mathew	15
Davis, William, Colonel	10	Donham, Joseph	13
Davis, Zachariah	37	Dopson, Joseph	24
Davis's Regiment	4	Doss, Joel	15
Davison, Hugh	38	Dottey, Jeremiah	54, 89
Davison, Joseph	61	Dottey, Sarah	54
Dawkins, Chloe	55	Dougharty, James	59
Dawson, Captain	16, 17	Dougherty, John	76
Dawson, Larkin	61	Douglas, David	2
Dawson, Richard	24	Douglas, John	55
Day, Josiah	73	Douglas, Joshua	13
De Traville, John B.	24	Douglas, Sherrard	37
Dean, Abner	15	Douglass, James	88
Deason, Enoch	44	Dove, Alexander	82
Dehay,	85	Dove, Jacob	24
Dehay, Andrew	4	Dover, John	22, 43
Deloach, Hardy	73	Dover, Zepha.	11
Deloach, Michael	72	Dowdle, James	22
Deloach, William	73	Doyal, John	84
Delough, William	67	Drake, John	55
Delstoche, Michael	22	Drayton, Thomas	15
Delwood, William	15	Driggers, Julius	24
Demsey, Jesse	11, 92	Drose, Mary	81
Dennis, Richard	83	Dubose, Elias	86
Depree, Samuel	89	Dudley, Thomas	78, 89
Derry, John, Lieutenant	20	Duggers, Julius	44
Devant, Ann	9	Duke, Edmund	45
Devant, Charles	37	Dumpard, John	81
Deveaus, Francis	37	Duncan, James	84
Dewees, John	73	Dunkin, John, Jr.	59
Dewitt, Reuben	81	Dunlap, James	89
Dial, Garret	37	Dunlap, John	29
Dial, Nathaniel	54	Dunn, James	88
Dick, Robert	20, 84	Dunnam, James	7
Dick, Thomas	37	Dupont, Charles	15
Dickey, John	87	Dupont, Cornelius	5
Dickison, Robert, Jr.	29	Dupont, Gideon	2
Dickson, James	81	Dupont, Josiah	20
Dickson, Joel	81	Durham, Arthur	29
Dickson, John	22	Dutoutle, John	48
Digmon, John	78	Eacheson, John	22
Dill, Nicholas	21	Eady, Henr	89
Dingley, Robert	38	*Eagle* Pilot Boat	48
Dixon, James	67	Eagle, Archibald	73
Dixon, William	61	Eargle, John	53
Dobbin, Thomas	88	Earle, Samuel	58
Dobbins, James	11, 59	East, Josiah	29
Dobbs, John	72	Eckles, William	48
Dodd, John	61	Eddingfield, William	76
Dodd, William	61	Eddins, John	15
Doeck, Thomas	67	Edds, John	15

Eddy, Henry	29	First Regiment State Troops	77
Edisto Company	86	Fishdam	84
Edmanson, Isaac	55	Fitzgerald, Charles	39
Edwards, Elizabeth	2	Fitzgerald, Philip	48
Edwards, John	4	Fitzpatrick, James	13
Eikesber, Mary	8	Flake, John	39
Eikester, Mary	8	Flanagan, Mrs.	13
Elder, James, Captain	50	Fleming, William	10
Ellerbie, William, Jr.	22	Flowers, Henry, Sr.	48
Elliott, Barnard	9, 15	Flowers, John	87
Elliott, Charles	84	Fogle, Barbara	8
Elliott, William	15, 24	Footrice, John	59
Elliotte, James	7	Forbes, Patrick	50
Ellis, Elizabeth	24	Ford, Edward	16
Endsworth, William	61	Ford, Elisha	45
Enoe, Jacob	37	Ford, Hezekiah	48
Eshworth, Benjamin	50	Ford, Nathaniel	29
Evans, John	22	Ford, Robert	29
Evans, Nathan	59	Ford, Stephen, Jr.	20
Evans, Nathaniel	37	Ford, Thomas	39
Evans, William	37	Foreman, George	37
Every, James	55	Forness, William	80
Ewbanks, John	61	Forr, George	55
Fail, Thomas, Lieutenant	24	Forris, George	39
Fairchild, Richard	44	Forster, John	9
Falker, Jacob	87	Founton, Zouston	86
Fanny, John	85	Fowler, John	29
Farmer, William	29	Fowler, Richard	29
Farned, Hannah	3	Fowler, William	29
Farr, Colonel	79	Foxworth, James	38
Farr, Thomas	1	Foxworth, Zachariah	29
Faulkenbery, Jacob	28	Franklin, Benjamin	10
Faulkner, John	13	Franklin, George	39
Faulkner, Thomas	83	Frasher, James	92
Favers, Theophilus	22	Frederick, James	22
Fear, Isham	86	Freeman, Captain	15, 16, 19
Feigge, Christian	48	Freeman, Henry	87
Felistion, John	57	Freeman, James	20, 78
Fell, John	44	Freeman, John	73
Felts, John, Captain	24	French, Michael	53
Fender, John	39	Fridig, Captain	24
Fender, William	39	Frierson, Robert	2
Ferguson, Elizabeth	7	Frigate *South Carolina*	43, 44, 48, 49, 77, 78
Ferguson, Samuel	7		
Ferry, William	81	Fritts, Henry	59
Field, Thomas	81	Frost, Captain	80, 89
Fields, Ab^m.	48	Fuller, Benjamin	48
Fields, Samuel	13	Fuller, Mess.	89
Fifth Regiment	87	Fulton, Thomas	73
Filend, Peter	22	Furr, John	59
Findley, Paul	29	Fynch, Daniel	67
Finkley, Charles	29	Gaddis, Christiana	84
Finlay, John	16	Gaddis, Christopher	4
Finley, John	45	Gage, James	67
Finnell, Ambrose	67	Gage, William	39
First Regiment	78, 87	Gaillard, Charles	28

Gaillard, John	90	Giles, Robert	16
Gainey, William	22	Gill, Captain	7
Gale, Ransom	44	Gillam, James	26
Galton, John, Sr.	45	Gillam, Major	49
Gamball, Major	38	Gillaspie, James	67
Gambell, William	73	Gillelan, Elenor	22
Gamble, John	45	Gillespie, Andrew	16
Garbet, George	39	Gillet, Aaron	48
Garden, Colonel	21, 24, 71 –	Gilmore, Edward	13
	76, 88	Gilmore, James	57
Garden's Regiment	83	Ginn, Gootsberry	78
Gardiner, John	51	Ginn, Madric	73
Gardner, William	13	Ginn, Mesheck	30
Gardon, Joseph, Captain	86	Giroud, David	24
Garey, William Bayley	45	Gist, General	81
Garlant, William	12	Givens, James	43
Garman, James	61	Glading, James	44
Garner, Richard	16	Glenn, James	29
Garnett, Joseph	73	Glenn, Joseph	29
Garrineau, Peter	16	Glover, Fredrick	39
Garsington, Christopher	30	Glyn, Colonel	56
Gartman, John	65	Glyn, Thomas	81
Garven, John	79	Goan, Gideon	83
Garvey, Michael	29	Godbold, James	29
Garvin, Captain	56	Goddard, Francis	2
Gasque, Thomas	44	Goddin, Ann	3
Gassert, John	24	Goebel, John	48
Gaston, Thomas	88	Good, Ernes	39
Gates, Christian	24	Goodby, William	39
Gates, Jacob	24	Gooden, Henry	44
Gearry, Thomas, Jr.	55	Goodman, David	22
Geary, John	29	Goodman, Henry	44
Geary, Thomas	45	Goodman, William	23
Gee, Charles	45	Goodwin, Harris	29
Geeseling, William	61	Goodwin, John	65
Gentry, Cain	16	Goodwin, Lewis	84
Gentry, Richard	52	Goodwin, William	61
Georgetown Garrison	9, 47	Goodwyn, Colonel	46
Georgetown Hospital	83	Goowin, Abel	48
Gerardeau, Peter	1	Gore, Captain	89
Gessindaner, Henry	24	Gore, John	55
Getty, Henry	39	Gore, Margaret	77
Gexson, Samuel	55	Gore, Rachel	10
Gibbes, Wᵐ	90, 93	Gorman, John	87
Gibbons, Michael	23	Gortman, John	53
Gibbs, James	52	Gotee, Henry	79
Gibbs, Robert	86	Gouge, John	38
Gibson, David	39	Gough, Francis	39
Gibson, James	44, 92, 93, 94	Gough, John	23
Gibson, Roger	13	Goulding, William	59
Giddens, James	1	Gourdine, Theodore	18
Giddens, John	1	Gowen, David	67
Gieger, John	26	Goyen, John	23
Gilbert, Uriah	22	Grad, William	59
Gilchrist, John	4	Graham, Charles	23
Giles, Colonel	48, 82	Grains, Henry	44

Grant, John	2	Hager, Simon	58
Grant, Mary	2	Haggard, Jonadab	16
Grant, William	88	Hagin, David	81
Granville County Regiment	9, 78 – 80	Haik, John	90
Grassett, Colonel	79	Hail, Henry	7
Gray, Captain	10, 47	Haild, James, Captain	62
Gray, James	18, 48, 77, 79	Hainey, Robert	62
Gray, John	58, 84	Hall, Daniel	1
Gray, John, Captain	45	Hall, Howard	23
Gray, Lt.	22, 23	Hall, Hugh	16
Green, Ab^m.	23	Hallman, John	65
Green, Bryant	45	Ham, Littleton	62
Green, Drury	78	Ham, McIlberry	62
Green, Isaac	42	Hambrey, Drury	68
Green, Jacob	29	Hamilton, Benjamin	32
Green, Peter	55, 91, 93	Hamilton, David	30
Green, William	8	Hamilton, James	43
Greene, General	44, 76, 80, 81, 82, 84, 85, 88, 89	Hammett, John	50, 52
		Hammon, S., Colonel	43
Greenwood's Wharf	18, 45	Hammond, Charles	32
Greer, William	26	Hammond, Colonel	54
Gregory, John	58	Hammond, S., Colonel	14, 76, 77, 80, 87
Grier, Joseph	4		
Grier, Samuel	4	Hammond, Samuel	32
Griffies, Edward	85	Hampton, H., Colonel	22, 82
Griffin, Anthony	29	Hampton, Hy., Colonel	48
Griffin, Benjamin	44	Hampton, J. Captain Company	58
Griffin, James	16	Hampton, J. Captain	57, 58
Griffin, Lane	16	Hampton's Cavalry	21
Griffin, Samuel	48	Hampton's Regiment	85
Griffin, William	16	Hancock, John	4
Griffith, Ezekiel	29	Hanna, Captain	7, 11, 26, 48
Griffith, Joshua	26	Hanna, James	89
Griffith, William	55	Hanna, William, Jr.	7
Griffiths, Edward	86	Hanna, William, Sr.	7
Grigg, Daniel	50	Hannah, Captain	7
Griggs, Daniel	67	Hannah, James	16
Grigsbey, Enoch	39	Hannah, Richard	10
Grim, John	53	Hannah, Robert, Jr.	71
Grimball, John, Lieutenant	48	Harbison, William	59
Grimes, James	84	Harbour, Walter	18
Grimesley, John	39	Harden, Colonel	20, 21, 23, 24, 42, 71 – 73, 76, 77
Grimsley, George	2		
Grindrat, Henry	23		
Griner, Mrs.	1	Harden, John	31
Grinet, John	44	Hardyman, Thomas	3
Grove, Francis	2	Hargrove, Charles	32
Guerard, Jacob	6	Harkins, John	48
Guinn, Richard	45	Harlen, Elizabeth	77
Guinton, Moses	50	Harley, Joseph	77
Gunter, Charles	29	Harling, Samuel	32
Gunter, William	29	Harman, Ab^m.	25
Gwen, William	45	Harman, Clarke	13
Hackins, Francis	55	Harper, Hance	7
Hadger, Charles	81, 84	Harrard, Hardy	16
Hagartee, John	7	Harrel, John	21

Harris, Ezekiel	32	Henderson's Brigade	7, 8, 22
Harris, James	78	Henley, Samuel	84
Harris, Jesse	10	Henning, Thomas	4
Harris, John	16	Henry, James	62
Harris, Moses	43	Henson, Obediah	23
Harris, Robert	89	Herd, Captain	17, 19
Harris, Thomas	11, 67	Herlong, Jacob	8
Harris, Timothy	4, 78	Hermon, Ab^m.	40
Harris, Timothy	78	Herrin, William	81
Harris, West	68	Herring, William	45
Harrison, Thomas	7	Hesse, George	80
Harrol, Jonathan	59	Hewey, James	12
Harron, James	50	Hext, Thomas	30
Hart, Jacob	7	Heyward, Daniel	24
Harter, Nicholas	8	Heyward, James	44
Hartsfield, James	4	Heyward, Thomas, Jr.	24, 77
Hartsuch, John	30	Heyward, Thomas, Sr.	78
Harvey, Charles	31	Hicklin, Arthur	84
Harvey, Evan	32	Hicklin, Isaac	85
Harvey, Thomas	83	Hicklin, John	30
Haselton, William	30	Hicks, Colonel	84, 87, 89, 90
Hasford, Samuel	24	Hicks, John	43
Hassan, George	25	Hier, Christopher	25
Hatcher, Benjamin	48	Hightower, Thomas	68
Hatcher, Benjamin, Captain	25	Hill, Adam	17
Hatcher, David	40	Hill, Colonel	7, 21, 39, 49, 89
Hatcher, John	32	Hill, Isaac	32
Hatcher, Robert	32	Hill, Thomas	25, 89
Hatcher, William	51	Hill, William	65, 88
Hatton, James	56	Hill's Regiment	10
Haulman, George	53	Hillery, John	76
Hawkins, Francis	55	Hillhouse, Captain	12
Hawkins, James	79	Hilton Head Company	83
Hawkins, Philip	79	Hilton, Amey	83
Hay, Charles	16	Hilton, James	30
Hay, James	59	Hinclin, William	86
Hay, John	43	Hindley, Edward	81
Hayes, Colonel	43	Hodge, David	73
Hayse, Jacob	62	Hodge, Henry	87
Hazelheart, John	57	Hodges, Benjamin	31
Hazleton, Richard	28	Hodges, James	81
Hearne, William	59	Hodges, John	89
Hearrens, Fredrick	40	Hodges, Robert	48, 79
Heartley, Amos	4	Hog, Thomas	32
Heaton, Salathiel	62	Hogan, John	31
Hedgewood, James	32	Hogg, George	30
Helms, Mary	23	Hogg, James	25
Hem, James	68	Hogg, John	25
Hembree, Joel	88	Hogg, William	3
Hemphill, Alexander	57	Hogwood, Reuben	17
Henderson	6	Holcom, John	68
Henderson, Archibald	10	Holcom, Joseph	68
Henderson, Captain	12	Holcum, Elisha	61
Henderson, General	2, 8, 9, 47, 78	Holcum, Moses	87
Henderson, Joseph	89	Holland, John	17
Henderson, William, General	12	Hollingsworth, Joseph	31

Hollingsworth, Zebulon	57	Husband, John	38
Hollingsworth, Zebulon, Jr.	57	Huse, John	40
Hollis, Lt.	23	Hustess, John	3, 92
Holloway, Obediah	32	Hutchinson, John Elias	43
Holman, Mary	1	Hutchinson, Robert	31
Holmes, James	24	Hutchinson, Thomas	17
Holmes, John	31	Hutchinson, William	43
Holsenback, William	32	Hutson, David	17
Holsey, William	24	Hutson, James	17
Hood, John	40	Hutson, Joseph	30
Hood, William	7, 18	Hutson, Nathaniel	17
Hoofman, Martin	30	Hutson, Robert	17
Hooker, Edward	55, 68	Hutson, Samuel	32
Hope, George	83	Hutson, William	17
Hopkins Regiment	85	Huxford, Harlow	21
Hopkins, Colonel	44, 77, 83 – 86	Hyrne, Henry	2
Hopkins, Jesse	43	Impfinger, John	86
Horn, Mrs.	4	Inabner, Margaret	30
Hornsby, Moses	23	Independent Company	77
Horry	20, 65, 78	Irby, Robert	40
Horry, Colonel	23, 42, 84	Irwin, Captain	17, 19
Horry, P. Colonel	20, 21, 39, 85, 88, 89	Irwin, John, Captain	45
		Izard, Ralph, Jr.	3
Horsekead, John	55	Jackson, James	79
Hort, William	93	Jackson, John	40, 62
Horton, Robert	5	Jackson, Jordan	62
Houston, John	2, 25	Jackson, Major	18
Houze, James	45	Jackson, Stephen	40
Howard, Edward, Jr.	84	Jackson, William	59
Howard, James	62	Jacob, Joshua	59
Howard, John	81	Jacobs, Shadrack	59
Howard, Thomas	62, 68	James, Alexander	77
Howe, Jane	43	James, Benjamin	40
Howe, William	88	James, John, Major	77
Howell, Jospeh	68	James, William	40
Hudgins, Ambrose	81	Jant, John	55
Hudson, Robert	48	Jay, John	65
Hudson, William	81	Jayroe, Peter	5
Huey, James	80	Jeffers, Samuel	7
Huger, Benjamin	4	Jefferson, John	10
Huger, Isaac	21	Jenkins, Benjamin	33
Huger, Isaac, Jr.	1	Jenkins, Captain	23
Huger, Isaac, Sr.	1	Jenkins, John	40, 55
Huger's Regiment	87	Jenkins, Reuben	87
Huggins, Joseph	4	Jenkins, William, Captain	42
Huggins, Rebecca	48	Jennings, John	33, 92
Hughes, Matthew	62	Jetter, Cornelius	62
Hughes, Samuel	10, 52	John, We	40
Hughes, William, Captain	30	Johnson, Jacob	14
Hull, William	23	Johnson, James	41
Hulsey, James	68	Johnson, John	10, 26
Humphry, David	43	Johnson, Mathew	31
Hunter, Andrew	31, 80	Johnson, Thomas	58
Hunter, H. Colonel	49	Johnston, Alexander	65
Hunter, Henry	1	Johnston, Barnet	81
Hunter, Robert	32	Johnston, Charles	45

Johnston, Jacob	41	Kelley, Daniel	25
Johnston, James	31, 68, 76, 86	Kellsall, Agnes	5
Johnston, John	8, 17, 26	Kelly, Amos, Captain	25
Johnston, Lewis	78	Kelly, Captain	24
Johnston, Martha	81	Kelly, G., Captain	25
Johnston, Nathan	79	Kelly, James	7
Johnston, Robert	31	Kelly, Joseph	74, 85
Johnston, Thomas	55	Kelsey, James	7
Joice, John	73	Kennedy, John	45, 56, 91, 93
Joice, William	73	Kennedy, Thomas	57
Jolley, Benjamin	88	Kennedy, William, Sr.	89
Jolley, Joseph	28	Kennelley, Elizabeth	8
Jolly, Joseph	84	Kent, Charles	48
Jolly, Lewis	84	Kerby, Archibald	43
Jones, Bartley	33	Kerr, John, Sr.	7
Jones, Benjamin	33, 68	Kershaw, Colonel	11, 12, 30, 44, 48, 89
Jones, Captain	11		
Jones, Charles	33	Kershaw, E., Colonel	89
Jones, Henry	33	Kershaw's Regiment	85
Jones, Hiram	52	Keville, Benjamin	68
Jones, Isaac	21	Key, Tandy	33
Jones, James	80	Kilgore, Captain	46
Jones, John	17, 57	Kilgore, Colonel	71
Jones, L. William	83	Killpatrick, Captain	45
Jones, Matthew	33, 68	Kimball, Colonel	12, 14, 30, 32, 38, 41, 44, 81
Jones, Richard	48, 79		
Jones, Richard	79	Kimball's Regiment	85
Jones, Robert	79	Kindermier, Henry	23
Jones, Simeon	81	Kindrick, Palmer	62
Jones, Thomas	57	Kinesler, Christian	43
Jones, Thomas, Captain	50	King, John	23
Jones, Vincen	90	King, Kerby	7
Jones, William	79	King, Thomas	89
Jonican, James, Sr.	33	Kinnard, Martin	56
Jonican, Moses	33	Kinslow, John	30
Jordan, Adam	17, 55	Kirk, Gideon	74
Jordan, Moses	25	Kirk, James	31
Jordan, Robert	43, 48	Kirk, William	74
Jordan, Thomas	52	Kirkland, John	40, 74
Jowers, John	40	Kirkland, Reuben	73
June, Peter	5	Kirkland, Richard	73
Kalts, Martin	59	Kirkland, Susanna	8
Kalts, Michael	59	Kirkling, James	40
Kays, Michael	82	Kirkwood, Hugh	79
Keagler, Andrew	8	Kithcart, Samuel	69
Keal, Abraham	9	Kitts, Francis	17
Kean, John	77	Knave, William	62
Kearsey, Levi	68	Knight, James	74
Kearsey, Randolph	68	Knox, Eleanor	48
Keath, Sarian	86	Knox, Isaac	86
Keating, John	84	Knox, James	53
Keel, William	90	Koker, Thomas	41
Keightley, Peter	87	Kolb, Colonel	46
Keith, Margaret	41	Koone, Henry	50
Keleaugh, John	7	Koone, John	50
Keller, George	8	Kuhn, Henry	78

Laboyteaux, John	78	Levingston, William	33
LaBruce, Thomas	20	Lewis, Benjamin	7
Lacey, Colonel	11, 14, 23, 46, 77, 81, 83, 89	Lewis, Captain	23, 81
		Lewis, George	8
Lacey's Regiment	6, 21, 85	Lewis, John	31, 45
Ladson, Thomas, Major	77	Lewis, Joseph	40
Lamar, Lewis	40	Lewis, Lanty	74
Lamar, Susanna	2	Lewis, Ross	31
Lamb, Ezekiel	5	Lewis, Rosser	33
Lane, Catherine	1	Lewis, William	46
Lane, Drury	41	Lewis, Winifred	9
Lang, James	31	Libolt, John	8
Lang, Willis	90	Liddle, Captain	15
Lankford, William	25	Liddle, James, Sr.	19
Lany, John	78	Liles, Captain	15
Laremore, James	90	Linam, George	85, 89
Larriey, John	74	Linn, John	85
Latta, William	86	Linn, Mary	14
Lattimore, John	49	Linquefield, Captain	82
Lauglen, Anthony	7	Lipham, Daniel	7
Lawrence, William	42	Little, John, Lieutenant	50
Laws, William	5	Littlejohn, Thomas	62
Lawsey, William	5	Littleton, Charles	56
Lawson, Benjamin	56	Livingston, Michael	59
Laycock, William	43	Livingston, William	48
Leach, John	33	Lockhart, Robert	49
Leach, Thomas	19	Logan, Thomas	11
Leacraft	90	Logue, Samuel	76
Leard, John	26	Long, James	46
Leathering, James	33	Long, Joshua	5
Leavell, Robert	56	Long, Thomas	50, 74
Leavolt, John	59	Loopers, William	33
Ledger, John	90	Loper, David	56
Lee, Abraham	8	Lott, John, Jr.	7
Lee, Colonel	18, 86	Love, James	14
Lee, Elliot	63	Love, John	14, 77
Lee, James	69	Low Craven Company	47
Lee, Lewis	84	Low Granville County Regt.	84
Lee, Nicholas	8, 76	Lowder, Zilpha	10, 92
Lee, Nicholas	8	Lowrey, Matthew, Sr.	33
Lee, Robert	33, 50	Lowry, Matthew	33
Leech, David	69	Lowther, George	79
Leech, John	19	Lucas, John	69, 82
Leecraft	93	Luckie, William, Jr.	19
Leeper, Robert, Jr.	87	Lunday, James	40
Lefever, John	40	Lupton, Mary	85
Legear, James	5	Lutis, John	65
Legislature	78	Lymbike, George	33
Lemar, Thomas, Jr.	33	Lynch, Thomas	5, 14
Lemire, Thomas	33	Lyon, Joseph	19
Lenier, Clemwood	63	Mabrey, Daniel	14
Lenud, Henry	38	Mackey, Thomas	14
Leonard, Abel	43	Mackie & Cameron	25
Lesley, John	14	Mackie, John	77
Levens, Richard	90	Mackleduff, Thomas	5
Leverett, Robert	89	Magary, Edward	19

Magens, Johannes	1	Matthews, Daniel, Sr.	33
Magill, John	31	Matthews, Isaac	33
Maham, Colonel	14, 18, 83	Mattocks, McKenzie	41
Major, John	41	Maxwell, Alexander	19
Maliel, Robert	56	Maxwell, John, Jr.	19
Malone, William	18, 65	Maxwell, Nicholas	19
Maner, Samuel	43, 74	Maxwell, Samuel	20
Maner, William	74	Maxwell, William	19
Mannon, Beasley	84	Mayers, Elijah	14
Marion, Gabriel	43	Mayfield, Robert	56
Marion, General	10 – 12, 14, 18, 21, 23 – 24, 44, 76, 82, 83	Mayfield, Samuel	80
		Maynard, William	50
Marion's Bridage	3, 4, 10, 17 – 21, 25, 28 – 32, 38, 39, 41 – 48, 78, 80 – 82, 84 – 86	McBee, Mathias	52, 69
		McCain, Alexander	77
		McCall, Charles	38
		McCall, Henry L.	46
		McCall, Henry	40
Marlor, William	41	McCall, James	50
Marsh, John, Jr.	85	McCall, John	87
Marsh, John, Sr.	82	McCall, Thomas	50
Marsh, Joshua	85	McCance, Charles	26
Marshal, Colonel	44, 45, 47, 48, 81	McCance, William	11
		McCants, Thomas	20, 84
Marshal, Daniel	34	McCarney, Owens	31
Marshal's Regiment	44	McCarty, Martha	69, 93
Marshall, Adam	78	McCauley, Captain	81
Marshall, Colonel	12, 28, 43, 77, 80, 81, 86 – 89	McCaw, Captain	16
		McCaw, William	38
Marshall, William	14	McCay, Cabton, Mrs.	82
Marshall's Regiment	78, 85	McCay, James	75
Marshel, Colonel	82	McCay, Joseph	84
Martin, Benjamin	90	McCay, Randal	79
Martin, Captain	22	McClaskey, Dennis	46
Martin, Edward	11, 85	McClearey, Robert	11
Martin, Edward, Captain	30, 41	McCleland, David	43
Martin, Elijah	33	McClellan, Samuel	13
Martin, James	5	McClelland, Robert	75
Martin, James, Jr.	14	McClendon, John	74
Martin, John	26, 45	McClendon, Wilson	34
Martin, John	45	McCleur, James	66
Martin, Peter	59	McClinton, John	46
Martin, Richard	46	McClinton, Robert	88
Martin, Robert	14, 46, 82, 92	McCluer, Captain	11
Martin, Roger	51	McCluney, William	85
Martin, William	23, 38	McClure, Captain	7
Martin, Zachariah	65	McClure, James	31
Mason, Thomas	82	McConnell, George	41
Massey, William	89	McCooll, Captain	13
Massingal, Joseph	54	McCooll, John, Captain	25
Maston, Thomas	10	McCord, John, Jr.	19
Matheney, James	14	McCord, John, Sr.	19
Mathews, Edmund	10	McCowen, Alexander	14
Mathews, James	14	McCowen, James	11
Mathews, James, Sergeant	79	McCoy, John	59
Mathews, Joseph R.	38	McCoy, Ruddin	46
Matley, John	56	McCracken, James	20

McCracken, John	5	McMillen, Bennet	34
McCracken, Robert	5	McMillen, James	34
McCrea, Joseph	85	McMullen, David	85
McCree, John	31	McNamar, Jesse	63
McCrery, Colonel	21	McNeal, Alexander	90
McCulloch, Samuel	78	McQueen, Alexander	18
McCullough, Samuel	26	McTeer, John	84
McDaniel, Daniel	49	McWattey, John	5
McDaniel, James	42	McWharter, Thomas	45
McDaniel, Matthew	31	McWilliams, James	71
McDavid, John	46	Meaners, John	34
McDead, James	31	Meggett, Margaret	3
McDonald, Absalom	33	Meggett, William	5
McDonald, Colonel	82	Meisereau, Joshua	77
McDonald, James	33	Mellett, Peter, Jr.	46
McDonald, Jehiel	33	Mellon, Nechanya	56
McDonald, John	33	Melson, David	34
McDonald, Martin	84	Melson, Samuel	34
McDonald, Thomas	31	Melven, George, Captain	20
McDougall, Alexander	56	Menuare, William	56
McDow, John	76	Merrick, Robert	41
McDowell, David	14	Messer, James	31
McDowell, William	50	Meyers, Margaret	5
McDugan, Alexander	56	Michael, William	63
McElworth, John	51	Michau, Daniel	20
Mc Fadden, Andrew	19	Micheau, Jacob	41
McFadden, Archibald	19	Middleton, Colonel	39
McFaddin, Patrick	46	Middleton, Henry	14
McFarsin, William	31	Middleton, Richard	38
McGarretty, James	21	Middleton, William	41
McGarrity, John	51	Miles, James	78
McGaw, Captain	17	Miles, John	34
McGee, Thomas	34	Miller, Adam	85
McGill, John	19	Miller, Hans	31
McGinney, Charles	3, 92, 93, 94	Miller, John	11, 92
McGloughling, George	31	Miller, John	33, 69
McGowen, James	42, 63	Miller, Mrs.	30
McGowen, Noble	34	Miller, Phillip	46
McHaffey, James	69	Miller, Robert	63
McHerd, John	50	Miller, William	1, 74
McIntosh, Alexander	87	Mills, Captain	7, 86
McIntosh, George	5	Mills, Henry	46
McKee, Adam	19	Millwee, Major	81
McKee, John	9	Minose, Domino	43
McKee, Thomas	69	Mires, Leonard	33
McKelduff, Adam	78	Mitchell, John	77
McKelveen, Mary	42	Mitchell, Solomon	19
McKendrick, Cath^l.	56	Mitchell, Stephen	83
McKenney, George	65	Mitchell, Thomas	19, 20
McKensey, Alex	42	Mixon, Francis	5
McLeland, Stephen	40	Mixon, Michael	5, 90
McLemore, Wright	56	Mixson, Michael	46
McLewrath, Robert	81	Mobley, Benjamin	87
McLilly, John	26	Mobley, Micaijah	77
McMahon, Patrick	80	Mocks, Andrew	33
McMichael, William	85	Mocks, Joseph	33

Moeboy, Matthew	69	Murfee, Moses	87
Moffett	12	Murfee, Ruduffe	92
Moffett, Captain	12	Murfey, Drury	18
Monday, William	34	Murphy, Colonel	22
Mongin, David	42	Murphye, Ruduff	82
Monks Corner	86	Murray, David	19
Montgomery, George	56	Murray, James	19
Montgomery, Henry	82	Murray, William	21
Montgomery, James	43	Murrel, William	20
Montgomery, Nathaniel	82	Murrell, William	38
Montgomery, William	85	Myers, Ab^m.	25
Moore, Colonel	11	Myers, John	8
Moore, Eliab	25	Myers, Joseph	30
Moore, James, Jr.	11	Myers, Richard	28
Moore, James, Lieutenant	74	Myles, William	40
Moore, John	19, 78	Myrick & Moody	41
Moore, John, Captain	80	Naramore, Edward	87
Moore, John, Jr.	74	Navill, Joseph	69
Moore, John, Sr.	74	Neal, Hugh	56
Moore, Joseph	19	Neal, Samuel	6
Moore, Levi	2	Neal, Thomas	3, 87
Moore, Lewis	74	Neaville, Joseph	51
Moore, Richard	34	Neel, Colonel	12, 49
Moore, Samuel	25	Neel, Hugh	26
Moore, Thomas	25	Neel, James	90
Moore, William	19, 79	Neel, Thomas	26
Moore's Independent Company	78	Neel, William	90
Moorehead, Edward	26	Neel's Regiment	22
Moorehead, William	11	Neeland, John	5
Morgan, Jesse	34	Neeland, William	2, 5
Morgan, Joseph	40	Neeley, Captain	12
Morison, John	40	Neely, John	12
Morlen, John	49	Neely, Robert, Jr.	11
Morreau, Mary	8	Neighbour, William	32
Morris, Burrel	45	Neil, Aaron	52
Morris, Garret	19	Neil, Moses	52
Morris, James	26	Neil, Thomas	40, 82
Morris, John	46	Neil's Regiment	6, 84
Morris, Thomas	26	Neilson, Isaac	18
Morrow, Joseph	11	Neilson, William	65
Morrow, Robert	69	Nell, William, Jr.	5
Morrow, Samuel, Jr.	11	Nelson, David	77
Morrow, William	19	Nelson, Robert	57
Moses, John	21	Nelson, Samuel	77
Moss, Stephen	85	Nesbit, Robert, Jr.	56
Moultrie, William	14	Nesmith, Nathaniel	25
Muckinfus, George	41	Nevelen, Jacob	8
Muckleduff, Adam	3, 5	Newman, Jonathan	5
Mucklewain, Mary	82	Newman, Thomas	80, 82
Muckleween, Henry	43	Niblin, Philip	8
Muldoon, James	88	Nicholls, Thomas	93
Mulherrin, Charles	19	Nichols, William, Sr.	34
Mullett, Gideon	9	Nickells, Thomas	11
Muncrief, Richard	2	Niel, Colonel	87
Murfee, Malachi	82	Niel, Elisha	22
Murfee, Morris	87	Nippers, Benjamin	34

Noble, Martin	30	Payne, Joseph	42
Noble, Thomas	14	Pearce, Dixon	40
Norrell, James	34	Pearce, John	42
Norrell, Mary	49	Pearce, John, Sr.	34
Norris, Agathy	49	Pearson, Edward	46, 48
Norris, Andy	19	Pearson, Enoch	56
Norris, Robert	19	Pearson, Major	80
Norton, William	38	Peek, Thomas	49, 79, 92
Norwood	19	Pegan, Captain	7
Norwood, Captain	16, 19	Pegues, Claudius, Jr.	87
Noveltown, Mrs.	86	Pelham, Edward	75
Nuble, Philip	8	Pen, Azariah	10
O'Benian, Ben	52	Pen, Elizabeth	30
O'Brian, William	38	Pendarvis, Josiah, Sr.	39
O'Neal, William	42	Pendarvis, Thomas	3
Oates, Martin	88	Peninton, Henry	88
Odam, B., Captain	83	Penney, Ann	39
Odam, Benjamin	38	Pennington, Jacob	83
Odam, Captain	83, 84	Pennington, William	34
Odam, Daniel	42	Perdriau, John	23, 28, 39
Offatt, Ezekiel	34	Perret, James	20
Ogelvie, Elijah	75	Perret, John, Sr.	18
Oliphant, Obediah	52	Perry, John	6, 91, 93
Oliver, Captain	32	Perry, Thomas	56, 77
Oliver, Peter	42	Person, Enoch	10
Oriack, James	59	Pettit, Joshua	69
Osburn, William	63	Pew, William	8
Otterson, Major	18	Peyre, John	23
Outlaw, Edward	40	Phegan, Philip	32
Overstreet, Jethro	49, 79	Phelpes, Moses	12
Owen, Archibald	27	Philips, James	86, 88
Owen, Captain	31	Phillips, Stephen	57
Owens, Benjamin, Jr.	42	Pickens, Captain	15 – 17, 19
Owens, Joshua	90	Pickens, General	8, 10, 22
Owens, Thomas	69, 75	Picket, Micajah	13
Page, Thomas	42	Pickett, Jonathan	81
Palmer, Charles	23	Pickett, Micaijah	82
Palmer, Elijah	34	Pickett, Thomas	77
Palmer, Thomas	42	Pierce, Hugh	52
Pardue, Joel	49, 93, 94	Pierson, Edward	10, 23
Park, Andrew	32	Pike, William	42
Parker, Daniel	18	Piles, Samuel	34
Parker, John	3, 11, 88	Pinion, Lewis	63
Parnell, William	34	Pister, Gasper	59
Parson, William	82	Pitman, John	34
Parsons, Captain	45	Pledger, Philip	42
Partin, Robert	43	Plunket, James	56
Patterson, Joseph	12	Plunket, Robert	56
Patterson, William	28	*Polly*	47
Patton, Benjamin	12	Ponpon Company	84
Patton, Colonel	88	Poole, John	32
Patton, Jacob	12	Pope, Captain	43
Patton, John	63	Popewell, Paul	75
Patton, William	63	Popwell, William	40
Paul, Mathew	10	Port, Benjamin	20
Pawley, Percival	77	Port, Benjamin, Jr.	6

Port, Peter	6	Read, James	9, 40
Postele, Colonel	84	Reams, Jeremiah	20
Postell, Colonel	8	Reaves, Burgess	6
Postell, James, Jr.	6	Recker, George	56
Postell, Major	81, 82	Reddish, Thomas	39
Potcher, Peter	57	Reed, Francis	8
Potter, Captain	7	Reed, Job	30
Potts, Thomas	25	Reed, Mary	2
Pouncey, Anthony	90	Reed, Murray	23
Pouncey, Roger	87	Reede, William	37
Pouncy, Roger	78	Rees, Charles	6
Pouncy, Samuel	40	Reeves, Ann	8
Powe	12, 13, 17, 18, 22, 25, 38, 39 – 41, 56, 57, 89	Reeves, James	30
		Reiley, David	82
		Reisinger, Thomas	57
Powell, John	75	Reynolds, Joseph	43
Powers, Francis	69	Rhodes, Henry	20
Powers, Giles	6	Rhodes, James	70
Prator, Philip	27	Rhodes, John	20
Price, Daniel	11	Rhodes, Solomon	20
Price, Henry	80, 88	Rice, James	47
Price, S., Captain	89	Rice, Thomas	57
Price, Samuel	20	Richards, James	2
Price, William	77	Richardson, Abraham	20, 92, 93, 94
Prince, Isam	83	Richardson, Benjamin	31
Pringle, William	46	Richardson, Colonel	82, 86
Printer, Margaret	28	Richardson, Edward	46
Pucket, Julany	51	Richardson, James	75
Puckett, William	28	Richardson, John	30, 71
Pullam, Robert	46	Richardson, William	82
Punch, Mary	85	Richey, James	82
Purkins, Willis	11, 92	Richison, Colonel	82
Purvis	54	Rickenbacker, Jacob	21
Purvis, Colonel	45, 49, 89	Ripley, Ambrose	37
Purvis's Regiment	30, 32 – 37, 39, 43, 45, 47 – 49, 54	Rippon, Isaac	3
		Ritchman, John	23
		Rittsendale, Martin	44
Putman, Barnet	51	River, William S.	46
Putteet, Tobias	51	Rivers, Benjamin	13
Quick, Thomas, Sr.	40	Rivers, John	8
Quinney, Joseph	21	Roach, James	82, 93
Rainey, Benjamin	84	Roachell, John	77
Rambee, Nicholas	30	Roberts, Abraham	82
Ramsay, Captain	21	Roberts, George	75
Ramsey, James	44	Roberts, Lewis	31
Ramsey, Robert	12	Roberts, William	78
Randals, Samuel	69	Roberts, Zachariah	82
Randolph, James	30	Roberts, Zeph[h].	78
Rapley, Richard Andrew	86	Robertson, Joseph	12
Rash, Adam	57	Robertson, William	6
Ratcliff, Elisha	80	Robins, William	85
Ravenal, Elizabeth	42	Robinson, Isaac	52
Ravencraft, William	30	Robinson, John	23
Ravo, Ab[m].	85	Robinson, Patrick	12
Rawlinson, John	82	Robison, Basdale	88
Raymond, Peter	42	Robison, Robert	26

Rochateer, Robert	26	Saunders, John	80
Roebuck, Colonel	55, 70, 79, 86 – 88	Saunders, Joshua	63
		Saunders, Mrs.	26
Roebuck, John	30, 70	Saunders, Roger Parker	3
Roebuck's Regiment	50 – 55, 57, 65 – 71, 83	Saunders, William	49
		Saunders, William, Jr.	53
		Saunders, William, Sr.	53
Rogan, Philip	26	Sausey, David	42
Roger, Mesh[k].	46	Savage, Benjamin, Jr.	63
Rogers, Alexander	58	Savage, Robert	63
Rogers, Daniel	43	Sawyer, John	47
Rogers, Felix	34	Schad, Abraham	83
Rogers, George	30	Scism, David	63
Rogers, John	42	Scott, Archibald	13
Rogers, Richard	63	Scott, Francis	41
Rogers, William	56, 71	Scott, James	37
Rohde, Levin Jorgen	1	Scott, Robert	41
Rolleson, Benjamin	20, 46	Scott, Thomas	82
Rosamond, Captain	19	Screven, Benjamin	89
Rose, John	80	Scrimsher, Robert	34
Rosell, George	79	Scrimsler, John	92
Ross, Andrew	80	Scriven, Elisha	80
Ross, Isaac, Jr.	79	Seabrook, Joseph	77
Ross, Robert	90	Seales, George	66
Rouch, Thomas	31	Sealy, Biggin	9
Round O Company	81	Searson, William	2
Rouse, Deborah	40, 46	See, Abraham	8
Rouse, Sarah	6	See, Nichoas	8
Rowdus, Elizabeth	39	Seeley, James	34
Rowe, Edward	6	Seelton, Robert	64
Rowland, David	90	Sellars, John	12
Ruff, George	59	Sessions, Solomon	6
Rumph, Captain	21, 24, 47	Sharber, Arthur	75
Rumph, David	8	Sharp, Francis	27
Rush, Benjamin	63	Shaw, William	12
Rushen, Matthew	49	Sheaver, Francis	21
Rusk, David	81	Shierer, Jacob	59
Russel, William	51	Shipman, Edward	34
Russell, Andrew	59	Shippy, Samuel	53
Russell, James	80	Shockley, John	64
Russell, Michael	82	Shockley, Thomas	85
Russell, Nathaniel	90, 93	Shoemaker, Sampson	42
Russell, William	40, 59	Shrewsberry & Lawrence	9
Saltus, Samuel	4	Siege of Augusta	83
Saltzer, Jacob	85	Simmons, Vincen	82, 93, 94
Sanders, Margaret	47	Simmons, William	70
Sanders, William	5, 14	Simons, Jesse	32
Sandiford, Samuel	12	Simons, M., Colonel	85
Sandlen, Daniel	8	Simons, Peter	21, 28, 39
Sansum, John	5	Simpson, John	51
Sap, Caleb	58	Simpson, William	43
Sap, Henry	58	Sims, Joseph	39, 92, 93, 94
Sap, John	58	Singleton, Benjamin	21
Sap, Shadrack	58	Singleton, Colonel	44
Saunders, Charles	18	Singleton, John	6, 77, 84
Saunders, Cornelius	53	Singleton, William	6
Saunders, James	11		

Singley, Rachel	56	Stafford, Richard	42
Singuefield, Francis	34	Stallions, Malachi	34
Sinkfield, Francis	56	Standard, Captain	41, 85
Sisson, Fred[h].	47	Stanley, John	22
Skillen, William	46	Starke, Thomas	37
Skipper, Amos	41	Starks, Henry	17
Slack, John	32	State Cavalry	21
Sleigh, George	59	State Commissary	1, 2, 85
Sleigh, Jacob	59	Stawlsworth, William	35
Sly, Charles	47	Stead, Benjamin	20
Smiley, David	34	Stearns, Aaron	37
Smiley, William	57	Steel, Captain	7, 11, 12
Smith, Aaron	70	Steel, Joseph	75
Smith, Ab[m].	75	Steel, William	64
Smith, Benjamin	89	Steen, William	65
Smith, Christian	30	Stemwinder, Fredrick	32
Smith, Christopher	56	Sterling, Isaac	75
Smith, Daniel	34	Stevens, Baalam	35
Smith, Daniel, Lt.	11	Stevens, Burrell	27
Smith, Enoch	59	Stevens, Daniel	70
Smith, Francis	2, 20	Stevens, Isham	4
Smith, George	21, 46, 80	Stevens, John	4, 17, 37
Smith, Giles	70	Steward, Hardy	87
Smith, Henry	6	Stewart, Alexander	27
Smith, James	42	Stewart, Captain	22
Smith, James High	83	Stewart, James	23, 37
Smith, Joel	23	Stewart, Thomas	21
Smith, John	1, 42, 46, 82	Stivener, George	47
Smith, John Jacob M.	47	Stobo, Richard P.	47
Smith, Mary	18	Stock, William Clerk	56
Smith, Ralph	23, 88	Stocker, Samuel	30
Smith, Reuben	23	Stockman, Stoffle	59
Smith, Robert	30, 82	Stoker, John	35
Smith, Simon	46	Stoker, Matthew	35
Smith, Susanna	46	Stoker, Robert	35
Smith, William	39	Stokes, William	22
Snell, John	21	Stoll, David	42
Snellgrove, John	31	Stone, Benjamin	70
Snelling, John	46	Stone, Cathbert	53
Snipes & Ford	83	Storey, George	64
Snow, James	32, 92	Story, Anthony	64
Sommers, Humphrey	32	Stoutinburgh, William	42
Sommers, John	9	Strain, Captain	15, 17
Sords, John	51	Strange, John	87
South Carolina	43, 44, 48, 49, 77, 78	Strange, Mitchel	28
		Stricklan, William	6
Sowers, William	59	Stringer, John	87
Spears, David	17	Stringer, William	35
Spears, William	20, 87	Strobhar, John	84
Spence, James	85	Stroman, Jacob	2
Spiel, Jacob	30	Stuart, Isabel	47
Spivey, James	39	Stuart, Mary	47
Squires, Andrew	6	Stucker, Jacob	60
St. Helena Company	3	Sullivan, George	35
Stafford, Colonel	9	Sullivan, John	6, 47
Stafford, Eleazer	75	Sullivan, Owen	35

Sullivan, Patrick	70	Thomas, J., Jr., Colonel	50
Sumers, John	81	Thomas, James	75
Summerlin, James	35	Thomas, Jesse	41
Sumter	6	Thomas, Josiah	47
Sumter, General	7, 8, 11 – 14, 18, 22, 48, 49, 77, 81, 84 – 86	Thomas, Jr., Colonel	8, 14
		Thomas, Mary Lamboll	1, 22
Sumter's Brigade	4, 7, 8, 23, 38, 43, 45, 46, 58, 78, 83, 84	Thomas, Samuel	37
		Thomas, Tarbeyfield	35
		Thomas, William	56, 57
Sutton, Samuel	49	Thomas, William, Jr.	41
Sweet, Anthony	6	Thomas's Regiment	80
Sweetingburg, Aberhart	64	Thomason, Turner William	51
Swicard, George	2	Thompson, Charles	65
Swicard, Jacob	21, 92	Thompson, Colonel	71
Swinton, Hugh	46	Thompson, Elizabeth	57
Swinton, William	21	Thompson, James, Colonel	23
Taggart, John	84	Thompson, John	64
Tandy, Achilles	35	Thompson, Major	4, 78
Tankesley, Charles	58	Thompson, Moses	27, 70
Tankinsley, William	64	Thompson, Swan	53
Tanner, Benjamin	42	Thompson, Theophilus	53
Tanner, Lynn	49, 80	Thompson, William	76
Tanseller, Mary	8	Thomson, Alexander	78, 86
Tate	14, 26, 43, 48, 50, 57	Thomson, Colonel	32
		Thomson, James, Colonel	14
Tate, Captain	6, 7, 11, 12, 66, 71 – 73, 75, 88, 89	Thomson, Lewis	49
		Thomson, Nathan	47
		Thomson, William	12
Tayley, John	57	Thorn, Elizabeth	57
Taylor, Colonel	14, 29, 41 – 44, 46 – 48, 51, 76, 78, 86, 90	Thorp, Eleazer	17
		Tillman, William	77
		Tin, William	35
		Tippings, Philip	70
Taylor, Drury	70	Tison, John	51, 80
Taylor, George	37	Todd, Haywood	41
Taylor, James	76	Todd, John	35
Taylor, Jane	47	Todd, Richard	44
Taylor, John	57, 70	Tollenare, De Charles	47
Taylor, Lewis	64	Toller, Mary	30
Taylor, William	12	Tomlinson, Nathaniel	13
Taylor's Regiment	90	Tomlinson, William	41
Tearel, William	18	Tomplatt, John	21
Teate, Thomas	39	Towles, Captain	82
Temple, Jesse	70	Towles, Jane	89
Terry, George	6	Townsend, Henry	12
Thacker, Isaac	51	Towsen, John	57
Theus, Randolph	5	Trevres, John	49
Third Regiment	47, 78, 87	Trezevant, Isaac Stephen	9
Thomas, Edward	43	Trout, Adam	38
Thomas, A., Captain	24, 76, 81, 82	Trout, Daniel	37
Thomas, Anderson, Captain	24, 32	Trout, George	38
Thomas, Benjamin	35	Tucker, Benjamin	6
Thomas, Captain	80	Tucker, John	13
Thomas, Colonel	23, 54	Tucker, William	89
Thomas, Evan	27	Tuctrel, Thomas	76
Thomas, Gilshot	75	Tue, John D.	38

Turil, William	32	Waring, Benjamin	93
Turkenot, Mrs.	35	Warnock, Abraham	35
Turner, Amey	44	Warren, George	47
Turner, Captain	21, 28	Warren, John	18
Turner, John	35, 70, 87, 89	Warren, Joseph	41
Turner, Jonathan	70	Warren, Reuben	35
Tweedy, Robert	43	Warren, Robert	11, 92
Twewitts, Elijah	43	Wasdon, Elijah	35
Twigg, Colonel	56	Washington, Colonel	20, 80, 86
Tyet, Mary	57	Waterfield, James	90
Tyler, Samuel	78	Waters	54, 57, 65
Tyner, William	35	Waters, Bordwine	83
Tyrrel, William	87	Waters, Charles	82
Ulmer, Jacob	44	Waters, Colonel	55, 88, 89
Ulmer, John	78	Waters's Regiment	50, 53 – 60,
Underwood, George	53		64 – 66
Valentine, Nicholas	60	Watson, William	71
Vallo, Nicholas	23	Watt, Samuel	27
Van Marjenhoff, John	28	Watts, Jacob	35, 71
Vance, William	12	Watts, John	9
Varcene, William	89	Waxhaw Station	82
Varnon, John	77	Wayne, General	9, 42, 85
Veatch, James	90	Weams, Thomas	27
Veitch, John	78	Weams, William	27
Vernidoe, Henry	47	Weas, William	11
Vessels, Michael	57	Weaver, Aaron	35
Vicary, William, Sr.	27	Webb, John	47
Vince, Joseph, Captain	80	Weber, Nicholas	44
Vivian, John	32	Webster, Samuel	80
Volloton, Jeremiah	42	Webster, Samuel, Jr.	49
Wadkins, Abhabel	23	Weeks, Joseph, Jr.	64
Waide, John	32	Weeks, William	66
Waight, Ab^m.	32	Welch, Nicholas	64
Wakefield, Charles	70	Welch, Richard	83
Walker, Captain	7, 12	Welch, William	38, 47
Walker, Elijah	84	Welcher, Benjamin	77
Walker, George	41, 70	Wells, Jeremiah	35
Walker, Jeremiah	84	Wells, John	21, 60
Wall, Howell	23	Wells, Lewis	64
Wall, James	86	Wells, Matthew	2
Wallace, Captain	6, 11, 43	Wells, William	60
Wallace, James	35, 51	Wells, William, Sergeant	60
Wallace, Josiah	58	Wernald, William	38
Wallace, Michael	11	Werner, Jacob	9
Wallace, Robert	43	West, William	23
Wallen, Michael	65	Wheeler, John	41
Waller, Benjamin	90, 93	Wheeler, Mary	12
Walter, Jasper	8	Wheeler, William	64
Walter, Richard	5	Whicker, Henry	60
Walters, Mary	11	Whitaker, James	64
Walton, Nicholas	49	White, Allen William	49
Ward, Dickey	78	White, Andrew	27
Ward, Susanna	22	White, Anthony, Jr.	6
Warden, Captain	43	White, Colonel	83, 84
Ware, David	47	White, George	21
Wareing, William	71	White, James	71

White, Joseph	35, 57, 71
White, Samuel	38
White, Thomas	83
Whitefield, Rodia	87
Whitehead, Daniel	12
Whitfield, Benjamin	18
Whitfield, Thomas	23
Whitmire, Fredrick	64
Whitsworth, Fendol	71
Whitten, Philip	38
Whitter, Fendol	53
Whittington, Barnett	41
Whittles, Burrows	49
Wigg, W.	23, 24, 42
Wigg, Hazard William	14
Wigg, William	9
Wiggins, William	58
Wilburn, Richard	82
Wilcher, Benjamin	35
Wiley, John	27
Wiley, Peter	28
Wilhelm, Peter	66
Wilkins, Alexander	76
Willard, John	64
Willawer, John	19
Williams, Barwick	38
Williams, Colonel	81, 84
Williams, Daniel	38
Williams, David	41
Williams, Edward	85
Williams, Elizabeth	47
Williams, Ezekiel	2
Williams, Isaac	49
Williams, Jesse	41
Williams, John	32, 77, 80
Williams, Joseph	38, 78
Williams, Joshua	38
Williams, Michijah	83
Williams, Robert	47
Williams, Samuel	76
Williams, Thomas	39, 87
Williamson, General	79
Williamson, Henry	38
Williamson, Jesse	47
Williamson, Thomas	87
Williamson, Thomas, Jr.	41
Williamson, William	12
Willis, John	41
Willson, Captain	17, 18
Willson, Hugh	60
Willson, James	88
Willson, Robert	27
Wilson, Algernon	1
Wilson, Captain	18
Wilson, Henry	49
Wilson, Hughey	60

Wilson, James	14, 43, 89
Wilson, James, Jr.	22, 35
Wilson, James, Sr.	49
Wilson, Joel	92
Wilson, John	1
Wilson, Martha	47, 92
Wilson, Robert	49
Wilson, Thomas	35
Wilson, Ulman	23
Wilson, William	23
Wiltown Company	78
Wimberley, James	47
Winders, James	18
Windham, Amos	19
Windham, Jesse	18
Windham, Samuel	41
Wines, Samuel	41
Wingart, Michael	31
Winkler, Lewis	88
Winkler, Mrs.	42
Winn, Colonel	11, 14, 77, 82, 84, 86
Winn, General	25, 30, 31, 42, 87
Winn, Richard	1
Winn's Regiment	10, 46, 84, 86
Winyert, Mathias	32
Wise, James	18
Wise, Jonathan	47
Wise, William	76
Witherspoon, Gavin	39
Witherton, John	57
Wittaker, William	1
Wolton, Moses	35
Wommock, Captain	25, 46
Wood, Alexander	58
Wood, Alexander, Jr.	58
Wood, Benjamin	18, 90
Wood, Dempsey	3
Wood, Hickebud, Sergeant	60
Wood, John	1, 35, 60, 90
Wood, Lazarus	88
Wood, Thomas, Corporal	86
Wood, William	57
Wood, William, Captain	71
Woodard, Samuel	39
Woodberry, Richard	85
Woodcock, Robert	14
Woods, John	32
Woodward, Burbage	80
Woodward, John	77
Woolbank, Richard	64
Wooters Philip	89
Wooters, Lilly	22
Word, Thomas	58
Wragg, John	11

Wragg, William	22
Wray, Thomas	35
Wright, Christopher	35
Wright, George	87
Wright, Henry	12
Wright, John	82
Wright, Stephen	41
Wyley, William	12
Wyn, William	49
Yarborough, Ambrose	65
Yelding, Mary	49
Yonge, Francis	28
York, Richard	27
Young, Benjamin	1, 28
Young, Daniel	65
Young, Edward	53
Young, Isaac	65
Young, Jesse	65
Young, John	14
Young, Levi	65
Young, Matthew	60
Young, Richard	65
Young, Robert, Jr.	49
Young, William	71
Youngblood, Captain	28
Zann, Christopher	31
Zimmerman, Mary	42
Zinn, Horonomas	47
Zubly, John	35

www.ingramcontent.com/pod-product-compliance
Lightning Source LLC
Chambersburg PA
CBHW080243270326
41926CB00020B/4349

9 780788 450990